PETERSON'S®

SAT® PREP GUIDE ASAP:
THE ULTIMATE QUICK-STUDY
GUIDE TO MASTERING THE
SAT®

PETERSON'S®

About Peterson's®

Peterson's is everywhere that education happens. For over five decades, Peterson's has provided products and services that keep students and their families engaged throughout the pre-college, college, and post-college experience. From the first day of kindergarten through high school graduation and beyond, Peterson's is a single source of educational content to help families maximize their student's learning and opportunities for success. Whether a fifth-grader needs help with geometry or a high school junior could benefit from essay-writing tips, Peterson's is the ultimate source for the highest quality educational resources.

SAT® is a registered trademark of the College Board, which did not collaborate in the development of, and does not endorse, this product.

For more information, contact Peterson's, 3 Columbia Circle, Suite 205, Albany, NY 12203, 800-338-3282 Ext. 54229; or find us online at *www.petersons.com*.

Peterson's SAT® Prep Guide ASAP

ISBN 978-0-7689-4118-0

Printed in the United States of America

10 9 8 7 6 5 4 3 2 1   19 18 17

First Edition

Peterson's Practice Test for the SAT® Exam

Your purchase of *Peterson's SAT® Prep Guide ASAP* gives you access to **Peterson's Practice Test for the SAT® Exam**, a full-length online practice test with automatic scoring and detailed feedback to help you understand the concepts presented. Use this helpful tool to jump-start your test-prep journey and build confidence— even on a tight schedule. Access the test at *www.petersons.com/sat*.

TABLE OF CONTENTS

THE SAT® ESSAY

CHAPTER 1: ALL ABOUT THE SAT® EXAM

OVERVIEW

- How to Use This Book
- The SAT® Exam: An Overview
- Registering for the SAT® Exam
- Scoring
- Getting Ready for Test Day
- Summing It Up

Are you just getting started preparing for the SAT® exam but are short on time? If this sounds like you—and you can feel the clock ticking—then you need to make the *absolute* most of your time between now and test day to get ready for this all-important exam. This means making all the right decisions about how you'll spend your time—whether you have a few hours, a few weeks, or something in-between—preparing for it.

We *know* you're feeling the pressure of the clock, but here's the good news:

We completely get it, and we're here to help—FAST!

Peterson's *SAT® Prep Guide ASAP* is designed for students like you, who don't have much time to prepare but still want to get their best possible scores on test day. Consider this book your indispensible, last-minute SAT® study buddy, the no-nonsense test-prep coach that's going to help you make up for lost time and get in the best test-taking shape possible! This book provides quick, effective, and straightforward strategies, practice, and review to help you conquer the exam—no unnecessary information or time-consuming plans that take more time than you actually have.

Getting a good score on the SAT® exam isn't easy, but it is an important step to help ensure your academic future and achieve long-term success. So, even though it's late in the game, the *last thing* you want to have happen is to stumble on the test and leave your future options in the hands of fate.

So, if you're nervous, anxious, or stressing out because you think you've waited too long to study or you feel the pressure of the ticking clock and are worried that you don't have enough time to prepare effectively, take a deep breath and know that you've already started making wise decisions by using *SAT® ASAP* to prepare! This helpful book includes:

- **Quick yet complete coverage** of the structure and format of the SAT® exam— exactly what you need to know about the exam to get ready for test day.

- **Straightforward and effective review** of topic material for each section of the exam. Each chapter of this book cuts straight to the core with the most essential topics and concepts that you'll need to know.

- **Effective tips that *really* work** on the exam. You'll show up on test day confident and ready with proven time-saving strategies and advice for every section of the exam so you can get your absolute best scores possible in a short amount of time.

- **No-nonsense practice** for all types of questions that you may encounter on test day to get you in solid test-taking shape—fast!

Here's the message at the heart of *SAT® ASAP*: It's never too late to build your skills and get ready for success on test day, and this book will help you make the most of the time you have. No matter how much time that is, if you use it wisely, you can achieve your goals for the SAT®.

We'll keep things moving forward at a brisk pace, focusing on just what you need to reach your target score. So keep reading!

HOW TO USE THIS BOOK

Only *you* know exactly how much time you have between now and test day. It's *our* job to help you make the most of that time. We suggest two possible strategies for using this book and taking full advantage of the time you have.

THE FULL REVIEW STRATEGY

This approach gives you an *equal* amount of time for each section of the exam for a comprehensive review of the entire test. You'll also dedicate a chunk of time to taking a test-like diagnostic exam that will let you assess your strengths and weaknesses going in to your study period.

Step 1: List the number of days you have until test day: _____ days

Step 2: Take a few hours off the top—*no more than a day*—reading this chapter to learn just what you need to know about the SAT® exam, including registering, scoring, and getting comfortable with the general format of each test section.

Step 3: Take one day to find a quiet space and attack the Diagnostic Test in Chapter 2. The exam itself will take you 3 hours and 50 minutes if you complete the essay, and 3 hours if you do not. When you're done, allot the rest of the day's study time to reviewing all answer explanations and assessing where you need to focus your study.

Step 4: Build your study plan. First, set aside one full day if you plan to take the essay portion of the exam. Focus all of that day's efforts on reading Chapter 6 and making your way through the sample essay prompt.

Then, divide all of your remaining time (whether it be days or weeks) equally for each test section. Spend the time allotted for each section to read through the review chapter, answer all chapter practice questions, and go over the diagnostic questions that gave you the most trouble.

Step 5: Structure your study calendar. Now that you know the number of days you have to devote to topic review and question practice for each exam section, take some time to fill in a study calendar so you'll know exactly what prep you'll be tackling each day between now and test day. Structure your calendar to suit your study style—devote each day to a single test section, or divide your days so you can work on a section for a set number of hours and then switch things up—whatever keeps you interested, focused, and on track!

THE WEAKNESS TARGETING STRATEGY

This approach lets you allocate the time you have between now and test day to target your weak areas and build your skills where you need to most.

Step 1: List the number of days you have until test day: _____ days

Step 2: Take a few hours off the top—*no more than a day*—reading this chapter to learn just what you need to know about the SAT® exam, including registration, scoring, and getting comfortable with the general format of each test section.

Step 3: Assess your strengths and weaknesses. Rank each test section based on your strengths and weaknesses in each test subject. We recommend you use your class grades as a guide. Have you always gotten great grades in English classes but struggle in math? Are you a writing whiz? Using your academic history as a guide, rank each test section from 1 (weakest subject) to 4 (best subject).

SAT® Math Section: _____

SAT® Reading Section: _____

SAT® Writing and Language Section: _____

SAT® Essay Section (*Optional*): _____

Step 4: Take 1 day to find a quiet space to confirm your subject assessment by taking the Diagnostic Test in Chapter 2. The exam itself will take you 3 hours and 50 minutes if you complete the essay, and 3 hours if you do not. When you're done, allot the rest of the day's study time to review the detailed explanations of the questions you answered incorrectly and the questions that gave you the most trouble.

Now that you have an even clearer idea of what you need to work on, you can adjust your rankings as needed as you move through your study schedule and calendar. Your skill levels may shift, and your study plan should follow suit so that you're always spending your time working on your weakest areas.

Step 5: Build your study plan. Divide the number of days/hours you have to prepare among the test sections, splitting your time (days or hours) based on your rankings. You can divide your time however you see fit, as long as you're dedicating the majority of your time to improving your weak spots.

One example for allocating your time is as follows:

- ○ 40% of your time for the section you ranked 1

- ○ 30% of your time for the section you ranked 2

- ○ 20% of your time for the section you ranked 3

- ○ 10% of your time for the section you ranked 4 (*or keep this for the optional essay*)

Once you're comfortable with your initial study plan, fill in your initial study times for each test section.

SAT® Math Section: _____

SAT® Reading Section: _____

SAT® Writing and Language Section: _____

SAT® Essay Section (*Optional*): _____

Step 6: Structure your study calendar. Now that you know the amount of time you have to devote to topic review and question practice for each section of the SAT® exam, take some time to fill in a study calendar so you'll know exactly what SAT® prep you'll be tackling each day between now and test day. Feel free to structure your calendar to suit your study style—devote each day to a single test section or divide your days so you can work on a section for a set number of hours and then switch—whatever will keep you interested, focused, and on track!

Remember, as your skill levels shift, you should reweigh and rerank each test section so that you're always giving sufficient focus to your weakest test areas.

THE SAT® EXAM: AN OVERVIEW

The first step to doing well on the SAT® exam—even if you're short on time—is to have a good grasp on the structure and format of the test and the fundamentals you'll need to know. We *know* you're eager to get to the test practice and review, but having a thorough understanding of the exam from top to bottom will give you a real advantage—and put you ahead of the test-taking competition!

Consider your scores on the SAT® exam as an important component of your college admissions package. Along with your GPA, resume of extracurricular activities, letters of recommendation, and application and essay, your scores on this high-stakes test will be among the most important factors that college admissions panels will use to decide whether or not to grant you admission.

SAT® Scoring

Your SAT® score will range from a low of 400 to a perfect 1600. This score is composed of the following:
- A score ranging from 200 to 800 on the Evidence-Based Reading and Writing sections
- A score ranging from 200 to 800 on the Math section

Your essay score—if you choose to take this optional part of the exam—will be reported separately. You'll receive a score ranging from 2 to 8 for each of the three dimensions measured.

Your test scores will help college admissions panels determine if you're ready and capable of handling college-level coursework and whether you possess any specific aptitudes or deficits in any tested area. Your SAT® scores will also help your future college advisors make decisions regarding class-level placement.

The SAT® exam is carefully designed by recognized experts in the field of education to test your proficiency in the following core subjects, which you've studied throughout your academic career: **Reading, Writing and Language,** and **Math**. We'll delve into an in-depth analysis of each section of the exam—along with comprehensive review and practice—in later chapters of this book.

SAT® Exam Timing and Pacing

The SAT® exam is a **3-hour exam** consisting of **154 multiple-choice questions**. Add in an extra 50 minutes if you're taking the optional SAT® Essay.

Make sure you're comfortable with the format and timing of the exam and develop an effective test-taking pace *before* exam day, through thorough practice and review under timed and simulated test-like conditions!

Most of the questions are multiple choice, the kind that requires you to select the best option among several possible answer choices. You'll be composing an argumentative essay for the *optional* SAT® Essay if you choose to take it.

THE SAT® EXAM: CHANGING FOCUS

The SAT® exam underwent some critical changes in March 2016—everything from test length and scoring to test components and reporting were altered by the College Board, the official SAT® test makers. But don't worry, the information in this book reflects the *most current* test specs and information available. For a complete overview of how the test has changed, visit the official College Board website.

Some important features of the current SAT® exam are as follows:

- **Greater focus on real-world college and career readiness:** The College Board has made a concerted effort to have the SAT® exam focus on the knowledge and skills that are most essential for real-world college and career success.

- **Greater emphasis and focus on context:** The SAT® exam focuses on word meaning in context and the impact of word choice on shaping overall meaning and tone.

- **Greater assessment of command of evidence:** The Evidence-Based Reading and Writing section of the exam and the SAT® Essay measure your ability to analyze and interpret information from a variety of sources, including infographics, charts, graphs, tables, and text.

- **Math questions with a practical focus:** The Math section of the SAT® exam features questions in three key areas that have a practical application in the real world: Problem Solving and Data Analysis, Passport to Advanced Math, and Heart of Algebra.

- **Eye on science and history/social studies:** The SAT® exam gauges your ability to answer math, reading, and writing questions that are grounded in science, history, and social studies contexts.

- **Simplified scoring:** The College Board has simplified the SAT® exam scoring and instituted rights-only scoring—you simply earn points for correctly answered questions, *with no penalty for guessing*. There's no reason to leave any question unanswered.

Let's take a closer look at each section of the SAT® exam and what you can expect on test day. Remember, knowledge is power, and the more you know about this important exam, the better prepared you will be!

THE READING TEST

The Reading Test is one of two tests that comprise the Evidence-Based Reading and Writing section of the SAT® exam (the other being the Writing and Language Test). The Reading Test is a 65-minute exam that consists of 52 questions. It's designed to test your ability to synthesize and analyze information in a variety of practical contexts. The makers of the SAT® exam want to test your skills at engaging with thought-provoking, evidence-based discussions on topics with real-world relevance, and in answering questions based on the information you'll encounter.

On this section of the SAT® exam, you'll encounter a series of reading passages, some of which may appear as a paired set of passages, and will answer a series of multiple-choice questions based on either the reading or graphics that accompany them—this may include infographics, charts, graphs, tables, or other graphic media.

The passages are designed to test your real-world reading skills, which will serve you well throughout your academic and professional career. This is the breakdown of passage topics that you'll encounter on test day:

- One passage from a historically relevant U.S. founding document or a piece of text that inspired a great global conversation (such as the Declaration of Independence or a speech by Martin Luther King, Jr.)

- One passage from a recognized work of literature—either classic or contemporary—from anywhere in the world

- One passage from the social sciences about topics such as sociology, psychology, economics, or another branch of discipline

- Two science-based passages that represent and examine core concepts in biology, chemistry, earth science, or physics

Passages for history and science topic areas may appear alone or in pairs.

Although not a complete list, questions on the SAT® Reading Test will ask you to do the following:

- Analyze information provided in the passages.
- Interpret supplemental graphical material and how it relates to the passage.
- Draw conclusions based on information provided.
- Locate and assess information directly from the passages. These could include a word, a line, or a series of lines in the passage.
- Understand and identify implications based on the author's words.

The Reading Test is designed to measure whether or not you have the following reading skills: Command of Evidence, Words in Context, and Analysis in History/Social Studies and in Science.

Command of Evidence

The Reading Test will assess your ability to identify, understand, and draw conclusions from relevant contextual evidence presented in the reading passages or associated graphics, including how authors use evidence to bolster their claims.

Words in Context

On the SAT® exam, you'll need to understand and answer questions based on key words, phrases, and context clues that appear in the reading passages, including how these words help define and shape each author's style, meaning, and tone. Words in Context questions are carefully selected for their practical application—both in the classroom and the workplace.

Analysis in History/Social Studies and Analysis in Science

The passages and associated questions in these topic areas will gauge your ability to apply your existing reading skills to practical application in these fields. This includes such concepts as interpreting data, considering larger-scale implications, and examining hypotheses.

The SAT® Exam: *Not* a Memorization Exam!

Doing well on today's SAT® exam is not a race to remember as many facts, figures, and formulas as possible between now and test day.

It's designed to test your ability to process, analyze, and apply real-world information in various practical applications, on top of the knowledge you've acquired throughout your academic career—simply put, it's testing the everyday tools you'll need to succeed in college!

THE WRITING AND LANGUAGE TEST

The Writing and Language Test is one of two tests that comprise the Evidence-Based Reading and Writing section of the SAT® exam (the other being the Reading Test). The Writing and Language Test is a 35-minute exam that consists of 44 questions. This test is designed to gauge your ability to recognize errors in construction, language, style, organization, and grammar, and to make corrections as needed in an effort to improve the passages.

NOTE: Being able to effectively edit and proofread written material is a practical skill that will serve you well—both in college and the world of work.

In this section of the SAT® exam, you'll encounter a series of passages that can touch upon a variety of topic areas, including:

- Social sciences
- History
- Careers
- Science
- The humanities
- Nonfiction narratives

You'll be tasked with answering a series of multiple-choice questions based on either the reading or graphical material that accompanies them—this may include infographics, charts, graphs, tables, or other graphic media, just like on the Reading Test. Also similar to the Reading Test, no prior knowledge of the topics that the passages are based on is required—you just need a sharp editorial eye!

Here's a look at the types of questions you'll encounter on the SAT® Writing and Language Test.

Standard English Conventions

Some questions on the Writing and Language Test will correspond to underlined portions of text in the passage and will ask you to determine if the underlined text is correct as written (for which you'd select the NO CHANGE option), or if it requires revision—and if so, which choices among the answer options is correct. These questions typically focus on the fundamentals of good writing, including grammar, usage, style, and tone.

Expression of Ideas

Other questions will ask you to make decisions regarding the structure and organization of text within a paragraph or passage—again with an eye on improving the flow and impact of the writing.

Command of Evidence

You'll also encounter questions that will ask you to make decisions about how an author develops his or her ideas. This may entail adding or deleting information from the passage based on available contextual evidence, with the goal of sharpening an author's claims or bolstering a point of view with relevant supporting details.

Words in Context

You'll be tasked with making critical decisions regarding word choice throughout the passages on test day. Your job will be to ensure that the best possible word choices are deployed throughout the passages—based on available contextual evidence—for maximum impact and to improve style, tone, or syntax.

Analysis in History/Social Studies and Analysis in Science

As mentioned, the SAT® exam will assess your ability to apply your analytical and writing skills to improve passages based on topics in science, social studies, and history. Why? Because these skills will be essential for long-term success—not only in the classroom, but also in your professional life after graduation.

THE MATH TEST

The Math section of the SAT® exam is an 80-minute test that consists of 58 questions. It is designed to test your ability to answer practical math questions with a focus on the following skills:

- Using algebraic structure
- Using tools strategically
- Modeling
- Problem solving

The Math Test focuses on the following core foundational areas: Problem Solving and Data Analysis, Heart of Algebra, Passport to Advanced Math, and Additional Topics in Math. Let's take a closer look at each of these so you'll know what to expect on test day.

Problem Solving and Data Analysis

These questions will test your quantitative literacy and ability to answer questions that require significant quantitative reasoning and analytical thinking. You'll need to be able to do the following:

- Create conceptual representations of problems and consider relevant quantitative relationships.
- Examine various objects, including their properties and appropriate units of measure.
- Effectively deploy a range of mathematical operations to arrive at the correct answers.
- Analyze data sets including identifying patterns and deviations.

SAT® Math Test questions will include both multiple-choice and student-produced response types, also known as *grid-in questions*, where choices will not be provided and you will have to insert your own solution (which we'll cover in greater depth in Chapter 4). In addition, use of a calculator will be permitted for some questions, but will not always be recommended or needed to arrive at the correct answers.

The questions you'll likely encounter from this domain will require the following skills:

- Solving percentages, units, unit conversion, and measurement questions requiring either single-step or multi-step solutions
- Identifying rates, ratios, scale, and proportional relationships
- Interpreting scenarios involving linear and exponential growth
- Interpreting scatterplots and describing the relationships between variables using quadratic, linear, and exponential models
- Analyzing key features of graphs and graphical data
- Making inferences based on sample data provided

- Using statistics to analyze spread, center, and shape and to investigate measures of center
- Calculating conditional probability and using two-way tables to summarize relative frequencies and categorical data
- Evaluating data collection methods and reports to make inferences and draw conclusions

Heart of Algebra

Foundational algebraic concepts are clearly the focus here, including mastery of linear equations and systems. You'll need to be able to do the following:

- Analyze and conceptualize linear equations and inequalities using procedural algebraic skills.
- Solve algebraic equations and systems of equations.
- Demonstrate algebraic fluency, strategic thinking, and logical reasoning towards interpreting graphical and algebraic representations.

Just like the Problem Solving and Data Analysis section, questions from this domain will include both multiple-choice and grid-in questions. Again, use of a calculator will be permitted for some questions, but will not always be recommended or needed to arrive at the correct answers.

The questions you'll likely encounter from this mathematical domain will require the following skills:

- Interpreting, creating, simplifying, and solving one-variable linear expressions and equations with rational coefficients
- Interpreting, creating, simplifying, and solving one-variable linear equalities with rational coefficients
- Developing linear functions or equations to demonstrate linear relationships between two quantities
- Interpreting, creating, and solving systems of linear equalities in two variables
- Interpreting, creating, and solving systems of two linear equations in two variables
- Utilizing core algebraic principles to solve inequalities or linear equations in one variable
- Utilizing core algebraic principles to solve two linear equations in two variables
- Analyzing and interpreting constants and variables in expressions for linear functions
- Making connections and drawing conclusions between algebraic and graphical representations

Again, these are *not* new skills that you need to quickly master between now and test day. They're skills that you've been using in your math classes all along, likely to great success. Careful practice and review will help you succeed.

SAT® Math Question Types: Multiple-Choice and Grid-ins

On the SAT® Math Test, you'll encounter two types of questions:

- **Multiple-choice:** You'll select the correct answer choice from a series of choices. The majority of questions on the SAT® Math Test are in multiple-choice format.

- **Grid-ins:** You'll solve problems and enter your answers in grids, which are provided on your answer sheet. Here's what the grid looks like:

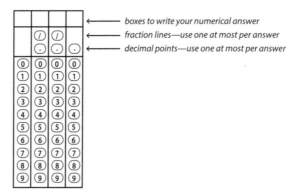

boxes to write your numerical answer

fraction lines—use one at most per answer

decimal points—use one at most per answer

Chapter 4 will cover both types of questions in greater depth—so keep reading!

Passport to Advanced Math

Some students cringe at the very notion of *advanced mathematics*. If this sounds like you, make the most of the math practice and review in this book and devote as much time as possible to prepare between now and test day.

This domain features analysis and manipulation of complex mathematical equations. It tests key skills that should be mastered before moving on to the study of advanced math concepts. You'll need to be able to do the following:

- Understand the structure of complex mathematical expressions.

- Analyze and manipulate complex mathematical expressions and deploy effective logic and reasoning skills to arrive at correct answers.

- Build and interpret functions.

Just like in the other domains, questions in this domain will include both multiple-choice and grid-in questions. Again, use of a calculator will be permitted for some questions, but will not always be recommended or needed to arrive at the correct answers.

The types of questions you'll likely encounter in this mathematical domain will require the following skills:

- Developing contextually relevant quadratic and exponential functions and equations

- Creating equivalent expressions involving rational exponents

- Determining the most suitable forms of various mathematical expressions

- Developing suitable equivalent forms of algebraic expressions

- Solving quadratic equations and one-variable equations that contain radicals or variables in fraction denominators

- Solving polynomial expressions using addition, subtraction, and multiplication

- Solving systems of linear equations and quadratic equations

- Rewriting simple rational expressions as needed using core mathematical operations

- Interpreting parts of nonlinear expressions

- Comprehending mathematical relationships between zeroes and polynomial factors and developing relevant graphs

- Understanding nonlinear relationships between variables when analyzing and interpreting graphs

- Using function notation to solve questions involving transformation and composition of functions

- Solving equations involving quantity of interest

The key to doing well on questions from this domain—and all mathematical domains on the SAT® exam—is thorough practice and review between now and test day, to make sure you're in top test-taking form!

ADDITIONAL MATH TOPICS

The designers of the SAT® exam have ensured that it covers a wide range of math concepts that relate to successful college and career readiness, including concepts in geometry and trigonometry. This domain also features both grid-in and multiple-choice questions. You'll need to be able to do the following:

- Use volume and measurement formulas to solve problems.

- Use the Pythagorean theorem and trigonometric ratios, including sine, cosine, and tangent, to determine lengths of triangle sides and angle measurements.
- Perform mathematical operations involving complex numbers.
- Make conversions between radians and degrees, use radians to determine arc length, and determine radian measure using trigonometric functions.
- Apply circle theorems to determine chord lengths, angle measures, sector areas, and arc lengths.
- Use concepts involving similarity and congruence to solve angle, triangle, and line problems.
- Understand and use knowledge of mathematical relationships between trigonometric ratios, right triangles, and similarity to solve problems.
- Use sine and cosine relationships to solve problems involving complementary angles.
- Develop and use two-variable equations to solve problems involving circles within coordinate planes.

Once again, a calculator is sometimes permitted, but not always recommended or needed.

Use your study time between now and test day—and the helpful practice and review provided in this book—to ensure that you have a firm grasp of these concepts and are ready for test-day success!

A Note About Calculators

Although the makers of the SAT® exam want to test your math skills and problem solving ability, they recognize the utility of calculators as practical tools in the real world.

Therefore, the SAT® Math Test is divided into two portions:

- **Math Test— No Calculator**
- **Math Test—Calculator**

Please note: Even when a calculator is permitted, that does not mean it's always recommended for use. Sometimes, your own problem solving abilities will help you arrive at the correct answers faster and more effectively than a calculator.

THE OPTIONAL ESSAY TEST

The optional SAT® Essay test is 50 minutes long and consists of a single essay-writing task, similar to a writing task that you'll encounter in a college-level writing course. You'll be tasked with:

- Reading a passage on a specific topic

- Explaining how effectively the author builds an argument in an effort to persuade readers regarding his or her point of view on the topic
- Using relevant contextual evidence from the passage to bolster your explanation and analysis

Your personal opinions on the topic provided will *not* affect your score, and you won't be asked to agree or disagree with a specific topic or position—only the quality of your ideas and writing matter will be evaluated. In addition, you will not be tasked with writing about a specific aspect of your personal experience.

NOTE: Although this is an optional test section, some colleges may require that you take it as part of your admissions application.

For a complete list of schools that recommend or require the SAT® Essay, visit the official College Board website: ***https://collegereadiness.collegeboard.org/sat/register/college-essay-policies***.

The Essay Prompt

The SAT® Essay prompt will ask you to read the passage provided and carefully consider how the author develops ideas and uses evidence to support his or her claims on the featured topic.

The ideas and evidence presented in the prompt include the use of relevant facts and examples, sound reasoning, and effective development of thoughts, as well as such persuasive elements as style, tone, and word choice.

Your essay will be a written response to the things you are being asked to consider within the prompt. All of the information you need to write a strong essay will be provided within the passage and prompt—no additional outside knowledge of the topic is needed.

The Essay Topics

The passage you'll encounter on test day can be based on a huge array of topic areas, so it's impossible to predict what topic you should expect to see. That said, there are some common passage elements that you can expect to see.

The passage you'll encounter will:
- Be written for a wide audience
- Articulate a specific point of view on a potentially complex subject
- Analyze ideas, trends, or debates in one or several of the following areas: arts and sciences; civic, cultural, or political life
- Utilize evidence and logical reasoning to support claims
- Always include information from published works

Your essay will be scored by two independent and experienced SAT® Essay readers, each of whom will grade your essay on a scale between 1 and 4 points in each of the following three categories:

1. **Writing:** Your essay demonstrates a well-crafted, focused, and on-target written response that addresses all aspects of the prompt and utilizes effective and appropriate elements of style, tone, word choice, and grammar.
2. **Reading:** Your essay demonstrates a thorough understanding of the passage and the connections between key details and ideas and an effective use of textual evidence.
3. **Analysis:** Your essay demonstrates a keen understanding of how the author of the passage constructed and developed his or her argument and uses sound evidence, reasoning, and other persuasive strategies to bolster claims.

REGISTERING FOR THE SAT® EXAM

Registering online for the SAT® exam is the quickest method—go to ***https://college-readiness.collegeboard.org/sat/register/online-registration-help***, follow the instructions, create a free online College Board account to get started and register, and find an appropriate testing center to meet your needs. You can also request makeup testing or get waitlisted online if you missed the registration deadline.

Visit the official SAT® website for additional information if you have special circumstances that need to be addressed or accommodated. This includes having a disability, being homeschooled, requiring a testing facility closer to home, being over 21 or under 13 years of age, or requiring Sunday testing.

If you have a special circumstance, you may need to register by mail (paper registration). Check out the College Board website for all the information you need, including deadlines: ***https://collegereadiness.collegeboard.org/sat/register/by-mail***.

REGISTRATION FEES

The fee for taking the SAT® exam without the optional Essay test is $45, which includes having your score report sent to you, your high school, and as many as four colleges of your choice. If you're taking the optional SAT® Essay test, the total fee is $57.

NOTE: You may be eligible for a fee waiver to help cover the cost of the SAT® exam. To find out if you're eligible, visit ***https://collegereadiness.collegeboard.org/sat/register/fees/fee-waivers***.

Other options and fees include:

- Additional score reports: $12
- Rush reporting of score reports: $31
- Phone registration: $15
- Changing the location or date of your test: $28

- Late registration (after the regular deadline but before the late registration deadline): $28

- Waitlist fee (if you are admitted on test day): $46

For a complete list of options and fees, visit ***https://collegereadiness.collegeboard.org/sat/register/fees***.

When and How Often Should I Take the SAT® Exam?

In the United States, the SAT® exam is given seven times a year—in October, November, December, January, March, May, and June. Select the test date that works best for you and your specific goals, and be sure to check out the registration deadlines on the official SAT® website.

It is important that you visit the official College Board website to review your complete options for taking and retaking the SAT® exam.

SCORING

Let's quickly review how the SAT® exam is scored. The exam does *not* penalize you for guessing or selecting a wrong answer. Simply put, you earn points for the questions you answer correctly. Therefore, it is important to answer *every* question on the test, even if you only guess. *Never* leave a question blank!

Your total score on the SAT® exam will be the sum of your scores on the two test sections: Evidence-Based Reading and Writing, and Math. Your score on each section will range from a low of 200 to a high of 800, with your total score ranging from 400 to a perfect 1600. If you decide to take the optional SAT® Essay, your score will not factor into your total score and will range from a low of 2 to a high of 8.

In addition, your SAT® score reports will include cross-test scores and subscores on a variety of tested categories. These subscores are designed to supply college admissions teams with additional information regarding your skills and capabilities, as well as assess your overall levels of college and career readiness.

You'll receive two **cross-test scores** based on selected questions in the Math, Reading, and Writing and Language tests (ranging from 10–40), that fall in the following two categories: **Analysis in History/Social Studies** and **Analysis in Science.** Your scores are designed to indicate your aptitude at analyzing texts and solving problems in these key subject areas.

You'll receive seven **subscores** (each ranging from 1 to 15) based on the following seven categories that fall within the test sections:

- **Math:** Problem Solving and Data Analysis, Heart of Algebra, and Passport to Advanced Math

- **Reading and Writing and Language:** Command of Evidence and Words in Context

- **Writing and Language:** Expression of Ideas and Standard English Conventions

Viewing and Reporting Your Test Scores

You'll be able to view your SAT® scores online by logging into your College Board account. After taking the test, you'll receive an e-mail when your scores are ready, with instructions for how to sign in to your online score report.

Scores are generally available for online viewing approximately three weeks after your test date and are sent to the colleges you've indicated while registering (up to four schools) around the same time. If there are additional institutions that you'd like to have your scores sent to, you can request additional reports.

We know you will be eager to find out your scores, but try to be patient when waiting for them to be posted. If you'd like additional information on rush score reporting, please visit the official College Board website.

Score Choice™ and SuperScoring

Have you heard about **Score Choice™**? If you've taken the SAT® exam multiple times, this program lets you select which scores you send to colleges (by test date), allowing you to make the best possible impression. Keep in mind that you can't select and combine section scores from one test day with section scores from another test day. In addition, some schools and scholarship programs require that you submit all of your scores.

However, some colleges allow you to take the SAT® exam multiple times and consider your best scores on each of the test sections. This is known as **superscoring,** and it may be a compelling reason to consider taking the SAT® exam more than once, especially if you did great on one test section but fell short of your perfect score goal on another.

For additional information on Score Choice™ and superscoring, visit ***https://collegereadiness.collegeboard.org/sat/scores/sending-scores/score-choice***.

For complete information regarding SAT® scoring policies and procedures, visit the official SAT® website.

GETTING READY FOR TEST DAY

We know that on test day you'll be ready to attack every SAT® exam section and question, but knowing the test day fundamentals and preparing for the big day—including selecting a test date and location, what to expect when you arrive at your test center, what to bring, and what to leave home—will help you avoid surprises, reduce anxiety, and stay ahead of the competition.

Getting ready for the SAT® exam is essential, but just as important is getting ready for what you'll encounter on exam day, so keep reading!

> 🔔 **ALERT:** For security purposes, you *must* provide an original, current, valid (unexpired), and legal photo ID in order to be admitted to the test center. A government-issued driver's license or non-driver ID, an official ID issued by your school, a passport, or a government-issued military or national identification card are acceptable examples.

CHOOSING YOUR TEST DAY AND LOCATION

When you register online or by mail, you'll be able to choose the test date and test center location that works best for you—so choose wisely! On your quest for a perfect score on the SAT® exam, be sure to choose a test date that:

- Allows you sufficient preparation time
- Is convenient for you
- Will not conflict with other activities on your schedule

The last thing you want on the day of this important exam is to be overbooked or racing around to the point of exhaustion. There are a limited number of test administrations each year, and considering just how important this test is, choose carefully and don't put it off until the last minute.

Also be sure that the location you choose to take the exam is convenient for you, and— this is important—make sure you know *precisely* how long it will take you to get to the testing center. Make a few practice runs, have a route as well as an alternate route to the test location just in case, and don't leave anything to chance. Be sure to take all possible factors into account to ensure you don't arrive late to the test center: traffic, adverse weather conditions, a detour to the gas station, etc. Showing up late for the test is not a good strategy!

Visit the official SAT® website to find the best test location for you—and register as early as possible to avoid having your preferred test location fill up before you sign up: *https://collegereadiness.collegeboard.org/sat/register/find-test-centers*.

WHAT TO EXPECT, WHAT TO BRING, AND WHAT TO LEAVE HOME

Test time starts between 8:30 a.m. and 9:00 a.m., and by this time you should be present and in your assigned seat. Plan to arrive early (doors open at 7:45 a.m.), giving you time to relax, get comfortable, and get settled into test-taking mode; you *definitely* don't want to have to deal with the stress of racing the clock to avoid missing the start of the test, and you will *not* be admitted to take the test if you arrive late.

When you arrive at your test center, the staff will check your photo ID and admissions ticket, admit you into the room, bring you to your assigned seat, and provide you with the required test materials.

Be sure to pay close attention to the test supervisor assigned to your chosen test center. He or she will be in charge of reading key test instructions and answering questions, letting you know when to start and stop each test section, when test breaks start and end (there will be one 10-minute and one five-minute break during the test), and collecting your test materials when the test is finished.

Your Test Day Checklist

Use the following helpful checklists to make sure you come to your test center appropriately prepared!

Must Haves: Make absolutely certain that you bring the following items with you on test day:

- A printed copy of your admissions ticket
- Acceptable photo ID
- Sharpened No. 2 pencils with erasers
- An approved calculator (keep reading for more information regarding acceptable calculators to bring)

Nice to Haves: Consider bringing the following optional items to help maximize your test-taking experience:

- A watch (without an alarm) to help pace yourself through each test section
- A sweater to help you adapt to the test center temperature if the room is cold
- Extra calculator batteries, in case of emergency
- A drink or snack (to have during break time only)

Don't Have: *Do not* bring the following items with you to the test room—you will absolutely not be able to use them:

- The following electronic devices: smartphone, cell phone, iPad or tablet, laptop, digital watch, camera, and any audio device and headphones
- Reading material, textbooks, reference materials (including dictionaries and other study aids), and outside notes
- Protractors, compasses, or rulers
- Extra scratch paper of any kind
- Highlighters, colored pens and pencils, or correction tape/fluid`

CALCULATORS AND THE SAT® EXAM

Here's everything you need to know about using a calculator on test day:

- You may use an approved calculator on the Math—Calculator portion of the test only.

- Calculators will not be provided to you; you must bring your own—and no sharing will be permitted.

- Bring a calculator that uses batteries, not a power cord.

- Bring any 4-function, scientific, or graphing calculator for use on test day, as long as it does not violate any of the rules listed below. Visit the official test website for a list of acceptable calculators: ***https://collegereadiness.college-board.org/sat/taking-the-test/calculator-policy***.

- You are responsible for the proper functioning of your calculator, and you are allowed to bring a spare calculator and batteries.

- If you bring or attempt to use a prohibited device on test day, you'll be dismissed from the exam and will not receive a test score.

The following calculators are *not* permitted for use on the SAT® exam:

- Any calculator with built-in or downloaded computer algebra system functionality.

- Handheld, tablet, or laptop computers, or any device that can access the Internet or has audio/recording/camera capabilites.

- Calculators built into smartphones, cell phones, or any other electronic communication devices.

- Calculators with a typewriter keypad.

- Electronic writing pads or pen-input devices.

SUMMING IT UP

- The SAT® exam consists of three main sections, each designed to measure practical skills that are essential for college and career success: **Evidence-Based Reading and Writing** (which contains both the **Reading** and **Writing and Language** tests), **Math,** and the optional **Essay,** for a total of 154 questions (155 with the Essay).

- You will have **3 hours** to complete the test (if you choose to take the SAT® Essay, add another 50 minutes).

- **The Reading Test** lasts 65 minutes and consists of 52 questions. **The Writing and Language Test** lasts 35 minutes and consists of 44 questions. **The Math Test** lasts 80 minutes and consists of 58 questions.

- Your scores on the SAT® exam will be among the most important factors that college admissions panels will use to make admissions decisions. It also gives colleges a good idea of your skills in each tested area and will help guide decisions regarding class level placement.

- The **maximum total score** you can achieve on the SAT® exam is **1600** (800 for each test section).

- The **optional SAT® Essay** is scored on a scale from 1 to 4, and the maximum score you can get is **8**, which reflects the sum of your scores from two independent essay readers.

- In addition to your total score, you'll also receive a comprehensive series of **subscores** and **cross-test scores.** You'll receive seven subscores based on the following seven domains (each ranging from 1 to 15):
  - **Math:** Problem Solving and Data Analysis, Heart of Algebra, and Passport to Advanced Math
  - **Reading and Writing and Language:** Command of Evidence and Words in Context
  - **Writing and Language:** Expression of Ideas and Standard English Conventions

- You'll receive two **cross-test scores** based on selected questions in the Math, Reading, and Writing and Language tests (ranging from 10–40), in the following two areas: **Analysis in History/Social Studies** and **Analysis in Science.**

- There is **no penalty for guessing or choosing an incorrect answer** on the SAT, so you should answer every question.

- Registering online for the SAT® exam is the quickest method—go to ***https://collegereadiness.collegeboard.org/sat/register***, follow the instructions, and create an online account to get started and register.

- Make sure you're fully aware of all applicable test fees, based on your specific testing and reporting needs.

- Choose the test date and location that works best for you, and make sure you register before the deadline.

- Make sure you have at least one, and preferably an alternate, route to your test location that will get you there with plenty of time to spare.

- Be sure to arrive at the test center well before test time; the test typically begins between 8:30 and 9:00 a.m.

- Make sure you're fully aware of what you *must bring*, *can bring*, and *cannot bring* with you on test day, as well as calculator guidelines.

- SAT® scores are generally reported to your chosen colleges and available for online viewing approximately three weeks after your test date.

- It's your responsibility to request that the College Board sends your score report to each college that you're interested in applying to; this includes the colleges you indicate while registering for the test (up to four), as well as any additional schools later on.

- Your best approach to doing well on the SAT® exam is to get plenty of practice and review between now and test day and to target your weakest areas for improvement. Use this book as your helpful guide throughout your journey to test day success!

CHAPTER 2: THE DIAGNOSTIC TEST

INTRODUCTION TO THE DIAGNOSTIC TEST

Before you begin preparing for the SAT® exam, it's important to know your strengths and the areas where you need improvement. If you find the questions easy for the Reading Test, for example, it would be a mistake to dedicate hours to practicing them. Taking the Diagnostic Test in this chapter and then working out your scores will help you determine how you should apportion your study time.

PREPARING TO TAKE THE DIAGNOSTIC TEST

If possible, take the test in one sitting. Give yourself at least 4 hours to complete the Diagnostic Test. The actual test lasts 3 hours and 50 minutes, and you'll be allowed to take two short breaks—you may even want to have some healthy snacks nearby for a quick break you'll want to take. Simulating the test this way will give you an idea of how long the sections are and how it feels to take the entire test. You will also get a sense of how long you can spend on each question in each section, so you can begin to work out a pacing schedule for yourself.

First, assemble all the things you will need to take the test:

- At least three No. 2 pencils
- A calculator with fresh batteries
- A timer
- The answer sheets and the lined paper for the essay—provided on the following pages

Set a timer for the time specified for each section, which is noted at the top of the first page of each test section. Stick to that time so you are simulating the real test. At this point, it's as important to know how many questions you can answer in the time allotted as it is to answer questions correctly.

Section 1: Reading Test

1. Ⓐ Ⓑ Ⓒ Ⓓ   12. Ⓐ Ⓑ Ⓒ Ⓓ   23. Ⓐ Ⓑ Ⓒ Ⓓ   33. Ⓐ Ⓑ Ⓒ Ⓓ   43. Ⓐ Ⓑ Ⓒ Ⓓ

2. Ⓐ Ⓑ Ⓒ Ⓓ   13. Ⓐ Ⓑ Ⓒ Ⓓ   24. Ⓐ Ⓑ Ⓒ Ⓓ   34. Ⓐ Ⓑ Ⓒ Ⓓ   44. Ⓐ Ⓑ Ⓒ Ⓓ

3. Ⓐ Ⓑ Ⓒ Ⓓ   14. Ⓐ Ⓑ Ⓒ Ⓓ   25. Ⓐ Ⓑ Ⓒ Ⓓ   35. Ⓐ Ⓑ Ⓒ Ⓓ   45. Ⓐ Ⓑ Ⓒ Ⓓ

4. Ⓐ Ⓑ Ⓒ Ⓓ   15. Ⓐ Ⓑ Ⓒ Ⓓ   26. Ⓐ Ⓑ Ⓒ Ⓓ   36. Ⓐ Ⓑ Ⓒ Ⓓ   46. Ⓐ Ⓑ Ⓒ Ⓓ

5. Ⓐ Ⓑ Ⓒ Ⓓ   16. Ⓐ Ⓑ Ⓒ Ⓓ   27. Ⓐ Ⓑ Ⓒ Ⓓ   37. Ⓐ Ⓑ Ⓒ Ⓓ   47. Ⓐ Ⓑ Ⓒ Ⓓ

6. Ⓐ Ⓑ Ⓒ Ⓓ   17. Ⓐ Ⓑ Ⓒ Ⓓ   28. Ⓐ Ⓑ Ⓒ Ⓓ   38. Ⓐ Ⓑ Ⓒ Ⓓ   48. Ⓐ Ⓑ Ⓒ Ⓓ

7. Ⓐ Ⓑ Ⓒ Ⓓ   18. Ⓐ Ⓑ Ⓒ Ⓓ   29. Ⓐ Ⓑ Ⓒ Ⓓ   39. Ⓐ Ⓑ Ⓒ Ⓓ   49. Ⓐ Ⓑ Ⓒ Ⓓ

8. Ⓐ Ⓑ Ⓒ Ⓓ   19. Ⓐ Ⓑ Ⓒ Ⓓ   30. Ⓐ Ⓑ Ⓒ Ⓓ   40. Ⓐ Ⓑ Ⓒ Ⓓ   50. Ⓐ Ⓑ Ⓒ Ⓓ

9. Ⓐ Ⓑ Ⓒ Ⓓ   20. Ⓐ Ⓑ Ⓒ Ⓓ   31. Ⓐ Ⓑ Ⓒ Ⓓ   41. Ⓐ Ⓑ Ⓒ Ⓓ   51. Ⓐ Ⓑ Ⓒ Ⓓ

10. Ⓐ Ⓑ Ⓒ Ⓓ   21. Ⓐ Ⓑ Ⓒ Ⓓ   32. Ⓐ Ⓑ Ⓒ Ⓓ   42. Ⓐ Ⓑ Ⓒ Ⓓ   52. Ⓐ Ⓑ Ⓒ Ⓓ

11. Ⓐ Ⓑ Ⓒ Ⓓ   22. Ⓐ Ⓑ Ⓒ Ⓓ

Section 2: Writing and Language Test

1. Ⓐ Ⓑ Ⓒ Ⓓ   10. Ⓐ Ⓑ Ⓒ Ⓓ   19. Ⓐ Ⓑ Ⓒ Ⓓ   28. Ⓐ Ⓑ Ⓒ Ⓓ   37. Ⓐ Ⓑ Ⓒ Ⓓ

2. Ⓐ Ⓑ Ⓒ Ⓓ   11. Ⓐ Ⓑ Ⓒ Ⓓ   20. Ⓐ Ⓑ Ⓒ Ⓓ   29. Ⓐ Ⓑ Ⓒ Ⓓ   38. Ⓐ Ⓑ Ⓒ Ⓓ

3. Ⓐ Ⓑ Ⓒ Ⓓ   12. Ⓐ Ⓑ Ⓒ Ⓓ   21. Ⓐ Ⓑ Ⓒ Ⓓ   30. Ⓐ Ⓑ Ⓒ Ⓓ   39. Ⓐ Ⓑ Ⓒ Ⓓ

4. Ⓐ Ⓑ Ⓒ Ⓓ   13. Ⓐ Ⓑ Ⓒ Ⓓ   22. Ⓐ Ⓑ Ⓒ Ⓓ   31. Ⓐ Ⓑ Ⓒ Ⓓ   40. Ⓐ Ⓑ Ⓒ Ⓓ

5. Ⓐ Ⓑ Ⓒ Ⓓ   14. Ⓐ Ⓑ Ⓒ Ⓓ   23. Ⓐ Ⓑ Ⓒ Ⓓ   32. Ⓐ Ⓑ Ⓒ Ⓓ   41. Ⓐ Ⓑ Ⓒ Ⓓ

6. Ⓐ Ⓑ Ⓒ Ⓓ   15. Ⓐ Ⓑ Ⓒ Ⓓ   24. Ⓐ Ⓑ Ⓒ Ⓓ   33. Ⓐ Ⓑ Ⓒ Ⓓ   42. Ⓐ Ⓑ Ⓒ Ⓓ

7. Ⓐ Ⓑ Ⓒ Ⓓ   16. Ⓐ Ⓑ Ⓒ Ⓓ   25. Ⓐ Ⓑ Ⓒ Ⓓ   34. Ⓐ Ⓑ Ⓒ Ⓓ   43. Ⓐ Ⓑ Ⓒ Ⓓ

8. Ⓐ Ⓑ Ⓒ Ⓓ   17. Ⓐ Ⓑ Ⓒ Ⓓ   26. Ⓐ Ⓑ Ⓒ Ⓓ   35. Ⓐ Ⓑ Ⓒ Ⓓ   44. Ⓐ Ⓑ Ⓒ Ⓓ

9. Ⓐ Ⓑ Ⓒ Ⓓ   18. Ⓐ Ⓑ Ⓒ Ⓓ   27. Ⓐ Ⓑ Ⓒ Ⓓ   36. Ⓐ Ⓑ Ⓒ Ⓓ

Section 3: Math Test—No Calculator

1. Ⓐ Ⓑ Ⓒ Ⓓ   4. Ⓐ Ⓑ Ⓒ Ⓓ   7. Ⓐ Ⓑ Ⓒ Ⓓ   10. Ⓐ Ⓑ Ⓒ Ⓓ   13. Ⓐ Ⓑ Ⓒ Ⓓ

2. Ⓐ Ⓑ Ⓒ Ⓓ   5. Ⓐ Ⓑ Ⓒ Ⓓ   8. Ⓐ Ⓑ Ⓒ Ⓓ   11. Ⓐ Ⓑ Ⓒ Ⓓ   14. Ⓐ Ⓑ Ⓒ Ⓓ

3. Ⓐ Ⓑ Ⓒ Ⓓ   6. Ⓐ Ⓑ Ⓒ Ⓓ   9. Ⓐ Ⓑ Ⓒ Ⓓ   12. Ⓐ Ⓑ Ⓒ Ⓓ   15. Ⓐ Ⓑ Ⓒ Ⓓ

Section 3: Math Test—No Calculator

16.   17.   18.   19.   20.

Section 4: Math Test—Calculator

1. (A) (B) (C) (D)   7. (A) (B) (C) (D)   13. (A) (B) (C) (D)   19. (A) (B) (C) (D)   25. (A) (B) (C) (D)

2. (A) (B) (C) (D)   8. (A) (B) (C) (D)   14. (A) (B) (C) (D)   20. (A) (B) (C) (D)   26. (A) (B) (C) (D)

3. (A) (B) (C) (D)   9. (A) (B) (C) (D)   15. (A) (B) (C) (D)   21. (A) (B) (C) (D)   27. (A) (B) (C) (D)

4. (A) (B) (C) (D)   10. (A) (B) (C) (D)   16. (A) (B) (C) (D)   22. (A) (B) (C) (D)   28. (A) (B) (C) (D)

5. (A) (B) (C) (D)   11. (A) (B) (C) (D)   17. (A) (B) (C) (D)   23. (A) (B) (C) (D)   29. (A) (B) (C) (D)

6. (A) (B) (C) (D)   12. (A) (B) (C) (D)   18. (A) (B) (C) (D)   24. (A) (B) (C) (D)   30. (A) (B) (C) (D)

31.   32.   33.   34.   35.

36.   37.   38.

Section 5: SAT® Essay

_____

_____

_____

_____

_____

_____

_____

_____

_____

_____

_____

_____

_____

_____

_____

_____

_____

_____

_____

_____

_____

_____

_____

_____

_____

_____

_____

_____

_____

Diagnostic Test—Answer Sheet

_____

_____

_____

_____

_____

_____

_____

_____

_____

_____

_____

_____

_____

_____

_____

_____

_____

_____

_____

_____

_____

_____

_____

_____

_____

_____

_____

_____

_____

_____

_____

_____

_____

_____

_____

_____

_____

Diagnostic Test—Answer Sheet

_____

_____

_____

_____

_____

_____

_____

_____

_____

_____

_____

_____

_____

_____

_____

_____

_____

_____

_____

_____

_____

_____

_____

_____

_____

_____

_____

_____

_____

SECTION 1: READING TEST

65 Minutes—52 Questions

TURN TO SECTION 1 OF YOUR ANSWER SHEET TO ANSWER THE QUESTIONS IN THIS SECTION.

DIRECTIONS: Each passage (or pair of passages) in this section is followed by a number of multiple-choice questions. After reading each passage, select the best answer to each question based on what is stated or implied in the passage or passages and in any supplementary material, such as a table, graph, chart, or photograph.

Questions 1–10 are based on the following passages and supplementary material.

Passage 1 was taken from the book A Practical Treatise on the Hive and Honey-bee, *by Rev. Lorenzo Lorraine Langstroth. L.L. Langstroth is considered by many to be the Father of American Beekeeping.* A Practical Treatise *was first published in 1857 and is still in print today.*

Passage 2 is excerpted from the article, "Honey Bee Health and Colony Collapse Disorder," provided by the Agricultural Research Service and the United States Department of Agriculture.

Passage 1

Age of Bees

The queen bee will live four, and sometimes, though very rarely, five years. As the life of the drones is usually cut short by violence, it is not easy to ascertain its precise limit. The workers are supposed to live six or seven months. Their age
Line depends, however, very much upon their greater or less exposure to injurious influ-
5 ences and severe labors. Those reared in the spring and early part of summer, and on whom the heaviest labors of the hive must necessarily devolve, do not appear to live more than two or three months, while those which are bred at the close of summer, and early in autumn, being able to spend a large part of their time in repose, attain a much greater age.

10 . . . [Bees] appear to die rather suddenly, and often spend their last days, and sometimes even their last hours, in useful labors. . . . The age which individual members of the community may attain, must not be confounded with that of the colony. Bees have been known to occupy the same domicile for a great number of years. I have seen flourishing colonies which were twenty years old. . . .

---

15   In some cases, the bees must take down and reconstruct the old combs, for if they did not, the young issuing from them would always be dwarfs . . . . That they do not always renew the old combs must be admitted, as the young from some old hives are often considerably below the average size. On this account, it is very desirable to be able to remove the old combs occasionally, that their place may be
20 supplied with new ones.

It is a great mistake to imagine that the brood combs ought to be changed every year. In my hives, they might, if it were desirable, be easily changed several times in a year; but once in five or six years is often enough; oftener than this requires a needless consumption of honey to replace them, besides being for other
25 reasons undesirable. . . .

Passage 2

Honey Bee Health and Colony Collapse Disorder

Honey bees, which are a critical link in U.S. agriculture, have been under serious pressure from a mystery problem: Colony Collapse Disorder (CCD), which is defined as a dead colony with no adult bees or dead bee bodies but with a live
Line queen and usually honey and immature bees still present. No scientific cause for
5 CCD has been proven.

But CCD is far from the only risk to the health of honey bees and the economic stability of commercial beekeeping and pollination operations in the United States. Since the 1980s, honey bees and beekeepers have had to deal with a host of new pathogens from deformed wing virus to nosema fungi, new parasites, pests like
10 small hive beetles, nutrition problems from lack of diversity or availability in pollen and nectar sources, and possible sublethal effects of pesticides. These problems, many of which honey bees might be able to survive if each were the only one, are often hitting in a wide variety of combinations and weakening and killing honey bee colonies. CCD may even be a result of a combination of two or more of these
15 factors and not necessarily the same factors in the same order in every instance.

Why Should the Public Care About What Happens to Honey Bees?

Bee pollination is responsible for more than $15 billion in increased crop value each year. . . . Commercial production of many specialty crops like almonds and other tree nuts, berries, fruits, and vegetables depend on pollination by honey bees. Almonds are completely dependent on honey bees for pollination.

20   The total number of managed honey bee colonies has decreased from 5 million in the 1940s to only 2.5 million today. At the same time, the call for hives to provide pollination services has continued to increase. This means honey bee colonies are being transported over longer distances than ever before.

Colony losses from CCD are a very serious problem for beekeepers. If losses
25 continue, it could threaten the economic viability of the bee pollination industry.
Honey bees would not disappear entirely, but the cost of honey bee pollination
services would rise, and those increased costs would ultimately be passed on to
consumers through higher food costs.

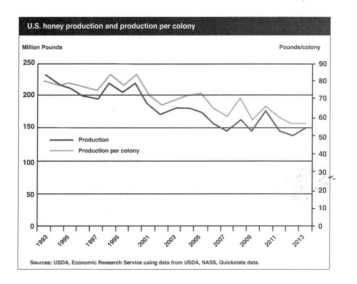

U.S. honey production and production per colony

Sources: USDA, Economic Research Service using data from USDA, NASS, Quickstats data.

---

1 What is the main idea of Passage 2?

A. Honey bees are dying and no one knows why.

B. Bees are an important part of our agricultural system.

C. CCD is a problem for beekeepers.

D. Bee colony collapse affects agriculture, food, and economics.

2 What is the distinction Langstroth makes between individual bees and colonies?

A. The queen bee is an individual that lives for several years in the same colony.

B. Individual bees live for only a short time, but their colonies are maintained for many generations.

C. The honeycombs are produced by the thousands of individual worker bees in a colony.

D. Bee colonies can't support all the individual worker bees, so they die within a few months.

3 Why are some bees in a colony undersized?

A. Bees hatched in old combs are smaller.

B. Bees hatched in the summer are smaller even though they live longer.

C. Bees affected by fungus infections are smaller.

D. Bees affected by nutritional problems are smaller.

4 How are the two passages different in their perspectives about bees?

A. Both discuss bee colonies, but only Passage 1 is concerned about the death of bees.

B. Passage 1 is concerned only about individual bees; Passage 2 describes concerns about the colonies.

C. Both passages discuss bee colonies, but only Passage 1 is focused on the bee population.

D. Passage 1 is written from personal observations; Passage 2 is a report of research about commercial bees.

5 What is the difference in tone between the two passages?

A. Passage 1 is cheerful but uninformative, and Passage 2 is pessimistic but informative.

B. Passage 1 is condescending but funny; Passage 2 is neutral.

C. Passage 1 is personal but matter of fact; Passage 2 is impersonal but worried.

D. Passage 1 is warm but angry, and Passage 2 shows no emotion.

6 According to Passage 1, how often should the combs be replaced?

A. Every six months

B. Several times per year

C. Every few years

D. Never

7 Which choice provides the best evidence for the answer to the previous question?

A. Lines 15–16 ("In some cases, ... always be dwarfs.")

B. Lines 18–20 ("it is very desirable ... new ones.")

C. Lines 21–22 ("It is a great mistake ... every year.")

D. Lines 22–25 ("In my hives, ... for other reasons undesirable.")

8 As used in line 11 of Passage 2, "sublethal" most nearly means

A. less than deadly.

B. not obvious.

C. secondary.

D. under the skin.

9 As used in line 9 of Passage 1, "repose" most nearly means

A. at peace.

B. hidden.

C. at rest.

D. undisturbed.

10 Based on the information from the passage and the graph, which of the following statements can reasonably be inferred?

A. Production per colony determines the level of total U.S. honey production.

B. Honey production in the United States will continue to decrease.

C. The greater the number of bees in the United States, the greater the amount of honey the United States produces.

D. If output per colony is low, increasing the number of colonies would increase overall output.

Questions 11–21 are based on the following passage.

At the beginning of the U.S. Civil War, Canadian-born Sarah Emma Evelyn Edmonds disguised herself as a man and enlisted in the Union army, where she served as a male field nurse. In this excerpt from her book, Nurse and Spy: Thrilling Story of the Adventures of a Woman Who Served as a Union Soldier, *she has "disguised" herself as an Irish female peddler, selling pastries to the army as she crossed enemy lines in order to spy on the Confederacy.*

With no medicine, no food, and consequently little strength, I was nearly in a state of starvation. My pies and cakes were spoiled in the basket, in consequence of the drenching they had received in crossing the river, and now I had no means
Line of procuring more. But something must be done; I could not bear the thought
5 of thus starving to death in that inglorious manner; better die upon the scaffold at Richmond, or be shot by the rebel pickets; anything but this. So I thought and said, as I rallied all my remaining strength to arrange my toilette preparatory to emerging from my concealment in the swamp.

It was about nine o'clock in the morning of the third day after crossing the
10 river, when I started, as I thought, towards the enemy's lines, … I traveled from that time until five o'clock in the afternoon, and was then deeper in the swamp than when I started. My head or brain was completely turned. I knew not which way to go, nor did I know east from west, or north from south.

It was a dark day in every sense of the word—and I had neither sun nor
15 compass to guide me. At five o'clock the glorious booming of cannon reverberated through the dense wilderness, and to me, at that hour, it was the sweetest and most soul-inspiring music that ever greeted my ear. I now turned my face in the direction of the scene of action, and was not long in extricating myself from the desert which had so long enveloped me.

20 Soon after emerging from the swamp I saw, in the distance, a small white house, and thither I bent my weary footsteps. I found it deserted, with the exception of a sick rebel soldier, who lay upon a straw-tick on the floor in a helpless condition. I went to him, and assuming the Irish brogue, I inquired how he came to be left alone, and if I could render him any assistance. He could only speak in a

25 low whisper, and with much difficulty, said he had been ill with typhoid fever a few weeks before, and had not fully recovered when General Stoneman attacked the rebels in the vicinity of Coal Harbor, and he was ordered to join his company. He participated in a sharp skirmish, in which the rebels were obliged to retreat; but he fell out by the way, and fearing to fall into the hands of the Yankees, he had crawled
30 along as best he could, sometimes on his hands and knees, until he reached the house.

He had not eaten anything since leaving camp, and he was truly in a starving condition. … exhausted as I was, I soon kindled a fire, and in less than fifteen minutes a large hoe-cake was before it in process of baking, and a sauce-pan of
35 water heating. … After searching about the premises, I found some tea packed away in a small basket, … My cake being cooked, and tea made, I fed the poor famished rebel as tenderly as if he had been my brother, and he seemed as grateful for my kindness, and thanked me with much politeness, as if I had been Mrs. Jeff Davis. …

40 After making my toilet and adjusting my wig in the most approved Irish style, I approached the sick man. … He was a man about thirty years of age, was tall and had a slight figure, regular features, dark hair and large, mournful, hazel eyes; altogether he was a very pleasing and intelligent looking man. … if I had had nothing more important to attend to, I should have enjoyed the privilege of caring for him
45 until he recovered. It is strange how sickness and disease disarm our antipathy and remove our prejudices.

There lay before me an enemy to the Government for which I was daily and willingly exposing my life and suffering unspeakable privation … and yet … I did not feel the least resentment, or entertain an unkind thought toward him personally,
50 but looked upon him only as an unfortunate, suffering man, whose sad condition called forth the best feelings of my nature, and I longed to restore him to health and strength; not considering that the very health and strength which I wished to secure for him would be employed against the cause which I had espoused.

11 What is Edmonds' relationship to the rebel soldier?

A. They are enemies.

B. They are old friends.

C. They are fellow travelers.

D. They are fellow soldiers.

12 What does her treatment of the soldier indicate about her character?

A. She is kind and caring.

B. She is fearful and obedient.

C. She is strong and willful.

D. She is patriotic and loyal.

13 Which of the following is the best description of the theme of the excerpt?

   A. War is terrible and causes pain and suffering on both sides.

   B. Prejudices are learned but can be overcome.

   C. War divides people and makes them enemies.

   D. People find humanity even in the midst of the horrors of war.

14 What was Edmonds's point of view about the Civil War?

   A. She was conflicted about it, because it inflicted such hardship on everyone.

   B. She thought it was a cause worth fighting for.

   C. She thought that wars were useless and not worth the pain and suffering.

   D. She thought it was destructive and pointless.

15 Why does Edmonds disguise herself as an Irish peddler?

   A. She liked to cook and wanted to sell her baked goods to hungry soldiers.

   B. She wanted to be recognizable as a woman for protection.

   C. She wanted to penetrate enemy lines without being suspected of being a Union soldier.

   D. It made her more identifiable as a Union spy.

16 Why does Edmonds refer to the sound of gunfire as "the sweetest and most soul-inspiring music"?

   A. It reinforced her love of being a soldier.

   B. She had been lost, and the gunfire indicated that she would be able to find her way.

   C. It meant that she would be able to get through enemy lines.

   D. She could follow it to spy on the rebels and find out what they were doing.

17 How does Edmonds create a mood of calm in the face of pending doom?

   A. Although she is fearful, her empathy toward the soldier overrides her fear.

   B. She advocates strength and courage in the face of danger.

   C. Her tone is matter of fact and steady as she relates her dire situation.

   D. She uses words that show empathy and show her to be a kind person.

18 Which choice provides the best evidence for the answer to the previous question?

   A. Lines 1–2 ("I was nearly in a state of starvation.")

   B. Lines 12–13 ("My head or brain … north from south.")

   C. Line 14 ("It was a dark day in every sense of the word.")

   D. Lines 40–41 ("After making my toilet … the sick man.")

19 Based on the context of the passage, we can infer that Mrs. Jeff Davis is

- **A.** Edmonds's married name.
- **B.** the soldier's mother.
- **C.** Edmonds's nursing mentor.
- **D.** the wife of a prominent Confederate official.

20 What does Edmonds mean when she says she did not want to die in "that inglorious manner" (line 5)?

- **A.** Death by starvation would be humiliating compared to death in battle.
- **B.** Starving to death would be respectable.
- **C.** Hanging would be a less painful death than starvation.
- **D.** Being shot in battle would make a better narrative.

21 As used in line 45, "antipathy" most nearly means

- **A.** fearfulness.
- **B.** animosity.
- **C.** good will.
- **D.** sympathy.

Questions 22–32 are based on the following passage and supplementary material.

This passage is excerpted from The Extermination of the American Bison *(1887) by William T. Hornaday. A taxidermist, Hornaday worked for the United States National Museum (now the Smithsonian Institution) where he took a census of the American bison (buffalo). He became alarmed at the extent of the vanishing herds, prompting his advocacy of conservation practices. Over his lifetime, Hornaday helped reintroduce and establish nine new bison herds, through the American Bison Society. He also tirelessly lobbied for new and better wildlife protection laws.*

     The causes which led to the practical extinction (in a wild state, at least) of the most economically valuable wild animal that ever inhabited the American continent, are by no means obscure. …

Line
5   The disappearance of the buffalo from all the country east of the Mississippi was one of the inevitable results of the advance of civilization. To the early pioneers who went forth into the wilderness to wrestle with nature for the necessities of life, this valuable animal might well have seemed a gift direct from the hand of Providence. During the first few years of the early settler's life in a new country, the few domestic animals he had brought with him were far too valuable to be killed
10 for food, and for a long period he looked to the wild animals of the forest and the prairie for his daily supply of meat. The time was when no one stopped to think of the important part our game animals played in the settlement of this country, and

even now no one has attempted to calculate the lessened degree of rapidity with which the star of empire would have taken its westward way without the bison,
15 deer, elk, and antelope. The Western States and Territories pay little heed to the wanton slaughter of deer and elk now going on in their forests, but the time will soon come when the "grangers" will enter those regions and find the absence of game a very serious matter.

Although the bison was the first wild species to disappear before the advance
20 of civilization, he served a good purpose at a highly critical period. His huge bulk of toothsome flesh fed many a hungry family, and his ample robe did good service in the settler's cabin and sleigh in winter weather. By the time game animals had become scarce, domestic herds and flocks had taken their place, and hunting became a pastime instead of a necessity.

25 As might be expected, from the time the bison was first seen by white men he has always been a conspicuous prize, and being the largest of the land quad-rupeds, was naturally the first to disappear. Every man's hand has been against him. While his disappearance from the eastern United States was, in the main, due to the settler who killed game as a means of subsistence, there were a few who made
30 the killing of those animals a regular business. This occurred almost exclusively in the immediate vicinity of salt springs, around which the bison congregated in great numbers, and made their wholesale slaughter of easy accomplishment. …

The disappearance of the bison from the eastern United States was due to its consumption as food. It was very gradual, like the march of civilization, and,
35 under the circumstances, absolutely inevitable. In a country so thickly peopled as this region speedily became, the mastodon* could have survived extinction about as easily as the bison. Except when the latter became the victim of wholesale slaughter, there was little reason to bemoan his fate, save upon grounds that may be regarded purely … sentimental. He served a most excellent purpose in the
40 development of the country.

The extirpation of the bison west of the Rocky Mountains was due to legitimate hunting for food and clothing rather than for marketable peltries. In no part of that whole region was the species ever numerous, although in the mountains them-selves, notably Colorado, within each reach of the great prairies on the east, vast
45 numbers were seen by the early explorers and pioneers. But to the westward, away from the mountains, they were very rarely met with, and their total destruction in that region was a matter of easy accomplishment.

There is reason to fear that unless the United States Government takes the matter in hand and makes a special effort to prevent it, the pure-blood bison will
50 be lost irretrievably through mixture with domestic breeds and through in-and-in breeding. … [I]t is clearly the duty of our Government to act in this matter, and act promptly, with a degree of liberality and promptness which can not be otherwise

than highly gratifying to every American citizen and every friend of science throughout the world.

* An animal that was related to the mammoth and that lived in ancient times

Map of the extermination of the American Bison to 1889

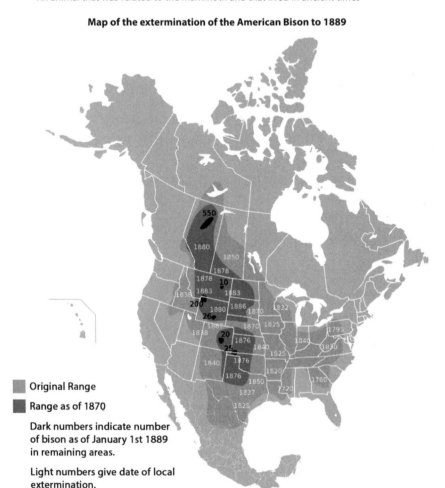

Original Range

Range as of 1870

Dark numbers indicate number of bison as of January 1st 1889 in remaining areas.

Light numbers give date of local extermination.

This map was adapted from a drawing by William Temple Hornaday in "Geographisches Handbuch zu Andrees Handatlas, Vierte Auflage, Bielefeld und Leipzig, Velhagen und Klasing, 1902."

22 What did Hornaday think about the disappearance of the bison?

   A. It was an inevitable by-product of the advancement of civilization.

   B. Its cause was baffling to him.

   C. It rid the continent of a dangerous pest.

   D. It was a minor problem with few consequences.

23 Why was Hornaday worried about the diminishing of game animals?

   A. He was concerned that they would become extinct.

   B. As a conservationist, he did not believe in hunting.

   C. He was concerned that settlers would be deprived of their only food source.

   D. As a conservationist, he wanted to study the similarities between bison and mastodons.

24 Which choice provides the best evidence for the answer to the previous question?

   A. Lines 5–8 ("To the early pioneers … hand of Providence.")

   B. Lines 35–37 ("In a … the bison.")

   C. Lines 41–42 ("The extirpation of the bison … marketable peltries.")

   D. Lines 48–50 ("There is reason to … lost irretrievably …")

25 Based on the map, how long did it take for the bison range in North America to be nearly eliminated?

   A. A quarter century

   B. A half century

   C. About a century

   D. A little over a century and a half

26 Which statement is the best description of the main idea of the excerpt?

   A. The government should outlaw bison hunting, except west of the Rocky Mountains.

   B. Bison are no longer important in America, having served their purpose in providing for settlers of the West.

   C. Bison understandably disappeared as the West developed, but the government should now intervene to prevent their complete extinction.

   D. People regret the slaughter of wild animals for sport.

27 Which of the following statements best represents Hornaday's view about bison?

   A. They should be preserved so that they don't become extinct.

   B. They can be hunted out of necessity, but should not be viewed as a prize.

   C. The government should intervene to help stem the tide of their disappearance.

   D. All of the above

28 Which is the most likely reason Hornaday would support the Endangered Species Act (1973), which protects endangered species and their habitats?

A. He was a taxidermist.

B. He did not condone hunting.

C. He thought the development of the West caused the disappearance of bison.

D. He was concerned about the extinction of wild animals.

29 Which choice provides the best evidence for the answer to the previous question?

A. Lines 1–3 ("The causes ...no means obscure. ...")

B. Lines 33–40 ("The disappearance of the ... development of the country.")

C. Lines 41–47 ("The extirpation of the bison ... a matter of easy accomplishment.")

D. Lines 48–54 ("There is reason to ... throughout the world.")

30 Why were bison so important in the development of the United States?

A. The bison was a particularly handsome quadruped and looked good on state flags.

B. The bison's large size made for excellent trophy hunting.

C. The bison's food and pelts were very useful at a crucial time for Western settlers.

D. The bison was more plentiful and more attractive than the elk.

31 As used in line 16, "wanton" most nearly means

A. uncontrolled.

B. unwelcome.

C. unsafe.

D. unpleasant.

32 As used in line 38, "bemoan" most nearly means

A. contest.

B. rejoice.

C. rue.

D. complain about.

Questions 33–42 are based on the following passage.

This passage was excerpted from 20,000 Leagues Under the Sea, *by the French author Jules Verne (1828–1905). Verne wrote science adventure stories that were among the first to be cast as science fiction. This book (1873) tells the story of three men whose ship is damaged when they find and attack the sea monster (whale) they had been looking for. In the upheaval, they mysteriously find themselves inside a submarine headed by Captain Nemo, an odd fellow who tells them that the existence of the submarine must remain a secret. He therefore can never let them leave, but they will all go on a voyage under the world's seas. Pierre Aronnax is a marine biologist and narrates the story. Conseil (French for counsel) is Aronnax's servant.*

The next day, the 22nd of March, at six in the morning, preparations for departure were begun. The last gleams of twilight were melting into night. The

cold was great, the constellations shone with wonderful intensity. In the zenith
Line glittered that wondrous Southern Cross—the polar bear of Antarctic regions. The
5 thermometer showed 120 below zero, and when the wind freshened it was most
biting. Flakes of ice increased on the open water. The sea seemed everywhere alike.
Numerous blackish patches spread on the surface, showing the formation of fresh
ice. Evidently the southern basin, frozen during the six winter months, was absolutely inaccessible. What became of the whales in that time? Doubtless they went
10 beneath the icebergs, seeking more practicable seas. As to the seals and morses
[walrus], accustomed to live in a hard climate, they remained on these icy shores.
These creatures have the instinct to break holes in the ice-field and to keep them
open. To these holes they come for breath; when the birds, driven away by the
cold, have emigrated to the north, these sea mammals remain sole masters of the
15 polar continent. But the reservoirs were filling with water, and the *Nautilus* was
slowly descending. At 1,000 feet deep it stopped; its screw beat the waves, and it
advanced straight towards the north at a speed of fifteen miles an hour. Towards
night it was already floating under the immense body of the iceberg. At three in
the morning I was awakened by a violent shock. I sat up in my bed and listened in
20 the darkness, when I was thrown into the middle of the room. The *Nautilus*, after
having struck, had rebounded violently. I groped along the partition, and by the
staircase to the saloon, which was lit by the luminous ceiling. The furniture was
upset. Fortunately the windows were firmly set, and had held fast. The pictures on
the starboard side, from being no longer vertical, were clinging to the paper, whilst
25 those of the port side were hanging at least a foot from the wall. The *Nautilus* was
lying on its starboard side perfectly motionless. I heard footsteps, and a confusion
of voices; but Captain Nemo did not appear. As I was leaving the saloon, Ned Land
and Conseil entered.

"What is the matter?" said I, at once.

30 "I came to ask you, sir," replied Conseil.

"Confound it!" exclaimed the Canadian, "I know well enough! The *Nautilus* has
struck; and, judging by the way she lies, I do not think she will right herself as she
did the first time in Torres Straits."

"But," I asked, "has she at least come to the surface of the sea?"

35 "We do not know," said Conseil.

"It is easy to decide," I answered. I consulted the manometer [pressure gauge].
To my great surprise, it showed a depth of more than 180 fathoms. "What does that
mean?" I exclaimed.

"We must ask Captain Nemo," said Conseil.

40 "But where shall we find him?" said Ned Land.

"Follow me," said I, to my companions.

We left the saloon. There was no one in the library. At the centre staircase, by the berths of the ship's crew, there was no one. I thought that Captain Nemo must be in the pilot's cage. It was best to wait. We all returned to the saloon. For twenty
45 minutes we remained thus, trying to hear the slightest noise which might be made on board the *Nautilus*, when Captain Nemo entered. He seemed not to see us; his face, generally so impassive, showed signs of uneasiness. He watched the compass silently, then the manometer; and, going to the planisphere [instrument for charting the stars], placed his finger on a spot representing the southern seas.
50 I would not interrupt him; but, some minutes later, when he turned towards me, I said, using one of his own expressions in the Torres Straits:

"An incident, Captain?"

"No, sir; an accident this time."

"Serious?"

55 "Perhaps."

"Is the danger immediate?"

"No."

"The *Nautilus* has stranded?"

"Yes."

60 "And this has happened—how?"

"From a caprice of nature, not from the ignorance of man. Not a mistake has been made in the working. But we cannot prevent equilibrium from producing its effects. We may brave human laws, but we cannot resist natural ones."

---

33 Which of the following is the best example of why the novel is science fiction?

A. The temperature was 120 degrees below zero.

B. After being hit, the ship lay still on its right (starboard) side.

C. The *Nautilus* traveled 1,000 feet below the ocean surface.

D. The men on board lived comfortably on the ship.

34 Which detail makes the story believable even though it is science fiction?

A. Charting direction by the stars

B. The fact that the submarine is secret

C. The circumstances by which they ended up aboard *Nautilus*

D. Descriptions of monsters in the sea

---

35 What is the best description of the mood of the story?

  A. Whimsical

  B. Foreboding

  C. Festive

  D. Mournful

36 Which of the following statements best describes the submarine?

  A. It was large, with several levels and rooms, including a library.

  B. It was small, with cramped quarters where everyone slept.

  C. It had large picture windows so the men could see under the surface of the ocean.

  D. It was large but felt cramped because there were no windows.

37 How does Nemo explain the cause of the submarine hitting something?

  A. Human error

  B. God's will

  C. Rough seas

  D. Natural laws of the universe

38 What does Nemo mean when he identifies this event as an accident as opposed to an incident (lines 52–53):

  A. This situation is more serious than a previous situation.

  B. Accidents are caused by nature, but incidents are not.

  C. The *Nautilus* is in immediate danger.

  D. The ship is stranded because of careless work.

39 The passage indicates that the *Nautilus* is currently

  A. in the Torres Strait.

  B. off the coast of Indonesia.

  C. somewhere near Antarctica.

  D. at the North Pole.

40 Which choice provides the best evidence for the answer to the previous question?

  A. Lines 16–18 ("At 1,000 feet … body of the iceberg.")

  B. Line 25–26 ("The *Nautilus* … perfectly motionless.")

  C. Lines 31–33 ("The *Nautilus* has struck… in Torres Straits.")

  D. Lines 47–49 ("He watched the compass silently, … the southern seas.")

41 As used in line 43, "berths" refer to a

  A. sleeping place.

  B. beginning of something new.

  C. kind of family.

  D. docking space for a ship.

42 As used in line 61, "caprice" most nearly means

  A. freakishness.

  B. inspiration.

  C. a steady hand.

  D. unpredictable change.

Questions 43–52 are based on the following passage.

When John F. Kennedy (1917–1963) took office in 1961, the country was in the midst of the Cold War, heavily competing with the Soviet Union in a race to dominate space. The Soviets had already succeeded in being first to send a man into space, but President Kennedy made it clear that the United States would be the leader. He took his proposal to Congress, vowing that before the end of the decade, the country would send a man to the moon and back. To many people at the time, the proposal seemed like science fiction. Killed by an assassin, the president did not live to see the country reach his goal.

Address at Rice University on the Nation's Space Effort

Delivered by President Kennedy on September 12, 1962, in Houston, Texas.

… Despite the striking fact that most of the scientists that the world has ever known are alive and working today, despite the fact that this Nation's own scientific manpower is doubling every 12 years in a rate of growth more than three times that *Line* of our population as a whole, despite that, the vast stretches of the unknown and
5 the unanswered and the unfinished still far outstrip our collective comprehension.

No man can fully grasp how far and how fast we have come, but condense, if you will, the 50 thousand years of man's recorded history in a time span of but a half-century. Stated in these terms, we know very little about the first 40 years, except at the end of them advanced man had learned to use the skins of animals to
10 cover [him]. Then about 10 years ago, under this standard, man emerged from his caves to construct other kinds of shelter. Only five years ago man learned to write and use a cart with wheels. Christianity began less than two years ago. The printing press came this year, and then less than two months ago, during this whole 50-year span of human history, the steam engine provided a new source of power.

15 Newton explored the meaning of gravity. Last month electric lights and telephones and automobiles and airplanes became available. Only last week did we develop penicillin and television and nuclear power, and now if America's new spacecraft succeeds in reaching Venus, we will have literally reached the stars before midnight tonight.

20 This is a breathtaking pace, and such a pace cannot help but create new ills as it dispels old, new ignorance, new problems, new dangers. Surely the opening vistas of space promise high costs and hardships, as well as high reward. …

We set sail on this new sea because there is new knowledge to be gained, and new rights to be won, and they must be won and used for the progress of
25 all people. For space science, like nuclear science and all technology, has no conscience of its own. Whether it will become a force for good or ill depends on man, and only if the United States occupies a position of pre-eminence can we help decide whether this new ocean will be a sea of peace or a new terrifying theater of war. I do not say that we should or will go unprotected against the hostile misuse of
30 space any more than we go unprotected against the hostile use of land or sea, but

I do say that space can be explored and mastered without feeding the fires of war, without repeating the mistakes that man has made in extending his writ around this globe of ours. ...

35   We choose to go to the moon. We choose to go to the moon ... (interrupted by applause) we choose to go to the moon in this decade and do the other things, not because they are easy, but because they are hard, because that goal will serve to organize and measure the best of our energies and skills, because that challenge is one that we are willing to accept, one we are unwilling to postpone, and one which we intend to win, and the others, too.

40   It is for these reasons that I regard the decision last year to shift our efforts in space from low to high gear as among the most important decisions that will be made during my incumbency in the office of the Presidency.

---

43 What is the most likely reason that Kennedy gave this speech?

A. To introduce the space program to the public

B. To warn the public of Soviet space aggression

C. To tell Congress to fund science and math

D. To connect the inspiring nature of space advancement with the interests of peace

---

44 Which of the following best represents the theme of the speech?

A. Science is moving at a very fast pace, and the United States is falling behind the Soviet Union.

B. The United States has the capacity to put a man on the moon and become the world leader in the new frontier of space exploration.

C. New scientific investigation of space exploration is the most important issue of our time.

D. We must put a man on the moon within the next decade.

45 Why does Kennedy talk about condensing time in paragraphs 2 and 3?

A. To show how science has advanced civilization throughout human history, and that landing a man on the moon will continue on that same path

B. To remind people that the most progress has been made in the most recent years of human civilization

C. To compare progress now with progress in the past

D. To illustrate what a time capsule can do when applied to science

---

46 Why did President Kennedy think the United States could meet what seemed like an impossible goal?

- **A.** He believed American scientist were better than Russian scientists.
- **B.** He thought that if all of the scientists in the United States worked together, they could beat the Soviet Union to the moon.
- **C.** He believed the growth of our scientific community and the natural quest for exploration of the unknown would lead to success.
- **D.** He thought the United States had the best conscience for nuclear science.

47 What argument does Kennedy use to support the idea that the space program for a moon landing will determine the future of the United States?

- **A.** The rapid increase in American scientists working toward a moon that landing will overwhelm the Soviet threat.
- **B.** Pure science has no loyalty to nations so whoever finds a solution first will emerge the new world leader.
- **C.** The United States will win the Cold War because Americans have always been bound by hard work.
- **D.** The United States has to be number one in order to determine whether space exploration will proceed peacefully or involve wars.

48 What is the effect of the use of repetition of specific words and phrases in Kennedy's speech?

- **A.** It ensures that the public understands his points.
- **B.** It emphasizes his ideas and helps inspire the audience.
- **C.** It proves that he knows the subject.
- **D.** It shows that idioms are useful for communicating important ideas.

49 Which line indicates that Kennedy wanted to make space the "new frontier"?

- **A.** Lines 6–8 ("No man ... a half-century.")
- **B.** Lines 23–25 ("We set ... all people.")
- **C.** Lines 26–29 ("Whether it ... of war.")
- **D.** Lines 34–39 ("We choose ... others, too.")

50 Which of the following shows that Kennedy thinks space travel is a high priority for the country?

- **A.** Lines 20–21 ("This is ... new dangers.")
- **B.** Lines 23–25 ("We set ... all people.")
- **C.** Lines 26–29 ("Whether it ... of war.")
- **D.** Lines 34–39 ("We choose ... others, too.")

51 As used in line 28, "theater" refers to

A. a place where dramas are performed.

B. a room for assemblies of people for a specific purpose.

C. a place where war games are played.

D. an area where battles take place.

52 As used in line 32, "writ" refers to

A. legal influence.

B. written documents.

C. power or authority granted by a written document.

D. written permission.

STOP

If you finish before time is called, you may check your work on this section only.
Do not turn to any other section.

SECTION 2: WRITING AND LANGUAGE TEST

35 Minutes—44 Questions

TURN TO SECTION 2 OF YOUR ANSWER SHEET TO ANSWER THE QUESTIONS IN THIS SECTION.

DIRECTIONS: Each passage below is accompanied by a number of questions. For some questions, you will consider how the passage might be revised to improve the expression of ideas. For other questions, you will consider how the passage might be edited to correct errors in sentence structure, usage, or punctuation. A passage or a question may be accompanied by one or more graphics (such as a table or graph) that you will consider as you make revising and editing decisions.

Some questions will direct you to an underlined portion of a passage. Other questions will direct you to a location in a passage or ask you to think about the passage as a whole.

After reading each passage, choose the answer to each question that most effectively improves the quality of writing in the passage or that makes the passage conform to the conventions of standard written English. Many questions include a "NO CHANGE" option. Choose that option if you think the best choice is to leave the relevant portion of the passage as it is.

Questions 1–11 are based on the following passage.

Industrial-Organizational Psychologists

In January 2014, the US Department of Labor released a list of the fastest-growing jobs in America. The results are somewhat surprising. Topping the list, with a projected growth rate over the next ten years of 53%, are industrial-organizational psychologists. **1** While the projected growth rate is somewhat misleading there are only about 160,000 industrial-organizational psychologists currently practicing in the United States the fact that the career field is expected to double over the next decade warrants some study of what the field entails.

According to the American Psychological Association, industrial-organizational psychology (I/O Psychology for short) is "the scientific study of human behavior in organizations and the work place." **2** The Society for Industrial and Organizational Psychology (SIOP) further defines this field as "the scientific study of working and the application of that science to workplace issues facing individuals, teams, and organizations." I/O psychologists help corporations and organizations make human resource decisions, engage employees, and increase overall work efficiency. The companies they work for often give I/O psychologists nice offices so people feel comfortable talking with them. **3**

---

4 Psychologists working in this field may screen company recruits, develop on-the-job training and development programs, conduct employee engagement surveys, provide performance feedback to employees, create coaching programs, help corporations with diversity training, and devise employee retention programs. **5** Companies such as Sara Lee, Merck, and the company Land O' Lakes employ and hire I/O psychologists to lead **6** their human resource departments. Says the SIOP, "Just as finance advises organizations how to maximize their financial **7** capitol, I/O psychologists teach organizations how to maximize their human assets." In the competitive world of corporate America, this can be a strategic advantage.

8 Furthermore, before rushing out in pursuit of a highly lucrative I/O psychologist position, potential candidates should consider the following information. First, while the average I/O psychologist makes an average $83,000 per year, qualified candidates for an I/O position must obtain a minimum of a master's degree in psychology. Many practicing I/O psychologists have a Ph.D. in the field. With costs of higher education rising, pursuing an advanced degree can be **9** rewarding.

Also, with greater demand comes greater supply. **10** Positions will be highly competitive and more and more candidates enter the field of I/O psychology. Compounding matters further, I/O psychology professor Rob Sitzer notes on the APA website that "This field has expanded so much in recent years that people from other fields, including MBA's and organizational development specialists, have also started moving into these work areas."

As competition for I/O psychology positions **11** intensify within the corporate arena, potential candidates must evaluate whether the cost of education is worth the gamble involved in landing a job.

1 **A.** NO CHANGE

B. While the projected growth rate is somewhat misleading there are only about (160,000) industrial-organizational psychologists currently practicing in the United States, the fact that the career field is expected to double over the next decade warrants some study of what the field entails.

C. While the projected growth rate is somewhat misleading, there are only about 160,000 industrial-organizational psychologists currently practicing in the United States; the fact that the career field is expected to double over the next decade warrants some study of what the field entails.

D. While the projected growth rate is somewhat misleading, there are only about 160,000 industrial-organizational psychologists—currently practicing in the United States —the fact that the career field is expected to double over the next decade warrants some study of what the field entails.

2 The writer is considering deleting the underlined sentence. Should the writer do this?

A. Yes, because it introduces a new idea that does not support the purpose of the paragraph.

B. Yes, because it repeats information that has already been provided.

C. No, because it provides relevant information that builds on the previous sentence.

D. No, because it establishes the main topic of the paragraph.

3 In order to improve cohesion and focus, the author is thinking about deleting the last sentence of this paragraph. Is this a good choice?

A. Yes, because it introduces a tangential detail that detracts from the focus of the paragraph.

B. Yes, because it is illogical and contradicts the previous sentence.

C. No, because it sets up the first sentence of the following paragraph.

D. No, because it is crucial to the main topic of the paragraph.

4 Which choice provides the most logical introduction to the sentence?

A. NO CHANGE

B. Child psychologists are hired to

C. Some of the jobs human resources people do is

D. Sara Lee hires psychologists to

5 **A.** NO CHANGE

B. Companies such as Sara Lee, Merck, and Land O' Lakes employ I/O psychologists

C. Companies such as Sara Lee, Merck, and Land O' Lakes employ and give jobs to I/O psychologists

D. Companies such as Sara Lee, Merck, and the company Land O' Lakes employ I/O psychologists

6 **A.** NO CHANGE

B. there

C. theirs

D. they're

7 **A.** NO CHANGE

B. Capitol

C. capital

D. capitalist

8 **A.** NO CHANGE

B. Subsequently,

C. However,

D. Therefore,

9 **A.** NO CHANGE

B. laughable

C. impossible

D. daunting

10 **A.** NO CHANGE

B. Positions will be highly competitive but more and more candidates enter the field of I/O psychology.

C. While more and more candidates enter the field of I/O psychology, positions will become highly competitive.

D. As more and more candidates enter the field of I/O psychology, positions will become highly competitive.

11 **A.** NO CHANGE

B. have been intensifying

C. intensifies

D. have intensified

Questions 12–22 are based on the following passage.

The First Nuclear Bomb

12 It was early in the morning in the hot New Mexico desert. Most people slept soundly in their beds, dreaming away the dawn of a new day. At 5:29 a.m., a blinding white light flashed across the New Mexico sky, followed by an explosion that shattered the sleepy silence, catapulting people from their beds. Authorities quickly responded to the concerns of citizens, many of **13** whom were clearing away debris from shattered windows. People were told that an ammunitions dump had exploded. The truth, however, was that the explosion had come from something much bigger.

On July 16, 1945, the US military tested a nuclear bomb it had been working on for the past four years. **14** The blast of the Fat Man, the most common name for the device generated heat four times greater than the interior of the sun. **15** It created a pressure of 100 billion atmospheres and could be seen up to 250 miles away. The force of the blast was equivalent to all of the bombs dropped on London by the Luftwaffe during the Blitz. Said physicist Robert Oppenheimer, the mastermind behind the project, "I am become death, the shatterer of worlds."

With a massive blast load equivalent to almost 18,000 tons of TNT, the explosion **16** damaged the tower enclosing the device; one mile away from the detonation point, the temperature was over 750 degrees Fahrenheit. **17** So much radiation poured into the atmosphere so much so that 50 years later radiation levels at the test **18** sight were still ten times greater than levels in surrounding areas.

The Manhattan Project—the code name given to the development of an atomic bomb—was a triumphant success. The US government spent nearly **19** $29 million on heavy water plants in their endeavor to beat the Germans to the bomb. When the Fat Man exploded over the desert on July 16, turning surrounding sand into glass, US military officials saw the opportunity to end WWII in **20** one felled swoop.

Only one month later, two atomic bombs, including one reconstructed from the wreckage of Fat Man, were dropped on Japan. The first fell on the city of Hiroshima. Days later, a second bomb fell on Nagasaki. Historians estimate that almost 350,000 people were killed as a result of these two bombs—**21** the only ever to be used nuclear weapons in warfare.

By 1949, the US government had stockpiled over 200 atomic bombs. By the end of the Cold War, the worldwide atomic weapons count was over 70,000. **22** For better or worse, the beginning of the atomic age was marked on July 16, 1945.

---

12 The writer is considering deleting the first sentence of this paragraph. Should the sentence be kept or deleted?

A. Kept, because it expresses the main topic of the paragraph.

B. Kept, because it sets the scene and provides sensory detail.

C. Deleted, because it contains information irrelevant to the paragraph.

D. Deleted, because it repeats information from later in the passage.

---

13 **A.** NO CHANGE

B. who

C. they

D. them

---

14 **A.** NO CHANGE

B. The blast of the Fat Man, the most common name for the device, sent out heat four times that found in the interior of the sun.

C. The blast, of the Fat Man the most common name for the device, sent out heat four times that found in the interior of the sun.

D. The blast of the Fat Man the most common name for the device, sent out heat four times that found in the interior of the sun.

---

15 In order to make sure she is including only the most relevant support for her argument, the author is considering deleting this sentence. Is this a good choice?

A. Yes, because it introduces an irrelevant detail that does not follow the focus of the paragraph.

B. Yes, because while relevant, it is illogical where it is placed in the paragraph.

C. No, because it expands and elaborates on the topic of the paragraph.

D. No, because while tangential, it provides an interesting detail that is worth keeping.

---

16 **A.** NO CHANGE

B. destroyed

C. injured

D. cracked

---

17 **A.** NO CHANGE

B. So much radiation poured into the atmosphere that 50 years later

C. So much radiation gushed and poured into the atmosphere that 50 years later

D. Radiation poured into the atmosphere, so much and so quickly, that 50 years later

---

18 A. NO CHANGE
  B. sights
  C. site
  D. sites

19 The writer is considering changing the underlined portion of the sentence. Which choice best fits in the context of the paragraph?

  A. NO CHANGE
  B. a total of $2 billion developing the atomic bomb
  C. $76 million to modify B-29 bombers to carry the bomb
  D. $3.3 trillion over the course of WWII

20 A. NO CHANGE
  B. one fallen swoop
  C. one foul swap
  D. one fell swoop

21 A. NO CHANGE
  B. ever to be used the only nuclear weapons in warfare.
  C. the only nuclear weapons ever to be used in warfare.
  D. the only ever nuclear weapons to be used in warfare.

22 A. NO CHANGE
  B. For better or worse, the start of the atomic age had been marked on July 16, 1945.
  C. For better or worse, the beginning of the atomic age was being marked on July 16, 1945.
  D. For better or worse, July 16, 1945, marked the beginning of the atomic age.

Questions 23–33 are based on the following passage.

Benefits of a Liberal Arts Degree

When I was a junior in high school, I had a road-map to success planned out. I would attend a large four-year university, study education, and get a teaching degree. It came as a surprise to me—and my family—when my thoughts turned away from that path and settled on something less concrete. After spending two weeks at a small Midwestern liberal arts college attending a special precollege camp, my eyes were opened to the larger possibilities of education. I liked being on my own, and I felt like an adult. Instead of looking at education **23** as a mean to an end, I suddenly saw education as an opportunity to build solid foundational skills in thinking and leadership that would transfer to any career field I chose to pursue. This is the philosophy that **24** lays at the heart of liberal arts education. **25**

Traditionally, liberal arts education referred to any four-year university program in which students studied a broad range of subjects. The traditional goal of liberal arts education was to develop well-rounded scholars and thinkers. Over time, that definition has evolved. **26** Today, the Association of American Colleges and Universities defines a liberal arts education as "learning that empowers individuals and prepares them to deal with complexity, diversity, and change." Liberal arts education helps students develop valuable **27** skills in communication leadership and complex problem solving that will transfer to any twenty-first-century career.

Critics of liberal arts education believe that the pursuit of a liberal arts degree puts students at a disadvantage in the workforce. With a greater national focus on and funding for STEM (science, technology, engineering, and math) programs, some argue that workers with a degree in a STEM-related field will earn more than a worker with a liberal arts degree. This point of view is heard frequently in circles where such debates take place. However, recent data from the Association of American Colleges disproves this argument.

According to the AACU data, workers with a degree in humanities and social sciences earn more, directly out of college, than workers with STEM degrees. Furthermore, 93% of employers surveyed state that they value a **28** workers ability to think critically, communicate clearly, and solve complex problems unrelated to a person's undergraduate major. **29**

When I was an undergrad at a liberal arts college, I was **30** coerced to take a variety of classes in fields that had nothing to do with my major. In doing so, I learned the principles of macroeconomics, the philosophies of major world religions, the psychological development of children and young adults, the science of plate tectonics, the intricacies of interpersonal communication, and **31** German-language basics. **32** While I has little need to converse in German, the critical thinking and problem-solving skills I developed when learning the language have served me well in all areas of my life. **33** It would blow your mind to know how many times I've used that knowledge!

23
A. NO CHANGE
B. as mean to an end
C. as meant to an end
D. as a means to an end

24
A. NO CHANGE
B. lies
C. has laid
D. lie

---

25 In order to make sure the essay is cohesive and focused, the author is considering deleting the last sentence. Is this a good choice?

A. Yes, because it introduces an irrelevant detail that does not follow the focus of the paragraph.

B. Yes, because while relevant, it is illogical when placed at the end of the paragraph.

C. No, because it elaborates on information presented and provides a useful transition to the main topic of the essay.

D. No, because while tangential, it provides an interesting detail that is worth keeping.

26 The writer is considering deleting the underlined sentence. Should the writer do this?

    A. Yes, because it provides unnecessary details that are irrelevant to the focus of the paragraph.

    B. Yes, because this information has already been provided.

    C. No, because it quotes a credible source that supports the paragraph's focus.

    D. No, because it introduces an important new idea.

27 **A.** NO CHANGE

    B. skills in communication, leadership, and complex problem solving

    C. skills, in communication, leadership and complex problem solving

    D. skills in communication leadership, and complex problem solving

28 **A.** NO CHANGE

    B. workers'

    C. worker's

    D. worker

29 The author would like to add one more piece of evidence to support her argument. Which choice best accomplishes that goal?

    A. The median earnings of engineering graduates are consistently higher than the earnings of all other degree holders.

    B. Workers with liberal arts degrees earn on average about $2,000 more per year than those who majored as under-graduates in professional or pre-professional fields.

    C. The unemployment rate for liberal arts graduates is 0.04 percent higher than the rates for those with a professional or pre-professional degree.

    D. Graduates with liberal arts degrees are overrepresented in social services professions such as social work or counseling.

30 **A.** NO CHANGE

    B. suppressed

    C. concussed

    D. required

31 Which choice provides the most relevant detail?

    A. NO CHANGE

    B. the basics of the German language

    C. German's language basics

    D. basic German

32 **A.** NO CHANGE
B. while I have little needs
C. while I have little need
D. while I has little needs

33 Which choice maintains the style and tone of the passage?

A. NO CHANGE
B. Would you believe it took me (such a dunce!) so long to learn something so simple?
C. It totally seems obvious today, but back then I had no idea what I was doing.
D. To this day, I am grateful for that all-important decision I made back in college.

Questions 34–44 are based on the following passage.

Concussions and Young Athletes

Each year, almost 300,000 sport-related injuries are reported. The majority of these injuries are concussions. Concussions are a form of traumatic brain injury that occurs when a sudden blow or jolt to the head causes the brain to rock back and forth, altering the way that the brain functions. **34** Between the ages of 15–24, concussions are the second leading cause of traumatic brain injury in young adults in the United States. New studies are underway investigating the link between concussions and long-term brain disease.

According to information from the Sports and Fitness Industry Association, participation in youth sports is on the decline, **35** rising 11% over the last 10 years. The leading factor in decreased participation is, says ESPN, a concern over injury. While steps have been put in place to protect young players from traumatic brain injury, many experts agree that more needs to be done. **36**

37 [1] Part of the dilemma in youth sports has always been the proper training of coaches, many of whom are volunteers. [2] Few states have certification requirements for youth sports coaches, and studies have found that many volunteer coaches have little knowledge of sports safety. [3] Most observers agree that training youth coaches better would greatly help young athletes. [4] As a result, some concerned policy makers believe that certification and training should be **38** optional for all youth coaches.

39 Training programs for youth sports coaches are now being offered by many colleges and universities. Critics argue that volunteer coaches have neither time nor money to participate in these programs. **40** However: formal college training is unnecessary in the implementation of a certification program—there are viable alternatives.

In an effort to address this issue, the Centers for Disease Control has **41** compelled a training booklet for youth football coaches that contains valuable information about recognizing and responding to possible traumatic brain injuries. The booklet notes that coaches should look for the following concussion symptoms in young athletes: glassy eyes, confusion, lack of balance and coordination, mood changes, and **42** improved focus.

The CDC also offers a five-step reintegration process for coaches to follow when bringing athletes back to the playing field following a concussion. The process begins with light aerobic activity and moves into heavier noncontact physical activity before allowing a participant to fully engage in the sports process.

In order to protect youth sports participants from traumatic brain injury, parents must take a proactive role as well. It is imperative that any player who suffers a possible concussion be immediately evaluated by a trained medical professional. For most athletes, symptoms disappear within ten days of the concussion. However, it is not uncommon for symptoms—**43** a bad headache, feeling fatigue, and getting dizzy— to last for several months. Parents must be advocates for their young athletes and make sure their children get the immediate and long-term care required. **44**

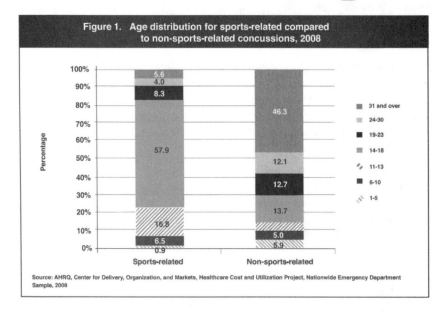

Figure 1. Age distribution for sports-related compared to non-sports-related concussions, 2008

Source: AHRQ, Center for Delivery, Organization, and Markets, Healthcare Cost and Utilization Project, Nationwide Emergency Department Sample, 2008

34 **A.** NO CHANGE

B. Concussions are the leading second cause of traumatic brain injury in young adults in the United States between the ages of 15–24.

C. In the United States, between the ages of 15–24, concussions are the leading second cause of traumatic brain injury in young adults.

D. In the United States, concussions are the second-leading cause of traumatic brain injury in young adults between the ages of 15–24.

35 Which choice provides information that best supports the claims made by this sentence and paragraph?

A. NO CHANGE

B. dropping 4% in five years

C. increasing since the early 2000s

D. but recovering steadily over the last 4 years

36 The author would like to add one more piece of relevant support to this paragraph. Which choice best accomplishes this goal?

A. According to a Boston University study, many former NFL players have thinking and memory problems.

B. The LA84 Foundation added criteria to its grant application stating that it would no longer provide support to community organizations that offered tackle football before age 9.

C. The New York City Council on Friday held a public hearing over a proposal to require doctors to be present at all youth games, and trainers or doctors at all full-contact practices.

D. From 2008 to 2013, the number of children ages 6 to 12 participating regularly in football fell 29 percent to 1.3 million, according to the Sports and Fitness Industry Association.

37 In order to improve the logic of this paragraph, this sentence should be placed

A. where it is now.

B. after Sentence 2.

C. after Sentence 3.

D. after Sentence 4.

38 **A.** NO CHANGE

B. difficult for

C. presented to

D. mandatory for

39 **A.** NO CHANGE

B. Many colleges and universities are now offering training programs for youth sports coaches.

C. Many colleges and universities to youth sports coaches are now offering training programs.

D. Training programs for youth sports coaches are among programs being offered by many colleges and universities.

40 **A.** NO CHANGE

B. However, formal college training is unnecessary in the implementation of a certification program—there are viable alternatives.

C. However—formal college training is unnecessary in the implementation of a certification program, there are viable alternatives.

D. However; formal college training is unnecessary in the implementation of a certification program; there are viable alternatives.

41 A. NO CHANGE
B. complied
C. compiled
D. compulsed

42 Which choice gives another supporting example that is most similar to the examples already in the sentence?

A. NO CHANGE
B. heavy coughing
C. existing diseases
D. memory loss

43 A. NO CHANGE
B. a headache, feeling fatigue and getting dizzy
C. like headaches, fatigue, and dizziness
D. like headaches, fatigue, and feeling dizzy

44 The author would like to add relevant and accurate support from the graph to her essay. Which choice best accomplishes this goal?

A. 6- to 18-year-olds account for more than 20% of all non-sports-related concussions.
B. Adults 31 and over account for 46.3% of all non-sports-related concussions.
C. Adults 31 and over account for less than 10% of all sports-related concussions.
D. 6- to 18-year-olds account for more than 80% of all sports-related concussions.

SECTION 3: MATH TEST—NO CALCULATOR

25 Minutes—20 Questions

TURN TO SECTION 3 OF YOUR ANSWER SHEET TO ANSWER THE QUESTIONS IN THIS SECTION.

DIRECTIONS: For **Questions 1–15,** solve each problem, select the best answer from the choices provided, and fill in the corresponding circle on your answer sheet. For **Questions 16–20,** solve the problem and enter your answer in the grid on the answer sheet. The directions **before Question 16** will provide information on how to enter your answers in the grid.

ADDITIONAL INFORMATION:

1. The use of a calculator in this section **is not permitted.**
2. All variables and expressions used represent real numbers unless otherwise indicated.
3. Figures provided in this test are drawn to scale unless otherwise indicated.
4. All figures lie in a plane unless otherwise indicated.
5. Unless otherwise specified, the domain of a given function f is the set of all real numbers x for which $f(x)$ is a real number.

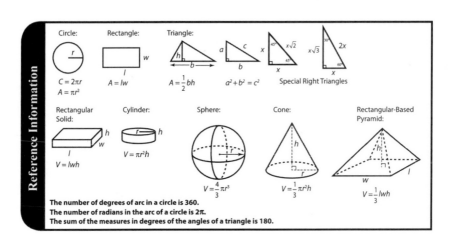

1 If $8x + 4 = 64$, then $2x + 1 =$

A. 12

B. 13

C. 16

D. 24

2 Which expression is equivalent to $(2x - 3)(3x + 2)$?

A. $6(x - 1)$

B. $6(x^2 - 1)$

C. $6x^2 - 5x - 6$

D. $6x^2 - 9x - 6$

3 Consider the equation $\sqrt{2x+8} = -x$. Which of the following are solutions?

I. -4

II. -2

III. 4

A. I only

B. II only

C. I and II only

D. I and III only

4 Given the system of equations $3x + 2y = 4$ and $6x - 3y = 6$, what does y equal?

A. 14

B. $\dfrac{14}{6}$

C. 2

D. $\dfrac{2}{7}$

5 $y = x^2 - 2x - 8$

The equation shown is graphed as a parabola on the coordinate plane. Which equivalent equation contains the x-intercepts of the parabola as constants or coefficients?

A. $y = x(x - 2) - 8$

B. $y = (x - 1)^2 - 9$

C. $y = (x - 4)(x + 2)$

D. $y + 9 = x^2 - 2x + 1$

---

6 $x^2 + y^2 = 25$

$x - y = 1$

If (v, w) and (r, s) are solutions of this system, what is the value of $|v + w| + |r + s|$?

A. 0

B. 7

C. 14

D. 2

---

7 A population of bacteria doubles every 8 days. If the initial population of bacteria is p_0, which equation can be used to model the population p after d days?

A. $p = p_0 (2)^{\frac{d}{8}}$

B. $p = p_0 (2)^{8d}$

C. $p = p_0 (8)^{\frac{d}{2}}$

D. $p = p_0 (8)^{2d}$

---

8 If $x \neq -2$, $\dfrac{3(x^2 - 4)}{x + 2} =$

A. $3x^2 + 4$.

B. $3x + 2$.

C. $3x - 2$.

D. $3x - 6$.

---

9 A student conducted an experiment with bean plants for a science fair. He measured the height of bean plants over the course of a week and found that he could model the growth of the plants with the equation $h = 0.15d + 0.85$, where h represents the height in centimeters and d represents the day of the experiment. What does the value 0.85 represent?

A. The initial height of the bean plants

B. The ending height of the bean plants

C. The change in the height of the bean plants each day

D. The total change in the height of the bean plants for the entire experiment

10 If $x - y = 10$ and $x + y = 20$, then what is the value of $x^2 - y^2$?

A. 400

B. 200

C. 100

D. 30

11 A cylindrical can with a base diameter of 4 inches and a height of 6 inches is $\frac{2}{3}$ full of juice. What volume of juice is in the can in cubic inches?

A. 12π

B. 16π

C. 36π

D. 64π

SHOW YOUR WORK HERE

12 The function $y = f(x)$ represents a parabola with vertex (2, 3). If $g(x) = f(x) + 4$, which ordered pair shows the vertex of the parabola $y = g(x)$?

A. (2, 7)

B. (2, −1)

C. (6, 3)

D. (6, 7)

SHOW YOUR WORK HERE

13 Tickets to a museum cost $5 for students and $12 for adults. If a group going to the museum will have at least 20 people and can spend no more than $200, which system of equations can be used to determine the number of students and adults that can go on the trip to the museum?

A. $5s + 12a \leq 200$
$s + a \leq 20$

B. $5s + 12a \geq 200$
$s + a \leq 20$

C. $5s + 12a \leq 200$
$s + a \geq 20$

D. $5s + 12a \geq 200$
$s + a \geq 20$

14 Which is equivalent to $(2 + i)(3 - i)$?

A. 6

B. 7

C. $5 + i$

D. $7 + i$

15 The points (0, 0) and (4, 0) are the endpoints of a diameter of circle O. Which equation represents circle O?

A. $(x + 2)^2 + y^2 = 4$

B. $(x + 2)^2 + y^2 = 16$

C. $(x - 2)^2 + y^2 = 4$

D. $(x - 2)^2 + y^2 = 16$

DIRECTIONS: For **Questions 16–20,** solve the problem and enter your answer in the grid, as described below, on the answer sheet.

1. Although not required, it is suggested that you write your answer in the boxes at the top of the columns to help you fill in the circles accurately. You will receive credit only if the circles are filled in correctly.

2. Mark no more than one circle in any column.

3. No question has a negative answer.

4. Some problems may have more than one correct answer. In such cases, grid only one answer.

5. **Mixed numbers** such as $3\frac{1}{2}$ must be gridded as 3.5 or $\frac{7}{2}$. If $3\frac{1}{2}$ is entered into the grid as $\overline{3\,|\,1\,/\,2}$, it will be interpreted as $\frac{31}{2}$, not $3\frac{1}{2}$.

6. **Decimal answers:** If you obtain a decimal answer with more digits than the grid can accommodate, it may be either rounded or truncated, but it must fill the entire grid.

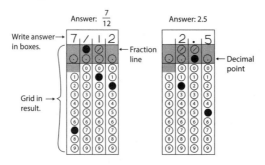

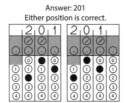

Answer: 201
Either position is correct.

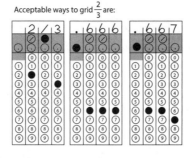

Acceptable ways to grid $\frac{2}{3}$ are:

16 Nigel can complete a task in 4 hours. Roger takes 6 hours to complete the same task. If they work together, they can complete the task in h hours, where $\left(\dfrac{1}{4}+\dfrac{1}{6}\right)h=1$. How many hours will it take to complete the task with Nigel and Roger working together?

17 Nick saves $85 per week from a side job. On the second week, he earns an extra $55 by doing some landscaping work for a neighbor. How many weeks are needed for Nick to save at least $900?

18 Two roads intersect at right angles. A pole is 30 meters from one road and 40 meters from the other road. How far (in meters) is the pole from the point where the roads intersect?

19 What is the x-intercept of the graph of $y - 2 = 5(x - 4)$?

20 Julia is painting a large wall at a constant rate. After working for 1 hour, she has 700 square feet left to paint. After working for 3 hours, she still has 500 square feet left to paint. If the area of the wall that still needs to be painted is modeled by the function $f(t) = at + b$, what is the value of b?

SECTION 4: MATH TEST—CALCULATOR

55 Minutes—38 Questions

TURN TO SECTION 4 OF YOUR ANSWER SHEET TO ANSWER THE QUESTIONS IN THIS SECTION.

DIRECTIONS: For **Questions 1–30,** solve each problem, select the best answer from the choices provided, and fill in the corresponding circle on your answer sheet. For **Questions 31–38,** solve the problem and enter your answer in the grid on the answer sheet. The directions **before Question 31** will provide information on how to enter your answers in the grid.

ADDITIONAL INFORMATION:
1. The use of a calculator in this section **is permitted.**
2. All variables and expressions used represent real numbers unless otherwise indicated.
3. Figures provided in this test are drawn to scale unless otherwise indicated.
4. All figures lie in a plane unless otherwise indicated.
5. Unless otherwise specified, the domain of a given function *f* is the set of all real numbers *x* for which *f(x)* is a real number.

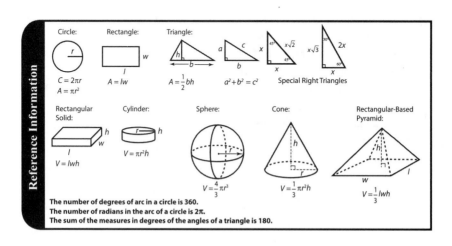

1. The normal sales tax in a city is 8.75%. A half-percent sales tax added last year increased tax revenue by $23 million dollars. What is the approximate combined revenue from the normal sales tax and half-percent sales tax, rounded to the nearest million dollars?

A. $201 million

B. $379 million

C. $403 million

D. $426 million

2. If $x \neq \dfrac{2}{3}$, then $\dfrac{6x^2 - 13x + 6}{3x - 2} =$

A. $3x - 2$.

B. $3x - 3$.

C. $2x - 6$.

D. $2x - 3$.

3. When Carlos drives to work at an average speed of 55 miles per hour, his commute takes 45 minutes. Which equation can be used to find the average speed at which Carlos must drive to decrease his commute time by 5 minutes?

A. $55x = 1{,}800$

B. $2{,}475 = 45(x - 5)$

C. $41.25 = \dfrac{2}{3}x$

D. $\dfrac{x}{40} = \dfrac{55}{45}$

SHOW YOUR WORK HERE

4 Houston, Texas, has an area of approximately 600 square miles and a population of approximately 2.2 million. Los Angeles, California, has a land area of approximately 469 square miles and a population of approximately 3.9 million. Approximately how much greater is the population density of Los Angeles than the population density of Houston?

SHOW YOUR WORK HERE

A. 152 people per square mile

B. 4,648 people per square mile

C. 6,558 people per square mile

D. 12,977 people per square mile

5 The graph of which of the following functions intersects all four quadrants?

A. $f(x) = 3(x + 2)^2 + 1$

B. $g(x) = (x - 4)^2 + 25$

C. $h(x) = (x - 4)^2 - 25$

D. $j(x) = -(x - 3)^2 + 4$

6 The graph shown represents the expected profit that can be generated by selling an item at different prices. At which price should the cost be set to generate the maximum profit?

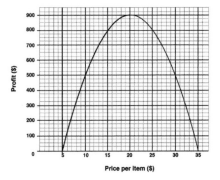

Price per Item ($)

A. $5

B. $20

C. $35

D. $90

7 Ocean waves start to break when the depth of the water, d, in feet, is approximately 1.3 times the height of the wave, h, in feet. If the waves on a given day range from 3 to 4 feet in height, which inequality represents the depth of the water at which the waves will break?

A. $1.7 < d < 2.7$

B. $2.3 < d < 3$

C. $3.9 < d < 5.2$

D. $4.3 < d < 5.3$

8 At a certain altitude, the speed of sound is approximately 740 miles per hour. How many feet will sound travel in 1 second at this altitude? [Round your answer to the nearest foot and use the relationship 1 mile = 5,280 feet].

SHOW YOUR WORK HERE

A. 505

B. 714

C. 1,084

D. 1,085

9 In the 2015 Canadian federal election, the Liberal Party won 184 seats in the House of Commons, and the Conservative Party won 99 seats. A total of 338 members were elected to the House of Commons. What percentage of the seats, rounded to the nearest percent, were won by parties other than the Conservative Party and the Liberal Party?

A. 16%

B. 30%

C. 47%

D. 55%

10 The number of buses, b, and cars, c, that a parking lot can hold is related by the inequality $10b + c < 100$. If the maximum number of buses is present, how many cars can still fit in the parking lot?

A. 0

B. 1

C. 9

D. 10

11 Which expression is equivalent to $2x^2\sqrt{5x}$?

SHOW YOUR WORK HERE

A. $\sqrt{10x^3}$

B. $\sqrt{10x^5}$

C. $\sqrt{20x^3}$

D. $\sqrt{20x^5}$

---

12 Which expression is equivalent to $(x+y)^2(x^2-y^2)$?

A. $x^4 - y^4$

B. $x^4 - 2x^2y^2 + y^4$

C. $(x+y)(x^3 - y^3)$

D. $(x+y)^3(x-y)$

---

13 In 2012, the gross domestic product (GDP) of the United States was approximately 16.2 trillion dollars. In 2013, the GDP was approximately 16.8 trillion dollars. If the GDP continues to grow at the same percentage rate, which function could be used to estimate the US GDP in trillions of dollars, $f(t)$, t years after 2012?

A. $f(t) = 16.2(0.964)^t$

B. $f(t) = 16.2(1.037)^t$

C. $f(t) = 16.2 + 0.964t$

D. $f(t) = 16.2 + 1.037t$

14
$$10x - 7y = 3$$
$$x - 1.4y = 1$$
For which value of x is the system of equations shown true?

A. -1

B. -0.4

C. 0.3

D. 1

15 A polynomial function $y = p(x)$ is graphed on the coordinate plane shown. Which expression must be a factor of $p(x)$?

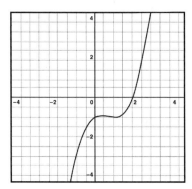

A. $x - 2$

B. $x - 1$

C. $x + 1$

D. $x + 2$

16 If the sum of the lengths of the edges of a cube is 48 inches, the volume of the cube in cubic inches is

A. 64.

B. 96.

C. 149.

D. 512.

17 A biologist recorded the weight, in grams, of hummingbird eggs in a sample. What is the mean weight of the sample to the nearest tenth of a gram?

Weight (g)							
1.4	1.1	1.3	1.3	1.3	1.1	0.7	0.6

A. 1.0

B. 1.1

C. 1.2

D. 1.3

18 A line drawn on the coordinate plane passes through the points (1, 3) and (5, 4). Which equation represents the line?

A. $y = -4x + 7$

B. $y = -\dfrac{1}{4}x + \dfrac{13}{4}$

C. $y = \dfrac{1}{4}x + \dfrac{11}{4}$

D. $y = 4x - 1$

19 The formula $F = \dfrac{9}{5}C + 32$ is used to convert temperatures from degrees Celsius to degrees Fahrenheit. Which of these equations is equivalent?

A. $C = \dfrac{5}{9}F - 32$

B. $C = \dfrac{5}{9}(F - 32)$

C. $C = \dfrac{9}{5}F + 32$

D. $C = \dfrac{9}{5}(F + 32)$

20 A survey of a random sample of 500 likely voters in a town finds that 60% intend to vote YES on Ballot Measure A, with a margin of error of 2%. If 8,000 people from the town vote, what is a reasonable estimate of the lowest number of YES votes for Ballot Measure A?

A. 4,000

B. 4,640

C. 4,960

D. 5,000

21 An object is launched into the air at a velocity of 40 meters per second. The velocity of the object, v, in meters per second, t seconds after it is launched can be found by using the equation $v = -9.8t + 40$. What does the -9.8 in the equation represent?

SHOW YOUR WORK HERE

A. The rate of change of the velocity

B. The number of seconds it takes for the object to travel 1 meter

C. The number of meters the object will travel in 1 second

D. The velocity of the object when it was launched

22 A political scientist gathered the data in the table to determine if there is a relationship between a person's opinion of a particular ballot measure and where that person lives. What fraction of the people in favor of the ballot measure live in rural areas?

	Rural	Urban
In Favor	40	45
Opposed	10	5

A. $\dfrac{2}{5}$

B. $\dfrac{4}{5}$

C. $\dfrac{8}{9}$

D. $\dfrac{8}{17}$

23 An airplane flies round trip between points A and B. Flying from point A to B, the airplane flies against a 50-knot wind and takes 4 hours to complete the trip. On the return trip, the airplane flies with the 50-knot wind and completes the trip in 3 hours. Which of the following equations can be used to solve for the speed of the aircraft in still air (in knots)?

SHOW YOUR WORK HERE

A. $\dfrac{3}{s+50} - \dfrac{4}{s-50} = 1$

B. $\dfrac{s+50}{3} = \dfrac{s-50}{4}$

C. $\dfrac{3}{s+50} + \dfrac{4}{s-50} = 1$

D. $3(s + 50) = 4(s - 50)$

24 Which equation could be used to generate a curve that models the data in the scatter plot shown?

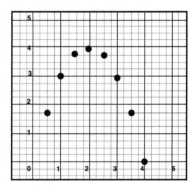

A. $y = -x^2 - 4$
B. $y = 2x(x - 4)$
C. $y = 4x - x^2$
D. $y = x^2 + 4$

25 If (h, k) is the vertex of the quadratic function $g(x) = -3x^2 - 12x - 10$, what is the value of k^h?

SHOW YOUR WORK HERE

A. -4

B. 4

C. $-\dfrac{1}{4}$

D. $\dfrac{1}{4}$

26 An airplane is flying toward an airport at a constant speed. Two hours after departure, the airplane is 900 miles away from the airport. Four hours after departure, the airplane is 200 miles from the airport. Which equation models the distance of the airplane from the airport, d, in miles, t hours after departure?

A. $d = 900 - 350t$

B. $d = 900 - 700t$

C. $d = 1,600 - 350t$

D. $d = 1,600 - 700t$

27 The Gross Domestic Product (GDP) of the European Union was approximately 13.9 trillion euros in 2014. That same year, the GDP of China was approximately 63.6 trillion yuan. If 1 euro was approximately equal to 7.7 yuan in 2014, what was the approximate ratio of the GDP of the European Union to the GDP of China?

A. 0.2

B. 0.6

C. 1.7

D. 4.6

28 A parabola graphed on the *xy*-coordinate plan has *x*-intercepts at $x = 2$ and $x = 4$, and a *y*-intercept at $y = 12$. Which equation represents the parabola?

A. $y = 2x^2 + 4x + 12$

B. $y = 1.5x^2 - 9x + 12$

C. $y = x^2 - 6x + 8$

D. $y = (x - 4)(x - 2) + 4$

29 Two pens and one notebook cost $8.50. One pen and two notebooks cost $9.50. Which equation shows the cost of one pen, *p*, and one notebook, *n*?

A. $p + n = 1.00$

B. $p + n = 6.00$

C. $p + n = 17.50$

D. $p + n = 18.00$

30 For a given function $f(x)$, $f(0) = 2$ and $f(3) = 0$. If a function $g(x)$ is defined so that $g(x) = -f(x)$, which statement **must** be true?

A. $g(-3) = 0$

B. $g(0) = 3$

C. $g(0) = -3$

D. $g(3) = 0$

> **DIRECTIONS:** For **Questions 31–38,** solve the problem and enter your answer in the grid, as described below, on the answer sheet.

1. Although not required, it is suggested that you write your answer in the boxes at the top of the columns to help you fill in the circles accurately. You will receive credit only if the circles are filled in correctly.
2. Mark no more than one circle in any column.
3. No question has a negative answer.
4. Some problems may have more than one correct answer. In such cases, grid only one answer.
5. **Mixed numbers** such as $3\frac{1}{2}$ must be gridded as 3.5 or $\frac{7}{2}$. If $3\frac{1}{2}$ is entered into the grid as $3\,|\,1\,/\,2$, it will be interpreted as $\frac{31}{2}$, not $3\frac{1}{2}$.
6. **Decimal answers:** If you obtain a decimal answer with more digits than the grid can accommodate, it may be either rounded or truncated, but it must fill the entire grid.

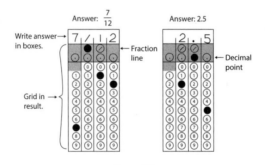

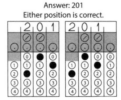

31 Machine A produces flue covers at a uniform rate of 2,000 per hour. Machine B produces flue covers at a uniform rate of 5,000 in $2\frac{1}{2}$ hours. After $7\frac{1}{4}$ hours, how many more flue covers has Machine A produced than Machine B?

SHOW YOUR WORK HERE

32 In the figure shown, *AB* is parallel to *ED* and *AC = BC*. If angle *E* is 50°, then what does *x* equal?

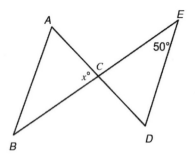

Figure not drawn to scale.

33 If 12 candies cost $1.70, how many of these candies can be bought for $10.20?

34 The density of steel is approximately 8 grams per cubic centimeter. What is the mass, in grams, of a steel plate that is 12 centimeters long, 12 centimeters wide, and 0.5 centimeter thick?

35 The populations of 5 of 6 New England states are given in the table. If the mean of the populations (in millions) of all 6 states is 2.41, what is the population (in millions) of Massachusetts?

SHOW YOUR WORK HERE

State	Population (in millions)
Connecticut	3.57
Maine	1.33
Massachusetts	?
New Hampshire	1.32
Rhode Island	1.05
Vermont	0.63

36 Gears A, B, and C are connected so that when gear A makes 5 revolutions, gear B makes 8 revolutions. When gear B makes 2 revolutions, gear C makes 3 revolutions. What is the ratio of revolutions of gear A to gear C?

37 A line passing through the point (2, 5) can be represented by the equation $y = -\dfrac{1}{2}x + b$. What is the value of b?

38 A school conducted a survey to determine whether students wanted to join either the Art Club or the Drama Club. The results are shown in the table below. What is the probability that a student who wanted to join the Drama Club also wanted to join the Art Club? Write your answer as a decimal.

		Drama Club	
		Yes	No
Art Club	Yes	50	50
	No	75	25

SECTION 5: SAT® ESSAY

50 MINUTES—1 ESSAY

Directions: The essay gives you an opportunity to show how effectively you can read and comprehend a passage and write an essay analyzing the passage. In your essay, you should demonstrate that you have read the passage carefully, present a clear and logical analysis, and use language precisely.

Your essay will need to be written on the lines provided in your answer booklet. You will have enough space if you write on every line and keep your handwriting to an average size. Try to print or write clearly so that your writing will be legible to the readers scoring your essay.

As you read the passage below, consider how John Bailey uses the following:

- Evidence, such as facts, statistics, or examples, to support claims.

- Reasoning to develop ideas and to connect claims and evidence.

- Stylistic or persuasive elements, such as word choice or appeals to emotion, to add power to the ideas expressed.

Adapted from "From Smokey Bear to Climate Change: The Future of Wildland Fire Management" by John Bailey, originally published by *The Conversation* on August 11, 2015. John Bailey is an associate professor of Silviculture and Fire Management at Oregon State University.

Current conditions in the West demonstrate that our US fire management system is struggling and approaching a state of crisis. Spending on fighting fires has climbed dramatically since the 1990s. And there is growing risk of more intense fires with each passing year, given the effects of climate change, accumulated fuels in the landscape, and our inability to extinguish all ignitions.

Our fire management system invariably leads managers to attempt suppression of nearly all wildland fires despite the natural, beneficial role of "good" fires. Ironically, our firefighting system is very efficient at extinguishing such "good" fires while, by default, creating the "bad" fires that have no historic precedents and create great losses.

. . .

Fire benefits

There is little doubt over the historic role of fire in forests throughout North America and much of the world. Fire has been a reality for millennia. Our ancestors recognized this fact, coexisted with fire, and actively set and spread fire to improve their lives for food, water, medicines, and safety.

Forest vegetation and animals evolved adaptations to fire; the forest as an ecosystem evolved with fire regimes of various frequencies, intensities, and spatial patterns that are fundamental to their structure, composition, and function.

For example, ponderosa pine and associated dry, mixed-conifer forests are **resistant** to fire. Historically, these forests burned once or twice per decade as low-intensity surface fires that maintained open forest conditions and grass understories, which promoted ensuing fires. A few trees were killed here and there, which made room for new individuals to grow into the main canopy, creating a forest that contained many ages, much like a multigenerational household.

In contrast, lodgepole pine forests are **resilient** to fire—destroyed but reborn. Whole mountainsides of such forests burned in spectacular fashion, but the blackened ground was soon covered with seeds, protected within the skeleton of their parents. The forest thereby regenerated in one big wave of children—like an elementary school!

Both resistance and resilience are valid strategies, and forests used these strategies in some mix for millennia.

Euro-American settlement largely put an end to that fundamental relationship between forests and fire. The expansion of towns and agriculture, fragmentation of the landscape, fire suppression, Smokey Bear, and a favorable climate pattern combined to limit fire during much of the 20th century. Fire histories from hundreds of research sites definitively show this change, and the forests changed with it.

Because of policies that prioritized fire suppression, there has been a consistent accumulation of fuels in most of our forests. This has created a structural continuity of those fuels across landscapes and from the forest floor to the canopy, as well as shifts in species composition.

The fuel problem

Now, the role of fire is changing as it re-exerts itself, despite our best efforts to continue suppressing it. Resistance mechanisms such as thick tree bark are no longer sufficient as fires burn hotter because of accumulated fuel. Large "mega-fires" threaten more resources and more human communities every year.

As a result, expenditures for suppression have grown. And because those efforts are largely successful, they tend to promote human settlement right up to the edge of vast forests. Our success in putting out wildfires thereby serves to extend the risk, driving a need for more suppression. But the accumulated fuel hazard—that is, the amount of fuel capable of burning—grows as fires are suppressed. And new risks associated with climate change, including drier and hotter conditions, are only projected to increase.

Landscapes are largely unalterable—vegetation will grow, die, and burn; and humans are not going to leave the forest edge. Therefore, there is only one way in this emerging crisis to break the cycle, which is to treat the continuously accumulating fuels.

. . .

More prescribed fires

A number of land management groups are launching more and larger forest restoration treatments, thinning the trees and removing fuel in order to turn this tide of built-up fuel. These efforts are commendable. But they are subsidized by state and federal taxes and produce little marketable material for a forestry industry that has largely disappeared in many locales. Therefore, these restoration efforts are too scattered and too small to make a difference in the landscape.

Instead, large wildland fires have been doing and will continue to do most of "the work" of draining the fuel reservoir. Our choice is between the current passive management of fire—suppressing when we can and otherwise minimizing the damage when mega-fires occur—or, instead, active management of fire.

Passive management fills the reservoir of fuel until it sporadically and dramatically drains large quantities in relatively uncontrolled fashions, which is our current trajectory.

Active management offers more controlled releases that will conserve more of our forest resources intact. This will mean a dramatic increase in deliberately ignited prescribed fires outside of the fire season and during periods of more moderate conditions within each fire season. It also means the use of prescribed fire tactics during wildland fire events to complement suppression activities.

> Write an essay in which you explain how John Bailey builds an argument to persuade his audience that the current US fire-management policy of suppression is not working and should be replaced with a policy of proactively setting controlled fires to remove accumulated fuel from forests. In your essay, analyze how Bailey uses one or more of the features listed above (or features of your own choice) to strengthen the logic and persuasiveness of his argument. Be sure that your analysis focuses on the most relevant features of the passage. Your essay should not explain whether you agree with the writer's claims, but rather explain how he builds an argument to persuade his audience.

STOP

If you finish before time is called, you may check your work on this section only.
Do not turn to any other section.

ANSWER KEYS AND EXPLANATIONS

SECTION 1: READING TEST

1. D	12. A	23. A	33. C	43. D
2. B	13. D	24. D	34. A	44. B
3. A	14. B	25. D	35. B	45. A
4. D	15. C	26. C	36. A	46. C
5. C	16. B	27. D	37. D	47. D
6. C	17. C	28. D	38. D	48. B
7. D	18. D	29. D	39. C	49. B
8. A	19. D	30. C	40. D	50. D
9. C	20. A	31. A	41. A	51. D
10. D	21. B	32. D	42. D	52. C
11. A	22. A			

READING TEST RAW SCORE [   ]
(Number of correct answers)

1. **The correct answer is D.** The overall idea of this passage is the impact that bee colony collapse is having on major industries. Choices A, B, and C are all statements that support the main idea.

2. **The correct answer is B.** Langstroth explains that the various bees in a colony have different life spans, most of them short, although the queen may live to be four or five years old. However, the colonies may continue through many generations over the course of years. The passage states that the queen lives for several years, but it does not specify if she always lives in one colony. Choice C is a true statement but it doesn't explain the relationship. Worker bees have a short lifespan; they do not die because of other bees in the colony (choice D).

3. **The correct answer is A.** Langstroth explains that the bees in a colony periodically reconstruct the honeycombs, and if they fail to do so, the offspring can be dwarfs. Bees hatched in the summer do live longer but are not necessarily different in size (choice B). Langstroth doesn't mention fungus infections or nutritional problems (choices C and D), probably because these are twenty-first–century problems.

4. **The correct answer is D.** Passage 1 is from a first-person perspective, by a beekeeper whose experience with bees informs the passage. Passage 2 is written in the third person and provides a more data-driven account of a specific contemporary problem with bees. Both passages are concerned with the death of bees, but from differing perspectives—the first in terms of a natural life cycle and the second in terms of an unnatural mass death in colonies (choice A). Passage 1 describes the role of individual bees but also discusses the colonies (choice B). Passage 1 does not discuss the overall bee population. This passage looks at the habits and lifecycle of the bee (choice C).

5. **The correct answer is C.** Passage 1 is written as a third-person narrative but switches to first person to inject the author's personal experience and authority. Passage 2 provides data that makes it impersonal, but it also expresses concern about the CCD problem. Passage 1 is neither particularly cheerful nor warm; it has a serious tone, though not angry and certainly not uninformative, making choices A and D incorrect. Passage 1 is neither condescending nor funny; it is a sober account of the author's observations, so choice B is also incorrect.

6. **The correct answer is C.** Langstroth states that it would be "very desirable to be able to remove the old combs occasionally" (lines 18–19), then specifies in the following paragraph that doing so every year would be "a great mistake" (line 21). He goes on to say that he finds changing his old combs out every five or six years "is often enough" (line 23). Choices A, B, and D are incorrect because they are directly contradicted in the text.

7. **The correct answer is D.** Lines 15–16 and 18–20 (choices A and B) explain merely the need to change the combs. Lines 21–22 (choice C) explain why Langstroth does not change his combs annually, though he could easily do so. Only lines 22–25 (choice D) explain Langstroth's rationale for changing his combs every few ("five or six") years and provide the best evidence to support the previous question's answer.

8. **The correct answer is A.** *Sublethal* is a combined form of the word *lethal* with the prefix *sub-*, meaning "less than." The word means "somewhat less than deadly," which in the context of the sentence means the pesticides have some risk of being lethal or deadly.

9. **The correct answer is C.** *Repose* means "at rest," though it can also convey being at peace or being concealed. However, in this context, neither of those meanings applies.

10. **The correct answer is D.** Unless the colonies begin producing more honey—which would require solving the problems related to bee health—the only way to increase

output is by establishing more colonies, which makes choice D the correct answer. Choice A is incorrect because in 1993, overall output was higher than output per colony, suggesting that output per colony is not the only factor that determines overall production. Choice B can't be inferred because there was actually an increase in honey production between 2012 and 2013. Choice C can't be inferred because, according to the passage, many bees are used for pollination rather than for honey production.

11. **The correct answer is A.** Although Edmonds treats the soldier kindly and is sympathetic to his plight, she is fighting on the Union side of the war, and the soldier is a "rebel," or a Confederate soldier, making them enemies in terms of the war (lines 47–48: "There lay before me an enemy … suffering unspeakable privation …"). They have no previous acquaintance, so they aren't friends (choice B), and he is hiding, not traveling (choice C). They are not fellow soldiers (choice D) because they are on different sides of the conflict.

12. **The correct answer is A.** Edmonds is patriotic, as evidenced by her efforts to fight in the war as a soldier, an unusual action, especially at the time—so unusual she had to disguise herself. However, when she encounters a sick and dying enemy soldier, she sees him as another human being who has needs, just like she does, and she treats him with respect and kindness, nursing his illness. This behavior shows her character to be empathetic and caring, in spite of their differences in outlook about the war.

13. **The correct answer is D.** The theme of the excerpt shows aspects of war from Edmonds's point of view. She is resolute and determined to serve the cause. In the midst of the deprivations brought on by the war, when she meets the Confederate soldier, her instinct for caring for other human beings kicks in, illustrating the idea that people can find common human ground, even in the worst of situations. The other choices are general statements that are true, but they do not reflect the idea of showing humanity in the face of danger.

14. **The correct answer is B.** Edmonds went out of her way to join the war effort at great risk to herself (lines 47–48: "to the Government for which I was daily and willingly exposing my life and suffering unspeakable privation") and speaks about the war as "the cause which I had espoused" (line 53). Despite her feelings of tenderness for the suffering rebel, she is indeed part of the war effort, so choice A is incorrect. There is no evidence in the text to support choices C or D.

15. **The correct answer is C.** The Irish peddler disguise was probably easier for Edmonds to pull off than her soldier disguise. However, her

—

—

plan to spy on the rebels would be less risky if the Confederates perceived her as simply an old woman selling baked goods, which they wanted anyway.

16. **The correct answer is B.** Edmonds had been horribly lost and feared she would not find her way in the dark. When she heard the cannons, she knew that she was not too far from a battlefield and would soon be able to work her way out of the woods toward enemy lines. It was not a guarantee that she would be able to get through the lines (choice D) or be successful at gathering intelligence about the enemy (choice C). But it did guarantee she would not have to spend the night lost in the dark woods (lines 17–19: "I now turned my face in the direction of the scene of action, and was not long in extricating myself from the desert which had so long enveloped me."). There is no evidence in the passage to support choice A.

17. **The correct answer is C.** Edmonds's memoir was written after the war and is written in the past tense. Although she describes the hardships, she narrates her story in a very matter-of-fact manner. She relates the events and circumstances without drama, even as she fears starvation (lines 5–8: "better die upon … in the swamp.") and meets a sick enemy soldier (lines 41–43: "He was a … intelligent looking man"). Though she displays strength, courage, and empathy (choices B and D), these qualities do not

necessarily convey a sense of calm. Choice A is incorrect because it is Edmonds's prejudices that are overridden with her compassion for the sick soldier, not her fear (lines 47–53: "There lay before me … which I had espoused.").

18. **The correct answer is D.** Edmonds manages to keep her tone even and matter of fact throughout the piece, even in the face of peril. Choices A, B, and C are all examples of this, though they show her in the direst of her circumstances. Choice D is the most compelling evidence of her narrative technique of maintaining calm and keeping her composure throughout the excerpt. That Edmonds is able to "make her toilet" and "adjust her wig" after three days of near starvation in a swamp—and in the presence of an enemy solder, sick or otherwise— best illustrates the overall tone of calm employed throughout the passage.

19. **The correct answer is D.** Jefferson Davis was the president of the Confederate States of America during the Civil War, but this knowledge is not necessary to understand that "Mrs. Jeff Davis" in the context of the passage is a figure the sick rebel soldier would have met with great relief and comfort. As we are not told the soldier's name, it would be foolish to assume we would be told his mother's name so indirectly (choice B). As there is no mention of Edmonds's husband or mentors elsewhere in the passage, we can rule out choices A and C,

thereby making choice D the most appropriate response.

20. **The correct answer is A.** Edmonds risked her life to spy behind enemy lines, "daily and willingly exposing [her] life" (lines 47–48), and envisioned that if she died, her death would be an honorable one, battling for her country and her cause. To starve alone in a swamp would seem inglorious, or humiliating, in comparison (lines 5–6: "better die … anything but this."). Choice B is directly contradicted in the text. There is no evidence in the passage to support choices C or D.

21. **The correct answer is B.** *Antipathy* means "strong dislike for something." Animosity is similar in that it refers to resentment or feelings of hostility.

22. **The correct answer is A.** Hornaday explicitly states this opinion in lines 33–34 ("The disappearance … civilization."). He goes on to explain exactly how Western settlers contributed to the bison's disappearance—i.e., in use of the animal for valuable food and pelts—and states that "The causes … are by no means obscure. …" (lines 1–3), so choice B is incorrect. Hornaday refers to the future absence of the animal as "a very serious matter" (line 18), so choice D is incorrect. There is no evidence to suggest he thought the bison was either dangerous or a pest (choice C).

23. **The correct answer is A.** Hornaday was worried about any animals in danger of becoming extinct, particularly the American bison. He states this worry (choice A) explicitly in lines 48–50: "There is reason to fear … lost irretrievably." While Hornaday was a conservationist, he was not anti-hunting (choice B) and describes settlers' hunting of the American bison in favorable terms (lines 20–23: "he served a good purpose … winter weather"). Though he makes one reference to the mastodon, there is no evidence to suggest he wanted to study the two animals together (choice D). He explains that the American bison was no longer the only food source in the region (lines 22–24: "By the time … instead of a necessity."), so choice C is incorrect.

24. **The correct answer is D.** Hornaday is most concerned that the American bison will become extinct, as expressed in lines 48–50. This is also one of the main ideas of the passage. Lines 5–8 and 41–42 (choices A and C) are expressions of solidarity for settlers having hunted the bison out of necessity during the period of Westward expansion. Lines 35–37 (choice B) compares the bison's ease of extinction with that of the mastodon; this is done for effect and does not express the main idea of the passage.

25. **The correct answer is D.** Looking at the dates shown on the map, the earliest elimination of the bison range was in 1720 (in the South),

and latest elimination was in 1886 (in the northern Great Plains area). That span is 166 years, which is the approximate equivalent of a century and a half.

26. **The correct answer is C.** The excerpt focuses on why the bison gradually disappeared, mostly as an inevitable consequence of Western expansion. Hornaday explains that hunting the bison is no longer required for subsistence (lines 22–24: "By the … instead of a necessity."), and advocates strongly for government intervention to stem the tide of disappearance and prevent the animal's outright extinction (lines 51–52: "[I]t is clearly the duty … promptness"). None of the other choices (A, B, or D) are supported by the text.

27. **The correct answer is D.** Hornaday's view of the bison is nuanced and complex. He discusses in the passage the difference between "legitimate hunting" and "wholesale slaughter" (lines 41–42 and line 38; choice B). He also suggests that the government must intervene to prevent the bison's extinction (line 51: "[I]t is clearly the duty … this matter"; choice C) and makes clear that protecting this animal is important and should be "highly gratifying to every American citizen and every friend of science throughout the world." (lines 53–54; choice A). All three views are clearly articulated, and equally crucial to the passage, so choice D is correct.

28. **The correct answer is D.** The Endangered Species Act was federal legislation designed to prevent the extinction of species of wild animals that are disappearing. Hornaday was very concerned about this problem in 1887 and urged the government to intervene. This is strong evidence he would support similar intervention in the following century. Though he did believe the development of the West contributed hugely to the disappearance of bison (choice C), it would not necessarily affect his opinion of the 1973 legislation. He makes clear in the passage that some subsistence hunting is "legitimate" (line 41), so choice B is incorrect. His career as a taxidermist is irrelevant to the question (choice A).

29. **The correct answer is D.** Choices A, B, and C express different aspects of Hornaday's view as to how the American bison came to be in danger of extinction. Only lines 48–54 (choice D) express his support of government intervention to solve the problem of extinction and his passion for the preservation of the species, which would seem robust enough to provide evidence of his hypothetical support of future conservation legislation.

30. **The correct answer is C.** Hornaday explains that the early Western settler must have looked upon the bison as "a gift direct from the hand of Providence" (lines 7–8) and later explains how the bison "served a good purpose at a highly critical

period … winter weather." Choice B is factually true, but irrelevant to the fact of Western expansion and the development of the country. There is no evidence in the text to support choices A or D.

31. **The correct answer is A.** *Wanton* means "uncontrolled" in this context. Hornaday refers to how people were indiscriminately killing wildlife in the West and says that it would eventually lead to a shortage of the game that they needed for food.

32. **The correct answer is D.** *Bemoan* means to express unhappiness or complain about something. In this case, Hornaday is clarifying that "[e]xcept when the latter became the victim of wholesale slaughter …" (lines 37–38), there was no reason to bemoan, or complain about, the fate of the bison, as it would not have been in vain. Choices A, B, and C are incorrect.

33. **The correct answer is C.** Submarines had not been invented when Verne wrote the book, so the idea of traveling by ship under the ocean was something people thought of as fiction, even though it turned out later to be a scientific achievement. Water temperatures in the Arctic could be –120 degrees, so choice A is incorrect. A ship that is hit could turn on its side and even right itself, depending on circum- stances, making choice B wrong. People can and did live comfortably on large ships (choice D)—they just

weren't submarines until long after this book was written.

34. **The correct answer is A.** The fact that the submarine's existence is secret, that the men don't know how they came to be on board, and that they cannot leave (choices B and C) are mysterious and defy verisimilitude. Sea monsters place the story in the realm of the fantastical (choice D). In the ship's navigation, however, Verne does not try to invent futuristic or mechanical devices; rather, he uses the nautical instruments that were available at the time to measure location, depth, and pressure, making the story seem real and credible.

35. **The correct answer is B.** The mood is foreboding, uncertain about the future and what will happen now that the ship has had an accident and appears to be stranded. The men express alarm and look to Captain Nemo for an answer. But he has none; his response is fatalistic— he says the laws of nature cannot be overcome. There is no sense of whimsy here (choice A), nor of any festivities (choice C). The men are not mournful (choice D); they express no great unhappiness or sadness, but there is a hint of darker things to come.

36. **The correct answer is A.** The Nautilus is described in detail through the eyes of the men as they wake up after the accident. They each have their own beds, with

enough space to be thrown to the middle of the room (line 20). There's a staircase and a saloon (living room) filled with furniture. There are windows (choice D), which did not break from the impact of the accident and which were not described as large or the equivalent of picture windows since the men could not tell whether or not the submarine had come to the surface.

37. **The correct answer is D.** Nemo explains that the accident was not human error (choice A), but nature, by which he means the laws of the seas and the universe (lines 61–63: "From a caprice of nature, not from the ignorance of man. … We may brave human laws, but we cannot resist natural ones."). He does not refer to God anywhere in the passage (choice B), and there is no indication that there were rough seas (choice C), as Aronnax describes how the ship "advanced straight" and was "floating" before the "violent shock" of the collision (lines 16–19).

38. **The correct answer is D.** The men compare this situation to a previous "incident," wherein the Nautilus turned over, but righted herself (lines 32–33: "I do not think she will right herself as she did the first time in Torres Straits."). When they consult Nemo, the captain clarifies that this situation is perhaps more serious and that the ship is actually stranded (lines 51–53: "… using one of his own expressions in the Torres

Straits: / "An incident, Captain?" / "No, sir; an accident this time."). He explicitly states that the accident was not from a mistake "in the working" (choice D) and that there was no immediate danger (choice C). There is no evidence in the text to support choice B.

39. **The correct answer is C.** Aronnax makes mention of the "great" cold (line 3), ice on the water (line 6), and the constellation the Southern Cross (lines 3–4: "In the zenith glittered that wondrous Southern Cross—the polar bear of Antarctic regions.") Later, Nemo "placed his finger on a spot representing the southern seas" (line 49) when trying to assess their position. The ship had previously been in the Torres Strait, but it is clear from context that it is no longer there (choice A). There is no evidence in the passage to support choices B or D.

40. **The correct answer is D.** The narrator has already described great cold, icy waters and a constellation of the "Antarctic regions," but when Captain Nemo consults his navigation tools and puts his finger on the southern seas (lines 47–49), he confirms this. Lines 16–18 (choice A) describe only the ship's depth and the kind of water they are in. Lines 31–33 (choice C) describe an earlier incident in the Torres Straits that occurred in the past. Lines 25–26 (choice B) describe only that the ship is motionless.

41. **The correct answer is A.** In the context of the sentence, *berths* refers to the kind of fixed bunk found on a ship—in this case, in the crew's quarters (lines 42–43: "At the centre staircase, by the berths of the ship's crew, there was no one"). The word *berths* could also refer to a ship's docking space (choice D), but in this context that meaning makes no sense, as the ship is underwater in the middle of the sea and nowhere near a port. Don't confuse *berth* with *birth*, a word with different meanings that could mislead you to select choices B or C.

42. **The correct answer is D.** *Caprice* implies something unpredictable and sudden, but not something out of the ordinary or freakish (choice A). Here, it refers to an act of nature that is unpredictable and can't be helped. It does not mean inspirational (choice B) or having a steady hand (choice C).

43. **The correct answer is D.** The speech cleverly connects the role of space exploration and the Cold War (lines 27–29: "and only if the United States ... terrifying theater of war.") and ties advancement in the sciences to winning that war. The public already knew about the space program (choice A), as evident in lines 40–41 ("the decision last year to shift our efforts in space from low to high gear"), and that the Soviets had already sent a man into space, aggressively or otherwise (choice B). Although the speech could be seen, in part at least, as a way to advocate for funding science and math, he does not explicitly mention funding (choice C). He focuses on his goal of getting a man on the moon, and being the first to do so "because there is new knowledge to be gained, and new rights to be won, and they must be won and used for the progress of all people." (lines 23–25).

44. **The correct answer is B.** Kennedy's theme is the urgency of advancing our scientific knowledge and how it will make putting a man on the moon possible and how achieving that feat will also push the country to be number one. He doesn't mention the Cold War specifically or name the Soviet Union or indicate that the United States is falling behind (choice A). Choice C does not explain why exploration is so important, and choice D is a main idea, not the theme.

45. **The correct answer is A.** The two paragraphs are designed to show how space is a new scientific frontier, one that needs to be explored and will in the future be compared to other great moments of scientific discovery, for example, laws of gravity and the steam engine. Although choice B is a true statement, Kennedy's objective was not to remind people of, but to rally them to support, his goal. The analogy he makes does more than simply compare progress of the past; it illustrates how mankind has reached this moment in history.

46. The correct answer is C. The first paragraph explains how the country has advanced recently, doubling the number of trained and educated scientists who were poised to explore space (lines 1–4: "most of the scientists ... our population as a whole"). He did not directly connect the scientists to the competition with the Soviet Union (choices A and B), nor did he connect the concept of conscience in space to the push for a moon landing (choice D). Rather, he connected the moon landing to something the country should want to do as a new challenge and a breakthrough in exploration that would, with some determination, lead to success (lines 35–39: "we choose to go to the ... we intend to win, and the others, too ...").

47. The correct answer is D. Kennedy argues that because space science "has no conscience of its own" (lines 25–26), the country that leads in such exploration will determine whether the outcome will be "for good or ill," that is, for positive and humane purposes or for war and tyranny, and he explicitly states the need for America to occupy "a position of pre-eminence" (lines 26–29: "Whether it will ... theater of war.") The increase in scientists in the United States is not directly related to the Soviet threat or the potential moon landing (choice A). Choices B and C do not refer at all to the space program and are therefore incorrect.

48. The correct answer is B. Using repetition in a speech places emphasis on the ideas conveyed and, as a literary device, is used to evoke passion in the audience. Kennedy uses it in several parts of the speech, for example, "despite the" in Paragraph 1, and "we choose to go" in the last part (lines 34–35). It does not change how people understand his words or show that he is particularly knowledgeable. The repetitive phrases are not idioms and are unrelated to them.

49. The correct answer is B. The "New Frontier" was the phrase used to describe Kennedy's policies. The words evoke the idea of a renewal of US expansion as part of the historical expansion of the land, only in this case, the frontier is outer space. Choice B refers to the benefits of exploration. His words here are metaphorical as they refer to space, not to the sea, but to the new ideas and knowledge gained from exploration.

50. The correct answer is D. Choice D shows the urgency of Kennedy's appeal—he does not want to postpone the effort. It is therefore a priority that needs to be attended to now, not later. Choice C explains a reason for his thinking, not a priority. Choice A refers to the pace of scientific achievements, showing that space exploration can also become part of that trajectory, but it does not indicate the priority of the policy he wants to adopt. Choice B explains why President

Kennedy considers space travel important, but it does not show the urgency he wants to convey in his speech.

51. **The correct answer is D.** A theater of war—as opposed to a theater where people are entertained—refers to the area in which a battle is waged. Here Kennedy opens the possibility that war could extend to space.

52. **The correct answer is C.** A *writ* refers to a formal written document, usually a legal document (for example, a writ of habeas corpus). But in this context, it refers to the authority or power granted by such documents. In the context of the sentence, a simple written document does not make sense. The word does not refer to either influence or permission.

SECTION 2: WRITING AND LANGUAGE TEST

1. C	10. D	19. B	28. C	37. A
2. C	11. C	20. D	29. B	38. D
3. A	12. B	21. C	30. D	39. B
4. A	13. A	22. D	31. B	40. B
5. B	14. B	23. D	32. C	41. C
6. A	15. C	24. B	33. D	42. D
7. C	16. B	25. C	34. D	43. C
8. C	17. B	26. C	35. B	44. D
9. D	18. C	27. B	36. D	

WRITING AND LANGUAGE TEST RAW SCORE
(Number of correct answers)

1. **The correct answer is C.** Choice C correctly identifies the nonrestrictive phrase and sets it off with commas. Choice A is incorrect because it is a run-on sentence. Choice B is incorrect because "160,000" is an essential element of the sentence. Choice D is incorrect because "currently practice in the United States" is separated from the rest of the nonrestrictive clause that begins with "there."

2. **The correct answer is C.** Choice C correctly suggests that this sentence should be kept because it is both relevant and builds on the previous sentence by further defining the field of organizational psychology. Choice A is incorrect because this sentence does not introduce a new idea. Choice B is incorrect because this sentence does not repeat information. Choice D is incorrect because the main topic of the paragraph is established by the previous sentence.

3. **The correct answer is A.** This paragraph is about defining the industry, not about what an I/O psychologist's workplace looks like, so choice A is correct, however interesting or relevant this detail might be in a longer passage. Choice B is incorrect because this detail could be seen to support the information in the paragraph, were there space to provide proper context for the argument. Choices C and D are incorrect.

4. **The correct answer is A.** Choice A correctly introduces organizational psychologists as the focus of the sentence and paragraph. Choice B

incorrectly talks about child psychologists. Choice C incorrectly talks about human resource employees. Choice D makes the sentence more specific than is necessary or correct.

5. **The correct answer is B.** Choice B correctly eliminates the redundant phrases "and the company" and "and hire." Choices A, C, and D are incorrect because they all contain redundancies.

6. **The correct answer is A.** Choice A is correct because the sentence requires a possessive determiner. Choice B is incorrect because *there* is an adverb. Choice C is incorrect because the plural is not required. Choice D is incorrect because it is a contraction of "they are."

7. **The correct answer is C.** Choice C is correct because *capital* means "worth" or "assets," which is what the author intends. Choice A is incorrect because *capitol* means a building in which a legislative body meets. Choice B is incorrect because when capitalized, it refers to the building in which the United States Congress meets in Washington. Choice D is incorrect because the word *capitalist* ("a person who favors capitalism") doesn't make sense in this sentence.

8. **The correct answer is C.** The previous paragraph describes plentiful corporate job opportunities for I/O psychologists. The sentence in question urges the reader to be cautious before assuming these opportunities will be available to him or her without having first a good number of qualifications. The word *however* (choice C) provides an appropriate transition to the qualification that the paragraph introduces. *Furthermore, subsequently*, and *therefore* (choices A, B, and D) would all serve to mislead the reader into thinking the information that follows in the new paragraph will continue in the same vein as the previous paragraph, which would be incorrect.

9. **The correct answer is D.** Only choice D supports the sentence's reference to the negative aspects of pursuing an advanced degree. Choice A is incorrect because it implies something positive, which is not the focus of the sentence. Choice B is incorrect because the author is not saying that education is ridiculous. Choice C is incorrect because it overstates the possible difficulty to which the author refers.

10. **The correct answer is D.** Choice D correctly uses the subordinating conjunction *as* to fix the sentence. Choices A and B are incorrect because the sentence requires a subordinating conjunction. Choice C is incorrect because the conjunction *while* implies a contradiction, which is not supported by the context of the sentence.

11. **The correct answer is C.** Choice C correctly uses the singular verb *intensifies*, which agrees with the singular noun *competition*. Choices

A, B, and D are incorrect because each of these choices is plural.

12. **The correct answer is B.** The sentence does not express the main idea of the paragraph (choice A), but is also not irrelevant to the paragraph (choice C), as it does a nice job of painting a picture for the surprising events of the first paragraph, which sets up the rest of the passage. Choice D is incorrect because the information is not repeated anywhere else in the passage.

13. **The correct answer is A.** Choice A is correct because an objective relative pronoun is required. Choice B is incorrect because *who* is in the subjective case. Choices C and D are incorrect because they are not relative pronouns.

14. **The correct answer is B.** Choice B accurately identifies a nonrestrictive element and uses commas to set it off. Choice A is incorrect because it omits a required comma after *device*. Choice C is incorrect because it incorrectly places a comma after *blast*. Choice D is not correct because it omits the comma after *Man*.

15. **The correct answer is C.** The sentence provides a concrete detail about the nuclear bomb, which is the focus of the paragraph. Choices A and B are incorrect because the sentence is relevant and correctly placed. Choice D is incorrect because the information is not tangential.

16. **The correct answer is B.** In the context of the passage, choice B best reflects the implied severity of the blast and does a better job of emphasizing that force. Choices A, C, and D are incorrect because they are too mild compared with the utter destruction described in the rest of the passage.

17. **The correct answer is B.** Choice B eliminates the redundant phrase "so much so." Choice A is incorrect because the phrase "so much so" is awkward and makes the sentence redundant. Choice C is incorrect because while it eliminates the original wordiness, it introduces the redundant terms *gushed* and *poured*. Choice D is incorrect because the phrase "so much and so quickly" is awkward and wordy.

18. **The correct answer is C.** Choice C is correct because *site* means "the place, scene, or point of an occurrence or event." Choice A is incorrect because *sight* refers to "the process, power, or function of seeing." Choice B is incorrect because it is the plural of *sight*. Choice D is incorrect because a plural is not required.

19. **The correct answer is B.** The main topic of the paragraph is the U.S. government's funding of the Manhattan Project in the interests of developing the atomic bomb. The most relevant statistic to this paragraph would be the overall amount it spent on that project (choice B). Choices A and C are

incorrect because they provide information that is too specific given the focus of this passage: choice A focuses on heavy water reactors alone, and choice C deals only with the transport of the bomb once developed. In choice D, it is unclear whether that spending total included other expenses beyond the purview of the bomb.

20. **The correct answer is D.** Choice D is correct because the conventional expression is "in one fell swoop," which has come to mean "in a single incident; as a single event; all at one time." Choices A, B, and C are incorrect because none of them is the correct expression.

21. **The correct answer is C.** Only choice C improves the clarity of the sentence and eliminates the syntax problems of the original. Choices A, B, and D are incorrect because they all have syntax problems.

22. **The correct answer is D.** Choice D eliminates passive voice problems and makes the sentence active. Choices A, B, and C are incorrect because they are all written in the passive voice.

23. **The correct answer is D.** Choice D accurately uses the conventional expression "as a means to an end," which describes those things that have little value except as they serve some larger goal. Choices A, B, and C are wrong because they all misuse the expression.

24. **The correct answer is B.** Choice B accurately uses the word *lies* to designate a thing that has a place in relation to something else. Choice A is incorrect because *lay* designates the action of placing or putting into a horizontal position. Choice C is incorrect because it is the present perfect tense of *lay*, which is wrong in this sentence. Choice D is incorrect because it is the plural verb form of *lie*.

25. **The correct answer is C.** Choice C is correct because this sentence connects liberal arts education, the topic of the essay, to the author's experiences choosing a course of study. Choices A and B are incorrect because the sentence should be kept, and it is neither irrelevant nor illogical. Choice D is incorrect because it is not tangential but central to the focus of the essay.

26. **The correct answer is C.** Choice C is correct because the sentence quotes from a credible source and develops the focus of the sentence by defining a key term. Choice A is incorrect because the details are relevant. Choice B is incorrect because this information has not been provided elsewhere. Choice D is incorrect because the definition provided expands on an idea that was presented previously.

27. **The correct answer is B.** Only choice B correctly places the comma in this part of the sentence. Choice A incorrectly omits all commas. Choice C incorrectly

places a comma after *skills*. Choice D incorrectly omits the comma that should be placed after *communication*.

28. **The correct answer is C.** The sentence requires a singular possessive noun, which choice C provides. Choice A is incorrect because it is not a possessive noun. Choice B is incorrect because the sentence requires a singular possessive noun, not a plural possessive noun. Choice D is incorrect because it is not a possessive noun.

29. **The correct answer is B.** Choice B elaborates on the idea that liberal arts majors make as much or more than those with STEM-related degrees. Choices A and C are incorrect because they provide examples that undermine the author's argument. Choice D is incorrect because its connection to the focus of the paragraph is unclear.

30. **The correct answer is D.** Choice D is correct because the author is talking about the requirements of his degree. Choice A is incorrect because it implies a threat that the context does not support. Choice B is incorrect because *suppressed* means "to prevent or stop," which does not make sense in this context. Choice C is incorrect because *concussed* means "to cause a concussion," which does not make sense in this context.

31. **The correct answer is B.** The rest of the choices in the long sentence are written in a parallel structure: "the _____ of _____." The best replacement for this selection (choice B) is written in the same structure as every other sentence item. Choices A and C are incorrect because they do not match this parallel structure. Choice D is closer, but still stands out as incorrect because it doesn't sync up with the rest of the sentence.

32. **The correct answer is C.** Choice C is the correct answer because it brings the singular subject into agreement with a singular verb. Choice A is incorrect because the plural verb does not agree with the singular *I*. Choice B is incorrect because, while it correctly uses "I have," it introduces an error by making "need" plural. Choice D is wrong because it erroneously adds an *s* to the word *need* and does not correct the original error.

33. **The correct answer is D.** Choice D maintains the conversational but formal tone of the essay. Choices A, B, and C are incorrect because they are all too informal.

34. **The correct answer is D.** Choice D eliminates misplaced and dangling modifier problems. Choices A, B, and C are incorrect because in each sentence it is unclear to what the phrase "between the ages of 15–24" refers.

35. **The correct answer is B.** Choice B is correct because it provides a statistic that supports the sentence and paragraph's focus on the decline in sports participation among youth. Choices A, C, and D are incorrect because they provide statistics that contradict the idea that sports participation is declining.

36. **The correct answer is D.** Only choice D provides information that supports the paragraph's focus on the decreasing number of youth athletes. Choice A is incorrect because it speaks to the focus of the previous paragraph, not this one. Choices B and C are incorrect because they highlight community responses to the problem, but this is not the focus of the paragraph.

37. **The correct answer is A.** The sentence introduces the topic of the paragraph by linking the previous paragraph's topic of youth sports to this paragraph's focus on youth coaching, so choice A is correct. Choices B, C, and D are incorrect because they create logical errors in the flow of information.

38. **The correct answer is D.** Choice D supports the paragraph's argument about the importance of training for youth coaches and communicates the need for stricter guidelines. Choices A and B are incorrect because they undermine the paragraph's concern over the issue. Choice C is incorrect because it is too soft, given the context of the paragraph.

39. **The correct answer is B.** Choice B correctly changes the original sentence from passive to active voice. Choices A and D are incorrect because they use the passive voice. Choice C is incorrect because it introduces a misplaced modifier.

40. **The correct answer is B.** Choice B is correct because it uses a comma after the subordinating conjunction *However* and a dash to emphasize the final clause. Choice A is incorrect because it misuses a colon. Choice C is incorrect because it misuses a dash. Choice D is incorrect because while a semicolon could be used after *program*, a semicolon is not used to follow a subordinating conjunction.

41. **The correct answer is C.** Choice C is the correct answer because *compiled* means "composed out of materials from other documents," which makes the most sense in the context of the sentence. Choice A is incorrect because *compelled* means "caused to do by overwhelming pressure." Choice B is incorrect because *complied* means "conformed, submitted, or adapted as required or requested." Choice D is incorrect because there is no such word as *compulsed*.

42. **The correct answer is D.** Choice D is correct because it is an example that relates to mental functioning. Choice A is incorrect because it

suggests an improvement in mental functioning. Choices B and C are incorrect because they are issues not related to brain injury.

43. **The correct answer is C.** Choice C correctly uses parallel structure to present the series. Choices A, B, and D are all incorrect because they fail to use parallel structure.

44. **The correct answer is D.** Only choice D provides relevant and accurate data from the chart. Choices A, B, and C are incorrect because, while they interpret the data correctly, the information they present is not relevant to the essay's focus on concussions in youth sports.

SECTION 3: MATH TEST—NO CALCULATOR

1. C	5. C	9. A	13. C	17. 10
2. C	6. C	10. B	14. D	18. 50
3. B	7. A	11. B	15. C	19. 3.6 OR 18/5
4. D	8. D	12. A	16. 2.4	20. 800

MATH TEST—NO CALCULATOR RAW SCORE
(Number of correct answers)

1. **The correct answer is C.** One simple way to solve this problem is to divide each side of the given equation by 4.

$$\frac{8x+4}{4}=\frac{64}{4}$$
$$2x+1=16$$

2. **The correct answer is C.** Use FOIL to multiply:

$$(2x-3)(3x+2)=6x^2+4x-9x-6$$
$$=6x^2-5x-6$$

3. **The correct answer is B.**

$$\sqrt{2x+8}=-x$$
$$2x+8=x^2$$
$$0=x^2-2x-8$$
$$0=(x-4)(x+2)$$
$$x=4, x=-2$$

Check the values in the original equation to rule out any extraneous solutions.

$$\sqrt{2(4)+8}=\sqrt{16}=4\neq-4$$
$$\sqrt{2(-2)+8}=\sqrt{4}=2=-(-2)$$

Only $x=-2$ is a solution of the equation.

4. **The correct answer is D.** To solve this system of equations for y, the first equation must be multiplied by 2.

$$3x+2y=4 \rightarrow 6x+4y=8$$
$$6x-3y=6 \rightarrow 6x-3y=6$$

Subtracting the two equations on the right gives $7y=2$. Therefore, $y=\frac{2}{7}$.

5. **The correct answer is C.** The form of the equation that shows the x-intercepts is the factored form. The parabola crosses the x-axis at $x=-2$ and $x=4$, and the factored form contains these numbers in the factors.

6. **The correct answer is C.** Solve the second equation for y, then substitute in the first equation and solve for x. Substitute the value of x to find y.

$$y = x - 1$$
$$x^2 + (x-1)^2 = 25$$
$$x^2 + x^2 - 2x + 1 = 25$$
$$2x^2 - 2x - 24 = 0$$
$$2(x-4)(x+3) = 0$$
$$x = 4, x = -3$$
$$y = 4 - 1 \rightarrow y = 3$$
$$y = -3 - 1 \rightarrow y = -4$$

The solutions are (4, 3) and (–3, –4).

So, identifying (4, 3) as (v, w) and (–3, –4) as (r, s) yields

$$|v+w| + |r+s| = |4+3| + |-3-4|$$
$$= 7 + 7 = 14$$

7. **The correct answer is A.** At $d = 8$, the population must have doubled, or $p = 2p_0$. Substituting 8 for d in choice A gives $p = p_0 (2)^{\frac{8}{8}} = p_0 (2)$. It is the only option for which the population doubles after 8 days.

8. **The correct answer is D.**

$$\frac{3(x_2 - 4)}{(x+2)} = \frac{3(x+2)(x-2)}{(x+2)}$$
$$= 3(x-2)$$
$$= 3x - 6$$

9. **The correct answer is A.** On day 0, the height of the bean plants is $h = 0.15(0) + 0.85 = 0.85$, so 0.85 represents the initial height of the bean plants.

10. **The correct answer is B.**

$$x^2 - y^2 = (x+y)(x-y) = 20 \times 10 = 200$$

11. **The correct answer is B.** The area of a circle is $A = \pi r^2$. Since the diameter is 4 inches, then the radius is 2 inches, and the area of the can's base is $A = \pi(2)^2 = 4\pi$. The volume of the can is $V = h \times A$. Since the can is only $\frac{2}{3}$ full, the volume of the juice is $\left(\frac{2}{3}\right)(6)(4\pi) = 4 \times 4\pi = 16\pi$.

12. **The correct answer is A.** The transformation $f(x) + 4$ will move all points 4 spaces upward. The point (2, 3) will move to (2, 7).

13. **The correct answer is C.** The total cost, $5s + 12a$, must be less than or equal to 200, while the number of people, $s + a$, must be greater than or equal to 20.

14. **The correct answer is D.** Multiplying the expressions results in:

$$6 + 3i - 2i - i^2$$
$$6 + i - (-1)$$
$$6 + i + 1$$
$$7 + i$$

15. **The correct answer is C.** The center of the circle is the midpoint of the diameter. (2, 0) is midway between (0, 0) and (4, 0). Since the diameter has a length of 4, the radius has a length of 2. The equation of a circle with center (h, k) and radius r is $(x - h)^2 + (y - k)^2 = r^2$. Substituting the values we know, the equation of the circle is $(x - 2)^2 + y^2 = 4$.

16. The correct answer is 2.4.

$$\left(\frac{1}{4}+\frac{1}{6}\right)h=1$$

$$\left(\frac{6}{24}+\frac{4}{24}\right)h=1$$

$$\frac{10}{24}h=1$$

$$h=\frac{24}{10}=2.4$$

17. The correct answer is 10. Let x be the smallest number of weeks needed to save $900. The following inequality describes this situation:

$$85x+55\geq900$$

$$85x\geq845$$

$$x\geq\frac{845}{85}$$

Since $850 \div 85 = 10$ and you can estimate that the right side is a bit smaller than 10, 10 weeks are needed to save $900.

18. The correct answer is 50.

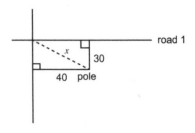

Using the Pythagorean theorem:

$$(30)^2 + (40)^2 = x^2$$

$$900+1,600=x^2$$

$$2,500=x^2$$

$$x=50$$

19. The correct answer is 3.6 or 18/5.

The x-intercept occurs where $y = 0$.

$$0-2=5(x-4)$$

$$-2=5x-20$$

$$18=5x$$

$$x=\frac{18}{5}=3.6$$

20. The correct answer is 800.

The rate of change is
$$a=\frac{700-500}{1-3}=\frac{200}{-2}=-100.$$ Using this value and the given values 1 for t and 700 for $f(t)$, solve for b:

$$700=-100\,(1)+b$$

$$700=-100+b$$

$$b=800$$

SECTION 4: MATH TEST—CALCULATOR

1. D	**9.** A	**17.** B	**25.** D	**32.** 80
2. D	**10.** C	**18.** C	**26.** C	**33.** 72
3. C	**11.** D	**19.** B	**27.** C	**34.** 576
4. B	**12.** D	**20.** B	**28.** B	**35.** 6.56
5. C	**13.** B	**21.** A	**29.** B	**36.** $\frac{5}{12}$
6. B	**14.** B	**22.** D	**30.** D	**37.** 6
7. C	**15.** A	**23.** D	**31.** 0	**38.** 0.4
8. C	**16.** A	**24.** C		

MATH–CALCULATOR TEST RAW SCORE [   ]
(Number of correct answers)

1. **The correct answer is D.** $23 million dollars is half of one percent of the total sales in the city, so 1% of the total sales is $46 million. The amount brought in by the normal tax is 8.75%, or 8.75(46) = 402.5 million. Add the half-percent tax to the normal tax to find the total: 23 + 402.5 = 425.5 ≈ $426 million.

2. **The correct answer is D.** Use long division to solve this problem:

$$3x-2\overline{\smash{\big)}6x^2-13x+6} \quad \begin{array}{r} 2x-3 \end{array}$$

$$\underline{6x^2-4x}$$
$$-9x+6$$
$$\underline{-9x+6}$$
$$0$$

3. **The correct answer is C.** Recall that distance = rate × time. Traveling at 55 miles per hour for 45 minutes is a distance of $55 \bullet \frac{45}{60} = 41.25$ miles. If his commute takes 5 minutes less, the new time will be 45 – 5 = 40 minutes. Again, distance = rate × time, so $41.25 = x \bullet \frac{40}{60}$, which reduces to $41.25 = \frac{2}{3}x$.

4. **The correct answer is B.** The population density of Houston is 2,200,000 people/600 square miles ≈ 3,667 people per square mile. The population density of Los Angeles is 3,900,000 people/469 square miles ≈ 8,315 people per square mile. 8,315 – 3,667 ≈ 4,648 people per square mile.

5. **The correct answer is C.** The vertex of $h(x) = (x - 4)^2 - 25$ is $(4, -25)$, which is in Quadrant IV. Since the coefficient of the squared term is positive, the graph opens upward. Also, the x-intercepts are $x = -1$ and $x = 9$. As such, the graph is as follows:

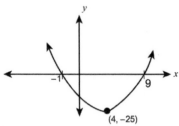

Figure not drawn to scale.

6. **The correct answer is B.** The maximum value occurs at the vertex of the parabola, which is at $(20, 900)$. The price to generate the maximum profit is the x-coordinate of that point.

7. **The correct answer is C.** The wave height can be represented by $3 < h < 4$. We are told that $d = 1.3h$, so multiply the inequality by 1.3 to obtain $3(1.3) < 1.3(h) < 4(1.3)$, or $3.9 < d < 5.2$.

8. **The correct answer is C.** There are $(60)(60) = 3,600$ seconds in one hour.

    (740 miles per hour)(5,280 feet per mile) = 3,907,200 feet per hour.

    3,907,200 feet per hour ÷ 3,600 seconds per hour ≈ 1,085 feet per second.

9. **The correct answer is A.** Parties other than the Liberal Party or

Conservative Party won $338 - 184 - 99 = 55$ seats. $55 \div 338 \approx 0.16 = 16\%$.

10. **The correct answer is C.** The maximum number of buses is 9 because we violate the constraint if $b = 10$. With 9 buses present, solve $10(9) + c < 100$, so $c < 10$. The largest whole number less than 10 is 9.

11. **The correct answer is D.**

$$2x^2\sqrt{5x} = \sqrt{4}\sqrt{x^4}\sqrt{5x}$$
$$= \sqrt{20x^{4+1}} = \sqrt{20x^5}$$

12. **The correct answer is D.** Factor out $(x^2 - y^2)$:

$$(x + y)^2(x^2 - y^2) = (x + y)^2(x + y)(x - y)$$
$$= (x + y)^3(x - y)$$

13. **The correct answer is B.** Assuming GDP growth at a constant percentage, an exponential model is appropriate. The approximate growth rate is $(16.8 - 16.2) \div 16.2 \approx 0.037$, and the initial value is 16.2. Substituting into the model for exponential growth, $f(t) = 16.2(1.037)^t$.

14. **The correct answer is B.** Multiply the second equation by 5 and subtract to eliminate the variable y, then solve:

$$10x - 7y = 3$$
$$-(5x - 7y = 5)$$
$$\overline{}$$
$$5x = -2$$
$$x = -\frac{2}{5} = -0.4$$

15. The correct answer is A. Since the polynomial function crosses the x-axis at $x = 2$, $x - 2$ must be a factor of the polynomial.

16. The correct answer is A. There are 12 edges on a cube, so each edge is 48 inches ÷ 12 = 4 inches. The volume of the cube is $(s)^3 = (4 \text{ inches})^3 = 64$ cubic inches.

17. The correct answer is B. To find the mean, add all of the values together and divide by the number of values:
$$\frac{1.4+1.1+1.3+1.3+1.3+1.1+0.7+0.6}{8}=1.1$$

18. The correct answer is C. The line has slope $m=\frac{4-3}{5-1}=\frac{1}{4}$. Using the point-slope form of the equation of the line, we can write $y-3=\frac{1}{4}(x-1)$, which simplifies to $y=\frac{1}{4}x+\frac{11}{4}$.

19. The correct answer is B. Begin by subtracting 32 from each side of the equation, then multiply both sides by $\frac{5}{9}$:
$$F=\frac{9}{5}C+32$$
$$F-32=\frac{9}{5}C+32-32$$
$$F-32=\frac{9}{5}C$$
$$\frac{5}{9}(F-32)=\frac{5}{9}\times\frac{9}{5}C$$
$$\frac{5}{9}(F-32)=C$$

20. The correct answer is B. Since the sample proportion is 60% with a margin of error of 2%, the

population proportion is likely to lie between 58% and 62%. To find 58% of 8,000 voters, multiply: (0.58)(8,000) = 4,640.

21. The correct answer is A. In a linear function, the coefficient of the constant term represents the rate of change of the function.

22. The correct answer is D. There were 40 + 45 = 85 respondents in favor of the ballot measure, and 40 of them lived in rural areas: $\frac{40}{85}=\frac{8}{17}$.

23. The correct answer is D. Let's represent the speed of the aircraft in still air. Using distance equals rate times time, we know that the distance from A to B is 4(s − 50), and the distance for the return trip (B to A) is 3(s + 50). Since these distances are equal, equate these expressions to get the equation 3(s + 50) = 4(s − 50).

24. The correct answer is C. The points are in a shape resembling a downward opening parabola, so a quadratic function with a negative second degree term is indicated. A zero at $x = 4$ shows that $x - 4$ is a factor, which shows that choice C is the correct answer.

25. The correct answer is D. Complete the square so that the vertex can be easily identified:

$$g(x) = -3x^2 - 12x - 10$$
$$= -3(x^2 + 4x) - 10$$
$$= -3(x^2 + 4x) + 4 \ -10 + 12$$
$$= -3(x+2)^2 + 2$$

So, the vertex is (–2, 2). So, $h = -2$ and $k = 2$. Thus, $k^h = 2^{-2} = \dfrac{1}{4}$.

26. The correct answer is C. The rate of change is $m = \dfrac{200 - 900}{4 - 2} = -350$. Using the point-slope form of the equation of a line, $d - 900 = -350(t - 2)$. Simplifying this equation results in $d = 1,600 - 350t$.

27. The correct answer is C. First, convert the currencies to the same unit (13.9 trillion euros)(7.7 yuan/euro) ≈ 107 trillion yuan. The ratio of the GDPs of the European Union and China is then $\dfrac{107}{63.6} = 1.682$, or approximately 1.7.

28. The correct answer is B. The x-intercepts mean that the quadratic function must have the form $y = a(x - 2)(x - 4)$. Multiplying this expression out leads to $y = ax^2 - 6ax + 8a$. The y-intercept, 12, must be $8a$, so $8a = 12$ means $a = 1.5$. Substituting 1.5 for a gives $y = 1.5x^2 - 6(1.5)x + 8(1.5) = 1.5x^2 - 9x + 12$.

29. The correct answer is B. First, set up the system of equations:

$$2p + n = 8.50$$
$$p + 2n = 9.50$$

Notice that if the two equations are added, the coefficients of p and n are the same. Use this fact to find the sum of p and n:

$$3p + 3n = 18 \rightarrow 3(p+n)$$
$$= 18 \rightarrow p + n = 18$$

30. The correct answer is D. Since $g(x) = -f(x)$, $g(3) = -f(3) = -0 = 0$.

31. The correct answer is 0.

Machine A: 2,000 /hr.

Machine B:

$$5,000 / \dfrac{5}{2} \text{ hr.} = 5,000 \left(\dfrac{2}{5} \right) = 2,000 / \text{hr.}$$

Since the rates are the same, they produce the same number of flue covers during any period of time. So Machine A has produced 0 more flue covers than Machine B.

32. The correct answer is 80.

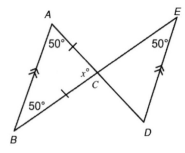

Figure not drawn to scale.

Since $ED \parallel AB$, angle E = angle B = 50°. (They are alternate interior angles.) Since $AC = BC$, angle A = angle B = 50°. (In a triangle, opposite equal sides are equal angles.). In triangle ABC:

$$50+50+x=180$$
$$x=80$$

33. The correct answer is 72. First, convert dollars to cents: \$1.70 = 170 cents and \$10.20 = 1,020 cents. Next, establish a ratio of candies to cents:

$$\frac{candies}{cents} : \frac{12}{170} = \frac{x}{1,020}$$
$$170x=12\,(1,020)$$
$$x=72$$

34. The correct answer is 576. Using the density formula, $D=\dfrac{m}{v}$, substitute the known values, $8=\dfrac{M}{72}$. To find the mass, multiply the density by the volume:

$$8\frac{g}{cm^3}\,(12cm\times12\ cm\times0.5\ cm)=576\ g$$

35. The correct answer is 6.56.

$$\frac{3.57+1.33+6.55+1.32+1.05+0.63}{6}=2.41$$
$$\frac{7.9+x}{6}=2.41$$
$$7.9+x=14.46$$
$$x=6.56$$

36. The correct answer is $\dfrac{5}{12}$. If gear C makes 3 revolutions when gear B makes 2 revolutions, gear C will make 12 revolutions when gear B makes 8 revolutions. Gear B makes 8 revolutions when gear A makes 5 revolutions, so gear C makes 12 revolutions when gear A makes 5 revolutions. The ratio of A to C is $\dfrac{5}{12}$.

37. The correct answer is 6. Substitute the values of x and y in the equation and solve for b.

$$5=-\frac{1}{2}(2)+b$$
$$5=-1+b$$
$$b=6$$

38. The correct answer is 0.4. 125 students wanted to join the Drama Club. Of those, 50 also wanted to join the Art Club. $50 \div 125 = 0.4$

SECTION 5: SAT® ESSAY

Analysis of Passage

Adapted from "From Smokey Bear to Climate Change: The Future of Wildland Fire Management" by John Bailey, originally published by *The Conversation* on August 11, 2015. John Bailey is an associate professor of Silviculture and Fire Management at Oregon State University.

1	Current conditions in the West demonstrate that our U.S. fire management system is struggling and	1	*The writer starts by clearly stating the seriousness of the situation he will be addressing: the need to change U.S. fire management.*
2	approaching a state of crisis. Spending on fighting fires has climbed dramatically since the 1990s. And there is growing risk of more intense fires with each passing year, given the effects of climate change, accumulated fuels in the landscape and our inability to extinguish all ignitions.	2	*Bailey underscores the urgency of the situation by identifying specific elements of the problem. As he does this, he uses evocative phrases: "a state of crisis," "climbed dramatically," "growing risks," and "more intense fires."*
3	Our fire management system invariably leads managers to attempt suppression of nearly all wildland fires despite the natural, beneficial role of "good" fires. Ironically, our firefighting system is very efficient at extinguishing such "good" fires while, by default, creating the "bad" fires that have no historic precedents and create great losses.	3	*The writer clearly explains the situation he will be addressing, in terms readers can easily understand: the current fire management system relies on suppressing wildland fires, including the "good" fires that are beneficial to nature. But by effectively extinguishing "good" fires, officials pave the way for "bad" fires that cause enormous damage. By introducing the terms "good fires" and "bad fires," the writer lays the foundation for his argument—a wildland fire can be a positive event.*

Fire benefits

4   There is little doubt over the historic role of fire in forests throughout North America and much of the world. Fire has been a reality for millennia. Our ancestors recognized this fact, coexisted with fire, and actively set and spread fire to improve their lives for food, water, medicines, and safety.

4   *The writer begins to support his argument by explaining that people have been interacting with fire for thousands of years, learning to coexist by deliberately setting fires to improve their lives.*

5   Forest vegetation and animals evolved adaptations to fire; the forest as an ecosystem evolved with fire regimes of various frequencies, intensities, and spatial patterns that are fundamental to their structure, composition, and function.

5   *The writer continues to support his argument with additional facts that show nature, too, "works" with fire. In fact, forests have evolved with fire events that are "fundamental to their structure, composition, and function." By making these statements, the writer underscores the beneficial role of fire in nature.*

6   For example, ponderosa pine and associated dry, mixed-conifer forests are **resistant** to fire. Historically, these forests burned once or twice per decade as low-intensity surface fires that maintained open forest conditions and grass understories, which promoted ensuing fires. A few trees were killed here and there, which made room for new individuals to grow into the main canopy, creating a forest that contained many ages, much like a multigenerational household.

6   *Bailey supports his claim that fire can be beneficial by providing a specific example: the positive relationship between fire and fire-resistant ponderosa pine ("and associated dry, mixed-conifer forests.")*

7 In contrast, lodgepole pine forests are **resilient** to fire—destroyed but reborn. Whole mountainsides of such forests burned in spectacular fashion, but the blackened ground was soon covered with seeds, protected within the skeleton of their parents. The forest thereby regenerated in one big wave of children—like an elementary school!

7 *The writer continues to support his claim that fire can be beneficial with a second example: fire-resilient lodgepole pine forests that are destroyed by fire but are reborn through seeds that are released from the burned trees. By giving these two examples, Bailey provides strong support for his claim that fire is beneficial —even forests that are destroyed by fire are often reborn.*

8 Both resistance and resilience are valid strategies, and forests used these strategies in some mix for millennia.

8 *The writer concludes this part of his argument by pointing out that both resistance and resilience are defenses against fire that work, and have worked, for thousands of years. In other words, nature "knows what it is doing."*

9 Euro-American settlement largely put an end to that fundamental relationship between forests and fire. The expansion of towns and agriculture, fragmentation of the landscape, fire suppression, Smokey Bear, and a favorable climate pattern combined to limit fire during much of the 20th century. Fire histories from hundreds of research sites definitively show this change, and the forests changed with it.

9 *Bailey now subtly suggests that nature may know what it is doing, but people don't. He points out that human settlement virtually ended the natural balance between fire and nature. People limited fire, and forests changed as a result. Bailey supports this claim by citing "fire histories from hundreds of research sites."*

10 Because of policies that prioritized fire suppression, there has been a consistent accumulation of fuels in most of our forests. This has created a structural continuity of those fuels across landscapes and from the forest floor to the canopy, as well as shifts in species composition.

10 *The writer further develops his argument by pointing out that fire suppression has led to an "accumulation of fuels in most of our forests." By saying this, he is establishing a cause-and-effect relationship that supports his argument: fire suppression leads to conditions that can result in bigger, more damaging fires.*

The fuel problem

11   Now, the role of fire is changing as it re-exerts itself, despite our best efforts to continue suppressing it. Resistance mechanisms such as thick tree bark are no longer sufficient as fires burn hotter because of accumulated fuel. Large "mega-fires" threaten more resources and more human communities every year.

11   *Bailey goes into more detail about why the accumulation of fuel is a problem: natural fire-resistant mechanisms such as thick tree bark are no longer effective because the accumulated fuel lets fires burn hotter. In addition, today's wildland fires grow into "mega-fires" that are harder to put out and cause more damage.*

12   As a result, expenditures for suppression have grown. And because those efforts are largely successful, they tend to promote human settlement right up to the edge of vast forests. Our success in putting out wildfires thereby serves to extend the risk, driving a need for more suppression.

12   *The writer continues to demonstrate cause and effect. With bigger fires occurring, people are spending more on—and getting better at—fire suppression. This leads to bigger, more destructive fires, which in turn lead to a desire for more suppression. And because we've become so good at suppression, people feel safe living at the "edge of vast forests."*

13   But the accumulated fuel hazard—that is, the amount of fuel capable of burning—grows as fires are suppressed.

13   *Bailey now drives home the need for a change in fire management policy: Suppression leads to ever more accumulated fuel, which in turn leads to bigger fires.*

14   And new risks associated with climate change, including drier and hotter conditions, are only projected to increase.

14   *Bailey adds additional support for his argument. In addition to bigger fires caused by suppression, we now face new risks from climate change, and these risks are "projected to increase."*

15   Landscapes are largely unalterable—vegetation will grow, die and burn; and humans are not going to leave the forest edge. Therefore, there is only one way in this emerging crisis to break the cycle, which is to treat the continuously accumulating fuels.

15   *The writer uses strong language to add urgency to his argument: "There is only one way" to stop this "emerging crisis"—get rid of the accumulating fuels.*

More prescribed fires

16 A number of land management groups are launching more and larger forest restoration treatments, thinning the trees and removing fuel in order to turn this tide of built-up fuel. These efforts are commendable. But they are subsidized by state and federal taxes and produce little marketable material for a forestry industry that has largely disappeared in many locales. Therefore, these restoration efforts are too scattered and too small to make a difference in the landscape.

16 *Bailey strengthens his credibility by conceding that there are some proactive efforts underway to eliminate accumulated fuel. However, he maintains the force of his argument by claiming they are "too scattered and too small to make a difference."*

17 Instead, large wildland fires have been doing and will continue to do most of "the work" of draining the fuel reservoir. Our choice is between the current passive management of fire—suppressing when we can and otherwise minimizing the damage when mega-fires occur—or, instead, active management of fire.

17 *The writer takes his argument to a new level by discussing what we can do. He defines and compares two approaches to fire control: the "current" passive management of fire and the active management of fire.*

18 Passive management fills the reservoir of fuel until it sporadically and dramatically drains large quantities in relatively uncontrolled fashions, which is our current trajectory.

18 *The writer describes what passive management achieves, using evocative words to paint a picture: it "sporadically and dramatically drains" large quantities in relatively "uncontrolled" fires.*

19 Active management offers more controlled releases that will conserve more of our forest resources intact.

19 *Bailey then describes what active management achieves: more controlled releases that conserve more of our forest resources. This description reinforces his argument that active management is the better policy. In this part of the essay, Bailey adds power to his ideas by echoing his earlier "good fire/bad fire" comparison. Here, passive management is bad; active management is good.*

20 This will mean a dramatic increase in deliberately ignited prescribed fires outside of the fire season and during periods of more moderate conditions within each fire season. It also means the use of prescribed fire tactics during wildland fire events to complement suppression activities.

20 *Bailey now clearly defines and describes what he means by active management. By doing this, he preempts a potential counterclaim that he is urging the irresponsible use of fire to manage forests.*

Sample Essays

The following are examples of a high-scoring and low-scoring essay, based on the passage by John Bailey.

HIGH-SCORING ESSAY

"Fighting fire with fire" is not just an expression; it's a real way to fight real fires. John Bailey examines the methods that are currently used to fight fires and explains why they have been so unsuccessful in recent years. Basically, we aren't fighting fire with fire, and it is backfiring on us. Bailey uses a variety of methods to teach us about the danger of wildfires, show us that current methods aren't working, and persuade us that we should be proactively setting controlled fires to remove accumulated fuel from forests, and thereby cutting down on the out-of-control wildfires that have become all too common in recent years.

The first step in persuading people to act is convincing them that a problem exists. Bailey's choice of words tells us just how dire the situation is. In the first paragraph, Bailey uses the words *struggling, crisis, dramatically, risk*, and *intense*. All of these terms ramp up the urgency of the situation, expressing the need for quick action.

Bailey then describes the current policy of suppressing all fires. He makes a distinction between bad fires that are fiercely destructive and good fires that benefit the environment. This distinction lays the groundwork for the idea of using a good fire to fight a bad fire.

In the Fire Benefits section, Bailey describes how nature uses fire to maintain a healthy ecosystem. The logical deduction is that we should use fire the same way to improve and maintain a healthy forest. The specific examples of mixed-conifer forests that are resistant to fire and lodgepole pine forests that are resilient to fire demonstrate that forests and fire can have a positive relationship. Trees in the forests have adapted to the occasional good fire. In fact, good fire rejuvenates a forest.

Bailey suggests that fire didn't become a problem in forests until people made it a problem. He follows the logical chain of events. 1) People built settlements that extended into the forests. Forest fires risked human lives and property. 2) The policy of suppressing all fires began. 3) Fuel collected in the forests.

In the Fuel Problem section, Bailey explains why the accumulation of fuel is such a big factor in forest fires. Using cause and effect, Bailey states that the abundance of fuel makes a fire burn hotter, so tree bark is not as effective as resisting the flames, and therefore the fire spreads faster and does more damage. He also notes that the drier weather conditions associated with climate change contribute to this increase in "mega-fires" as well, and these are only expected to get worse.

In the More Prescribed Fires section, Bailey examines the current passive methods of fire control and explains why something more is needed. Although he acknowledges the good intentions of the current effort, Bailey maintains that they are too scattered and small to make much of a difference. Currently, it is still the wildfires that are getting rid of most of the built-up fuel. Then Bailey makes the next logical leap: actively manage the problem by using good fires to destroy the fuel. This closes the circle of good fire versus bad fire introduced in the beginning of the article.

Bailey contends that this active management of setting controlled fires will conserve more of our forests and minimize damage to private property. Active fire setting can be done outside of the fire season, which will keep fires from spreading. Furthermore, the elimination of the overabundance of fuel during these intentionally set fires will help curb major fires from raging out of control during the dry season.

Overall, Bailey presents a conclusion that relies on facts and logic. The result is a very per-suasive argument for active management as a tool to reduce the danger and damage caused by uncontrolled wildfires.

LOW-SCORING ESSAY

John Bailey wrote an article entitled "From Smokey Bear to Climate Change: The Future of Wildland Fire Management." Bailey looks at the problem of big fires in American forests. He uses several techniques to help readers understand the problem and he presents a solution for the problem.

Bailey thinks there are too many wildfires that cause too much damage and kill too many people. During the summer, the news is full of stories about wildfires. Sometimes firefighters and other people are killed by wildfires.

Climate change (global warming) has caused a drought in California, which has made the spread of wildfires a challenge to the firefighters. Firefighters have been injured or killed while fighting fires there.

John Bailey thinks that a big problem causing wildfires is all the fuel lying around on the ground. He says that people should prevent wildfires like they used to in the old days. 1. Don't live in the woods. 2. Make sure the area has lots of water. 3. Start fires to burn the fuel that's lying around.

I think that those three things will help people prevent fires from starting and spreading so much. Bailey's arguments, which protect forests from wildfires, are reasonable and smart.

COMPUTING YOUR SCORES

Now that you've completed the diagnostic test, it's time to compute your scores. Simply follow the instructions on the following pages, and use the conversion tables provided to calculate your scores. The formulas provided will give you as close an approximation as possible on how you might score on the actual SAT® exam.

To Determine Your Practice Test Scores

1. After you go through each of the test sections (Reading, Writing and Language, Math—No Calculator, and Math—Calculator) and determine which questions you answered correctly, be sure to enter the number of correct answers in the box below the answer key for each of the sections.

2. Your total score on the practice test is the sum of your Evidence-Based Reading and Writing Section score and your Math Section score. To get your total score, convert the raw score—the number of questions you answered correctly in a particular section—into the "scaled score" for that section, and then calculate the total score. It sounds a little confusing, but we'll take you through the steps.

To Calculate Your Evidence-Based Reading and Writing Section Score

Your Evidence-Based Reading and Writing Section score is on a scale of 200–800.

1. Count the number of correct answers you got on the **Section 1: Reading Test.** Remember that there is no penalty for wrong answers. **The number of correct answers is your raw score.**

2. Go to **Raw Score Conversion Table 1: Section and Test Scores** on page 129. Look in the "Raw Score" column for your raw score, and match it to the number in the "Reading Test Score" column.

3. Do the same with **Section 2: Writing and Language Test** to determine that score.

4. Add your Reading Test score to your Writing and Language Test score.

5. Multiply that number by 10. This is your Evidence-Based Reading and Writing Section score.

To Calculate Your Math Section Score

Your Math score is also on a scale of 200–800.

1. Count the number of correct answers you got on the **Section 3: Math Test—No Calculator** and the **Section 4: Math Test—Calculator**. Again, there is no penalty for wrong answers. **The number of correct answers is your raw score.**

2. Add the number of correct answers on the Section 3: Math Test—No Calculator and the Section 4: Math Test—Calculator.

3. Use the **Raw Score Conversion Table 1: Section and Test Scores** on page 129 and convert your raw score into your Math Section score.

To Obtain Your Total Score

Add your score on the Evidence-Based Reading and Writing Section to the Math Section score. This is your total score on the diagnostic test, on a scale of 400–1600.

Subscores Provide Additional Information

Subscores offer you greater details about your strengths in certain areas within literacy and math. The subscores are reported on a scale of 1–15 and include Heart of Algebra, Problem Solving and Data Analysis, Passport to Advanced Math, Expression of Ideas, Standard English Conventions, Words in Context, and Command of Evidence.

Heart of Algebra

The **Heart of Algebra subscore** is based on questions from the **Math Test** that focus on linear equations and inequalities.

- Add up your total correct answers from these questions:
  - Math Test—No Calculator: Questions 1, 4, 9, 13, 16, 17, 19, 20
  - Math Test—Calculator: Questions 3, 5, 7, 10, 14, 18, 21, 23, 26, 29, 37
- Your Raw Score = the total number of correct answers from all of these questions
- Use the **Raw Score Conversion Table 2: Subscores** on page 131 to determine your **Heart of Algebra** subscore.

Problem Solving and Data Analysis

The **Problem Solving and Data Analysis subscore** is based on questions from the **Math Test** that focus on quantitative reasoning, the interpretation and synthesis of data, and solving problems in rich and varied contexts.

- Add up your total correct answers from these questions:
  - Math Test—No Calculator: None
  - Math Test—Calculator: Questions 1, 4, 6, 8, 9, 13, 17, 20, 22, 24, 27, 31, 33, 34, 35, 36, 38
- Your Raw Score = the total number of correct answers from all of these questions
- Use the **Raw Score Conversion Table 2: Subscores** on page 131 to determine your **Problem Solving and Data Analysis** subscore.

Passport to Advanced Math

The **Passport to Advanced Math subscore** is based on questions from the **Math Test** that focus on topics central to your ability to progress to more advanced math, such as understanding the structure of expressions, reasoning with more complex equations, and interpreting and building functions.

- Add up your total correct answers from these questions:
  - Math Test—No Calculator: Questions 2, 3, 5, 6, 7, 8, 10, 12, 14
  - Math Test—Calculator: Questions 2, 11, 15, 19, 25, 28, 30
- Your Raw Score = the total number of correct answers from all of these questions
- Use the **Raw Score Conversion Table 2: Subscores** on page 131 to determine your **Passport to Advanced Math** subscore.

Expression of Ideas

The **Expression of Ideas subscore** is based on questions from the **Writing and Language Test** that focus on topic development, organization, and rhetorically effective use of language.

- Add up your total correct answers from these questions in Section 2: Writing and Language Test:
  - Questions 2, 3, 4, 5, 8, 9, 12, 15, 16, 17, 19, 21, 25, 26, 29, 30, 31, 33, 35, 36, 37, 38, 42, 44
- Your Raw Score = the total number of correct answers from all of these questions
- Use the **Raw Score Conversion Table 2: Subscores** on page 131 to determine your **Expression of Ideas** subscore.

Standard English Conventions

The **Standard English Conventions subscore** is based on questions from the **Writing and Language Test** that focus on sentence structure, usage, and punctuation.

- Add up your total correct answers from these questions in Section 2: Writing and Language Test:
  - Questions 1, 6, 7, 10, 11, 13, 14, 18, 20, 22, 23, 24, 27, 28, 32, 34, 39, 40, 41, 43
- Your Raw Score = the total number of correct answers from all of these questions
- Use the **Raw Score Conversion Table 2: Subscores** on page 131 to determine your **Standard English Conventions** subscore.

Words in Context

The **Words in Context subscore** is based on questions from the **Reading Test** and the **Writing and Language Test** that address word/phrase meaning in context and rhetorical word choice.

- Add up your total correct answers from these questions in Sections 1 and 2:
  - Reading Test: Questions 8, 9, 20, 21, 31, 32, 41, 42, 51, 52
  - Writing and Language Test: Questions 7, 9, 16, 18, 24, 30, 38, 41
- Your Raw Score = the total number of correct answers from all of these questions
- Use the **Raw Score Conversion Table 2: Subscores** on page 131 to determine your **Words in Context** subscore.

Command of Evidence

The **Command of Evidence subscore** is based on questions from the **Reading Test** and the **Writing and Language Test** that ask you to interpret and use evidence found in a wide range of passages and informational graphics, such as graphs, tables, and charts.

- Add up your total correct answers from these questions in Sections 1 and 2:
  - Reading Test: Questions 6, 7, 18, 19, 29, 30, 39, 40, 49, 50
  - Writing and Language Test: Questions 2, 4, 12, 19, 26, 31, 33, 35, 42
- Your Raw Score = the total number of correct answers from all of these questions
- Use the **Raw Score Conversion Table 2: Subscores** on page 131 to determine your **Command of Evidence** subscore.

CROSS-TEST SCORES

The SAT® exam also reports two cross-test scores: Analysis in History/Social Studies and Analysis in Science. These scores are based on questions in the Reading Test, Writing and Language Test, and both Math Tests that ask you to think analytically about texts and questions in these subject areas. Cross-test scores are reported on a scale of 10–40.

Analysis in History/Social Studies

- Add up your total correct answers from these questions:
  - ○ Reading Test: Questions 11, 12, 13, 14, 15, 16, 17, 18, 19, 20, 21, 43, 44, 45, 46, 47, 48, 49, 50, 51, 52
  - ○ Writing and Language Test: Questions 12, 15, 16, 17, 19, 21
  - ○ Math Test—No Calculator: None
  - ○ Math Test—Calculator: Questions 1, 4, 9, 13, 20, 22, 27, 35
- Your Raw Score = the total number of correct answers from all of these questions
- Use the **Raw Score Conversion Table 3: Cross-Test Scores** on page 133 to determine your **Analysis in History/Social Studies** cross-test score.

Analysis in Science

- Add up your total correct answers from these sections:
- Reading Test: Questions 1–10, 22–32
- Writing and Language Test: Questions 35, 36, 37, 38, 42, 44
  - Math Test—No Calculator: Question 5
  - Math Test—Calculator: Questions 7, 8, 17, 19, 21, 23, 24
- Your Raw Score = the total number of correct answers from all of these questions
- Use the **Raw Score Conversion Table 3: Cross-Test Scores** on page 133 to determine your **Analysis in Science** cross-test score.

RAW SCORE CONVERSION TABLE 1: SECTION AND TEST SCORES

Raw Score	Math Section Score	Reading Test Score	Writing and Language Test Score	Raw Score	Math Section Score	Reading Test Score	Writing and Language Test Score
0	200	10	10	30	530	28	29
1	200	10	10	31	540	28	30
2	210	10	10	32	550	29	30
3	230	11	10	33	560	29	31
4	240	12	11	34	560	30	32
5	260	13	12	35	570	30	32
6	280	14	13	36	580	31	33
7	290	15	13	37	590	31	34
8	310	15	14	38	600	32	34
9	320	16	15	39	600	32	35
10	330	17	16	40	610	33	36
11	340	17	16	41	620	33	37
12	360	18	17	42	630	34	38
13	370	19	18	43	640	35	39
14	380	19	19	44	650	35	40
15	390	20	19	45	660	36	
16	410	20	20	46	670	37	
17	420	21	21	47	670	37	
18	430	21	21	48	680	38	
19	440	22	22	49	690	38	
20	450	22	23	50	700	39	
21	460	23	23	51	710	40	
22	470	23	24	52	730	40	
23	480	24	25	53	740		
24	480	24	25	54	750		
25	490	25	26	55	760		
26	500	25	26	56	780		
27	510	26	27	57	790		
28	520	26	28	58	800		
29	520	27	28				

CONVERSION EQUATION 1 SECTION AND TEST SCORES

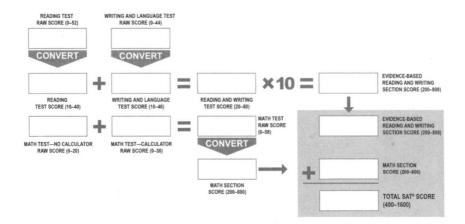

RAW SCORE CONVERSION TABLE 2: SUBSCORES

Raw Score (# of correct answers)	Expression of Ideas	Standard English Conventions	Heart of Algebra	Problem Solving and Data Analysis	Passport to Advanced Math	Words in Context	Command of Evidence
0	1	1	1	1	1	1	1
1	1	1	1	1	3	1	1
2	1	1	2	2	5	2	2
3	2	2	3	3	6	3	3
4	3	2	4	4	7	4	4
5	4	3	5	5	8	5	5
6	5	4	6	6	9	6	6
7	6	5	6	7	10	6	7
8	6	6	7	8	11	7	8
9	7	6	8	8	11	8	8
10	7	7	8	9	12	8	9
11	8	7	9	10	12	9	10
12	8	8	9	10	13	9	10
13	9	8	9	11	13	10	11
14	9	9	10	12	14	11	12
15	10	10	10	13	14	12	13
16	10	10	11	14	15	13	14
17	11	11	12	15		14	15
18	11	12	13			15	15
19	12	13	15				
20	12	15					
21	13						
22	14						
23	14						
24	15						

CONVERSION EQUATION 2 SUBSCORES

HEART OF ALGEBRA RAW SCORE (0–19)	EXPRESSION OF IDEAS RAW SCORE (0–24)	COMMAND OF EVIDENCE RAW SCORE (0–18)	PROBLEM SOLVING AND DATA ANALYSIS RAW SCORE (0–17)
CONVERT	CONVERT	CONVERT	CONVERT
HEART OF ALGEBRA SUBSCORE (1–15)	EXPRESSION OF IDEAS SUBSCORE (1–15)	COMMAND OF EVIDENCE SUBSCORE (1–15)	PROBLEM SOLVING AND DATA ANALYSIS SUBSCORE (1–15)

STANDARD ENGLISH CONVENTIONS RAW SCORE (0–20)	WORDS IN CONTEXT RAW SCORE (0–18)	PASSPORT TO ADVANCED MATH RAW SCORE (0–16)
CONVERT	CONVERT	CONVERT
STANDARD ENGLISH CONVENTIONS SUBSCORE (1–15)	WORDS IN CONTEXT SUBSCORE (1–15)	PASSPORT TO ADVANCED MATH SUBSCORE (1–15)

RAW SCORE CONVERSION TABLE 3: CROSS-TEST SCORES

Raw Score (# of correct answers)	Analysis in History/Social Studies Cross-Test Score	Analysis in Science Cross-Test Score	Raw Score (# of correct answers)	Analysis in History/Social Studies Cross-Test Score	Analysis in Science Cross-Test Score
0	10	10	18	28	26
1	10	11	19	29	27
2	11	12	20	30	27
3	12	13	21	30	28
4	14	14	22	31	29
5	15	15	23	32	30
6	16	16	24	32	30
7	17	17	25	33	31
8	18	18	26	34	32
9	20	19	27	35	33
10	21	20	28	35	33
11	22	20	29	36	34
12	23	21	30	37	35
13	24	22	31	38	36
14	25	23	32	38	37
15	26	24	33	39	38
16	27	24	34	40	39
17	28	25	35	40	40

CONVERSION EQUATION 3: CROSS-TEST SCORES

TEST	ANALYSIS IN HISTORY/SOCIAL STUDIES		ANALYSIS IN SCIENCE	
	QUESTIONS	RAW SCORE	QUESTIONS	RAW SCORE
Reading Test	11–21, 43–52		1–10, 22–32	
Writing and Language Test	12, 15, 16, 17, 19, 21		35, 36, 37, 38, 42, 44	
Math Test—No Calculator			5	
Math Test—Calculator	1, 4, 9, 13, 20, 22, 27, 35		7, 8, 17, 19, 21, 23, 24	
TOTAL				

ANALYSIS IN HISTORY/
SOCIAL STUDIES
RAW SCORE (0–35)

CONVERT

ANALYSIS IN HISTORY/
SOCIAL STUDIES
CROSS-TEST SCORE (10–40)

ANALYSIS IN SCIENCE
RAW SCORE (0–35)

CONVERT

ANALYSIS IN SCIENCE
CROSS-TEST SCORE (10–40)

CHAPTER 3: THE SAT® READING TEST

OVERVIEW

- A Brief Introduction to the SAT® Reading Test
- U.S. and World Literature Passages
- History and Social Studies Passages
- Science Passages
- Paired Passages and Informational Graphics
- SAT® Reading Question Types: A Closer Look
- Summing It Up

The first subject you will face on the SAT® exam is the Reading Test. SAT® Reading Test questions cover both the kinds of reading comprehension skills you've already been learning throughout your high school career (identifying main idea, author's purpose, making inferences, etc.) and the somewhat more complex concepts you'll need when you start college (analyzing word choice and text structure, synthesizing information across passages and between a passage and an informational graphic, etc.). This chapter will review every passage type and question type you will see on the SAT® Reading Test. Let's not waste another second and get right to it.

Reading Test Snapshot
- Test length: 65 minutes
- Number of questions: 52 multiple-choice questions

NOTE: For comprehensive information regarding the Reading Test, visit the official *website: https://collegereadiness.collegeboard.org/sat/inside-the-test/reading*.

A BRIEF INTRODUCTION TO THE SAT® READING TEST

The SAT® Reading Test is a 65-minute exam consisting of four passages of 500 to 750 words each, and one paired passage consisting of two shorter passages of roughly 350 words each. There are a total of 52 multiple-choice questions on the test.

 Taking a maximum of 1 minute and 15 seconds to answer each question will help you make the most of the 65 minutes you have to complete the SAT® Reading Test.

There are three different kinds of passages you'll read on the SAT® Reading Test: **U.S. and World Literature, History/Social Studies,** and **Science.** The following chart gives the basics of what these passages cover and how they will appear on the test.

Subject	Types and Topics	Subject-Related Passages	Associated Questions
U.S. and World Literature	Potential types of passages include: • Excerpts from classic and contemporary short stories and novels • Complete classic and contemporary short stories Genres/Types include: • Drama • Humor • Gothic fiction • Science fiction	1	10
History/ Social Studies	1 Social Science passage 1 Founding Document	2 (either two single passages or one single and one paired passage set)	21
Science	Potential science topics include: • Earth science • Biology • Chemistry • Physics	2 (either two single passages or one single and one paired passage set)	21

Each passage or paired passage set is accompanied by **10 or 11 multiple-choice questions**. One History/Social Studies passage and one Science passage will also include an **informational graphic** in the form of a chart, table, diagram, graph, or map. These passages will require you to answer two or three questions that test your ability to connect, or synthesize, ideas between the passage and the graphic.

Although you'll be reading different kinds of passages on the SAT® Reading Test, the different subjects will not require different reading skills. In fact, you might want to use the same active and close reading skills when reading all of these passages.

Follow this order when approaching any passage type you see on test day:

- **Step 1, Active Reading:** Read the passage quickly (a little more than a skim, but not word-for-word) to get a general idea of the main idea and where important details are. Taking notes will help you keep track of those details.

- **Step 2, Close Reading:** Read the questions to find out the details you'll really need to know in the passage, and go back to read the passage again carefully for the finer details.

Use What Works Best for YOU!

All of the tips, strategies, and techniques in this book are proven to be effective for tackling the SAT® exam—but you're a unique individual with a unique test-taking style. What works for someone else might not be the best strategy for you.

Your best approach—and one of the best pieces of advice we can offer you—is to try these strategies well in advance of test day to determine if they work well for you.

Bottom line: Use what works for you, and don't spend your time on what doesn't.

Try not to be intimidated by the variety of topics you will face on test day. It helps to keep in mind that **outside knowledge is never required on the SAT® Reading Test.** You will not have to be a historian to answer history questions or a scientist to answer science questions. All of the information you'll need to answer all 52 questions is contained in the passages and informational graphics. So don't waste time studying these topics before the exam. Focus on practicing answering genuine SAT-type questions.

There are five essential question types on the SAT® Reading Test:

1. Information and Ideas questions require you to make inferences, understand relationships, cite evidence, and identify main ideas, author's purpose, and themes.

2. Words in Context questions test your ability to identify the meaning of specific words within a passage.

3. Rhetoric questions require you to analyze word choice, text structure, point of view, arguments, and purpose.

---

4. Command of Evidence questions require you to find lines in the passages that support your answers to previous questions.

5. Synthesis questions require you to make connections between pairs of passages and passage/informational graphics pairs.

We'll discuss these question types in more detail later on in the chapter. Now we'll take a slightly closer look at all these passage and question types—we'll stick to the greatest hits, so you can get the essential idea of what you'll be facing on test day.

Memorization Is a Waste of Your Time!

There's no way to know what words you'll need to know to answer Words in Context questions, so don't bother trying to memorize vocabulary lists, even if they are supposedly words that commonly appear on the SAT® exam. The definitions you read may not even be the ones you'll need to know on the test since most wrong answer choices to Words in Context questions will actually define the vocab word correctly; they just won't define how the word is used in the context of the passage.

U.S. AND WORLD LITERATURE PASSAGES

The U.S. and World Literature passage is an excerpt from a classic or contemporary short story or novel, and you'll have to read only one on the SAT® exam. Don't expect a complete story, which would be challenging to tell in just 500 to 750 words. These passages may be more about giving you the impression of a particular character, setting a scene, or establishing a conflict. They may be told from the first-person point of view (when a story is narrated by a character in it) or the third-person point of view (when an unnamed narrator is describing the actions of others). The passage can represent any genre, but that does not really matter, because the same kinds of questions will be used regardless of whether you're required to read a dramatic, humorous, fantastical, or any other kind of story. Whether the story is an example of classic or contemporary literature is similarly irrelevant to the kinds of questions you'll have to answer.

 The literary passages on the SAT® Reading Test are fairly complex, so if you have time, you might want to do a bit of outside reading (for pleasure, even!) to flex your muscles when it comes to paying attention and understanding what you read.

Here's an example of the kind of U.S. and World Literature passage you can expect to read on the SAT® exam. Take the time now to familiarize yourself with this passage. Try reading it actively since you will be using it to answer some sample questions a bit later in this chapter.

This passage is excerpted from Sense & Sensibility *by Jane Austen.*

The family of Dashwood had long been settled in Sussex. Their estate was large, and their residence was at Norland Park, in the centre of their property, where, for many generations, they had lived in so respectable a manner as to
Line engage the general good opinion of their surrounding acquaintance. The late
5 owner of this estate was a single man, who lived to a very advanced age, and who for many years of his life, had a constant companion and housekeeper in his sister. But her death, which happened ten years before his own, produced a great alteration in his home; for to supply her loss, he invited and received into his house the family of his nephew Mr. Henry Dashwood, the legal inheritor of the Norland
10 estate, and the person to whom he intended to bequeath it. In the society of his nephew and niece, and their children, the old Gentleman's days were comfortably spent. His attachment to them all increased. The constant attention of Mr. and Mrs. Henry Dashwood to his wishes, which proceeded not merely from interest, but from goodness of heart, gave him every degree of solid comfort which his age
15 could receive; and the cheerfulness of the children added a relish to his existence.

By a former marriage, Mr. Henry Dashwood had one son: by his present lady, three daughters. The son, a steady respectable young man, was amply provided for by the fortune of his mother, which had been large, and half of which devolved on him on his coming of age. By his own marriage, likewise, which happened soon
20 afterwards, he added to his wealth. To him therefore the succession to the Norland estate was not so really important as to his sisters; for their fortune, independent of what might arise to them from their father's inheriting that property, could be but small. Their mother had nothing, and their father only seven thousand pounds in his own disposal; for the remaining moiety of his first wife's fortune was also
25 secured to her child, and he had only a life-interest in it.

The old gentleman died: his will was read, and like almost every other will, gave as much disappointment as pleasure. He was neither so unjust, nor so ungrateful, as to leave his estate from his nephew; but he left it to him on such terms as destroyed half the value of the bequest. Mr. Dashwood had wished for it
30 more for the sake of his wife and daughters than for himself or his son; but to his son, and his son's son, a child of four years old, it was secured, in such a way, as to leave to himself no power of providing for those who were most dear to him, and who most needed a provision by any charge on the estate, or by any sale of its valuable woods. The whole was tied up for the benefit of this child, who, in occa-
35 sional visits with his father and mother at Norland, had so far gained on the affec-tions of his uncle, by such attractions as are by no means unusual in children of two or three years old; an imperfect articulation, an earnest desire of having his own way, many cunning tricks, and a great deal of noise, as to outweigh all the value of

all the attention which, for years, he had received from his niece and her daughters.
40 He meant not to be unkind, however, and, as a mark of his affection for the three girls, he left them a thousand pounds a-piece.

Mr. Dashwood's disappointment was, at first, severe; but his temper was cheerful and sanguine; and he might reasonably hope to live many years, and by living economically, lay by a considerable sum from the produce of an estate
45 already large, and capable of almost immediate improvement. But the fortune, which had been so tardy in coming, was his only one twelvemonth. He survived his uncle no longer; and ten thousand pounds, including the late legacies, was all that remained for his widow and daughters.

HISTORY AND SOCIAL STUDIES PASSAGES

You will see two History/Social Studies passages on the SAT® Reading Test, and each is a different kind of passage:

> **1. A Social Science passage** focused on economics (the study of money), politics (the study of government), or sociology (the study of people and society).

> **2. A Founding Document** that may be an important document, such as the U.S. Declaration of Independence and the Bill of Rights, or a momentous speech by a major figure in United States history.

 Be sure to use the close reading technique on the History/Social Studies passages because they are likely to contain a lot of important details—dates, documents, important people, etc.

The Social Science passage will probably be an excerpt from a report, editorial, history book, or textbook. The Founding Document is more likely to be a complete text, since governmental documents and speeches tend to be on the shorter side. These passages may deal with events in U.S. history or more current events.

Here's an example of the kind of Social Studies passage you might encounter on the SAT® Reading Test. Try actively reading it and the sample Founding Document that follows, since you will be using these passages to answer some sample questions a bit later in this chapter.

This passage is excerpted from The Battle of Gettysburg *by Samuel Adams Drake.*

Stripped of the glamour which has made its every stick and stone an object of eager curiosity or pious veneration, Gettysburg becomes a very plain, mat-ter-of-fact Pennsylvania town, of no particular antiquity, with a very decided Dutch
Line flavor in the names and on the tongues of its citizens, where no great man has

5 ever flourished, or anything had happened to cause its own name to be noised abroad, until one day in the eventful year 1863—the battle year—fame was suddenly thrust upon it, as one might say, not for a day, but for all time. The dead who sleep in the National Cemetery here, or who lie in unknown graves about the fields and woods, and counting many times more than the living, help us to understand

10 how much greater was the battle of Gettysburg than the town which has given it its name.

Gettysburg is the market town—or borough, accurately speaking—of an exclusively farming population, planted in one of the most productive sections of the Keystone State. It is the seat of justice of the county. It has a seminary and

15 college of the German Lutheran Church, which give a certain tone and cast to its social life. In short, Gettysburg seems in all things so entirely devoted to the pursuits of peace, there is so little that is suggestive of war and bloodshed, even if time had not mostly effaced all traces of that gigantic struggle, that, coming as we do with one absorbing idea in mind, we find it hard to reconcile the facts of history

20 with the facts as we find them.

There is another side to Gettysburg—a picturesque, a captivating side. One looks around upon the landscape with simple admiration. One's highest praise comes from the feeling of quiet satisfaction with which the harmony of nature reveals the harmony of God. You are among the subsiding swells that the South

25 Mountain has sent rippling off to the east. So completely is the village hid away among these green swells that neither spire nor steeple is seen until, upon turning one of the numerous low ridges by which the face of the country is so cut up, you enter a valley, not deep, but well defined by two opposite ranges of heights, and Gettysburg lies gleaming in the declining sun before you—a picture to be long

30 remembered.

Its situation is charming. Here and there a bald ridge or wooded hill, the name of which you do not yet know, is pushed or bristles up above the undulating prairie-land, but there is not one really harsh feature in the landscape. In full view off to the northwest, but softened by the gauzy haze of a midsummer's afternoon,

35 the towering bulk of the South Mountain, vanguard of the serried chain behind it, looms imposingly up between Gettysburg and the Cumberland Valley, still beyond, in the west, as landmark for all the country round, as well as for the great battlefield now spreading out its long leagues before you; a monument more aged than the Pyramids, which Napoleon, a supremely imaginative and magnetic man himself,

40 sought to invest with a human quality in the minds of his veterans, when he said to them, "Soldiers! from the summits of yonder Pyramids forty ages behold you." In short, the whole scene is one of such quiet pastoral beauty, the village itself with its circlet of fields and farms so free from every hint of strife and carnage, that again and again we ask ourselves if it can be true that one of the greatest conflicts of

45 modern times was lost and won here.

Yet this, and this alone, is what has caused Gettysburg, the obscure country village, to be inscribed on the same scroll with Blenheim, and Waterloo, and Saratoga, as a decisive factor in the history of the nations. Great deeds have lifted it to monumental proportions. As Abraham Lincoln so beautifully said when dedi
50 cating the National Cemetery here, "The brave men, living and dead, who struggled here have consecrated it far above our power to add or detract. The world will little note, nor long remember, what we say here, but it can never forget what they did here."

Now here's a sample Founding Document in the form of an important speech:

The following is Franklin Delano Roosevelt's Fourth Inaugural Address.

Mr. Chief Justice, Mr. Vice President, my friends, you will understand and, I believe, agree with my wish that the form of this inauguration be simple and its words brief.

Line We Americans of today, together with our allies, are passing through a period
5 of supreme test. It is a test of our courage—of our resolve—of our wisdom—our essential democracy.

If we meet that test—successfully and honorably—we shall perform a service of historic importance which men and women and children will honor throughout all time.

10 As I stand here today, having taken the solemn oath of office in the presence of my fellow countrymen—in the presence of our God—I know that it is America's purpose that we shall not fail.

In the days and in the years that are to come we shall work for a just and honorable peace, a durable peace, as today we work and fight for total victory in war.

15 We can and we will achieve such a peace.

We shall strive for perfection. We shall not achieve it immediately—but we still shall strive. We may make mistakes—but they must never be mistakes which result from faintness of heart or abandonment of moral principle.

I remember that my old schoolmaster, Dr. Peabody, said, in days that seemed
20 to us then to be secure and untroubled: "Things in life will not always run smoothly. Sometimes we will be rising toward the heights—then all will seem to reverse itself and start downward. The great fact to remember is that the trend of civilization itself is forever upward; that a line drawn through the middle of the peaks and the valleys of the centuries always has an upward trend."

25   Our Constitution of 1787 was not a perfect instrument; it is not perfect yet. But it provided a firm base upon which all manner of men, of all races and colors and creeds, could build our solid structure of democracy.

And so today, in this year of war, 1945, we have learned lessons—at a fearful cost—and we shall profit by them.

30   We have learned that we cannot live alone, at peace; that our own well-being is dependent on the well-being of other nations far away. We have learned that we must live as men, not as ostriches, nor as dogs in the manger.

We have learned to be citizens of the world, members of the human community.

35   We have learned the simple truth, as Emerson said, that "The only way to have a friend is to be one."

We can gain no lasting peace if we approach it with suspicion and mistrust or with fear. We can gain it only if we proceed with the understanding, the confidence, and the courage which flow from conviction.

40   The Almighty God has blessed our land in many ways. He has given our people stout hearts and strong arms with which to strike mighty blows for freedom and truth. He has given to our country a faith which has become the hope of all peoples in an anguished world.

So we pray to Him now for the vision to see our way clearly—to see the
45 way that leads to a better life for ourselves and for all our fellow men—to the achievement of His will to peace on earth.

SCIENCE PASSAGES

You will see only two Science passages on the SAT® Reading Test, but there are four potential areas of focus:

1. Earth Science is the study of the planet Earth, its features, its history, and its future.

2. Biology is the study of human and animal life and bodies.

3. Chemistry is the study of elements, substances, and matter.

4. Physics is the study of motion and the properties of matter, including objects in our galaxy.

Remember that although science can be a complex and intimidating subject, you should still approach the Science passages on the SAT® Reading Test as you would all other reading passages. You will not be expected to perform complex equations or develop theories. You will just be required to comprehend and analyze the words, language, details, concepts, and ideas in the passages. As always, you must keep in mind that every bit of information you need to know to answer all the questions is contained within the given passages. The SAT® Reading Test assesses how well you comprehend information, not how well you remember science.

NOTE: Even a Science passage that includes an informational graphic with a lot of numerical information will not require you to perform complex equations.

Read the following sample biology passage. Try reading it actively, since you will be using this passage to answer some sample questions a bit later in this chapter.

This passage is excerpted from How Snakes Eat *by Catherine C. Hopley.*

The Hamadryad's appointed diet is one ring-snake per week; but "Ophi," as we now call him, is occasionally required—and with no sacrifice of his principles either—to eat an extra snake to satisfy the curiosity of some distinguished visitor.
Line Sometimes, too, colubers are plentiful, and two small ones are not too much for his
5 ten or twelve feet of appetite. This splendid serpent has rewarded care by remaining in perfect health, and growing several feet. He was between eight and nine feet long when he came, and is now not far short of twelve and proportionately larger in circumference. Sometimes during winter, when ring-snakes are scarce, "Ophi" is compelled to fast; for he is not then to be tempted with other food. During the
10 first year of his residence in the Gardens, the supply was good, and he ate no less than eighty-two fellow-creatures before the winter was well over. Towards spring, however, the supply ran short, and only two more remained for him. He had now fasted two entire weeks, and looked hungry and eager. The keeper offered him a guinea-pig, at which he took great offence, raising his hood and hissing angrily for
15 a long while. Eggs he declined, also a lizard and a rat, in great disgust. In India the Ophiophagi are said to feed on lizards and fish occasionally, but *our* Ophiophagus preferred to fast. At last one of the two ring-snakes was produced, and Ophio was to be regaled. It was the 31st of March, 1876, and he had been a denizen of the Gardens just one year. My note-book informs me that it was a lovely, soft spring day,
20 and that Ophio was quite lively. He had rejected frogs on his own account, but in the uncertainty of more ring-snakes arriving, he was now decoyed into eating half a dozen. Holland contrived that the snake destined for his dinner should answer the purpose of a feast, and had allowed it to eat as many frogs as it chose. Like the poor wretch who, doomed to the gallows, is permitted to fare sumptuously the
25 last morning of his life, the ring-snake ate three frogs, by which the Ophiophagus was to derive chief benefit; he, all unconscious of the cause of his victim's unusual plumpness, swallowed him speedily.

Soon after this Ophio doffed his winter coat entire, and having again fasted for ten days, was at once rewarded by the last remaining ring-snake in a similarly ple-
30 thoric condition, namely, with three more frogs inside him. Now and then during

the winter months the scarcity of ring-snakes has compelled the sacrifice of some far rarer colubers to Ophio's cannibal tastes. And yet each year we hear of hundreds of ring-snakes being ruthlessly killed in country districts, while at great cost and trouble others are purchased or brought from the Continent for the Hamadryad's
35 sustenance. Lord Lilford, one of the Ophidarium's best patrons, sometimes sends presents of game in the shape of ring-snakes to the Hamadryad.

Diet of a Garter Snake	
Frogs	85%
Invertebrates	11%
Mammals	4%

PAIRED PASSAGES AND INFORMATIONAL GRAPHICS

U.S. and World Literature passages always follow the same format: a single 500- to 750-word passage. History/Social Studies and Science passages are less consistent. They might appear as single 500- to 750-word passages, or they might appear as **paired passages.**

There will be one paired passage on the SAT® Reading Test in either History/Social Studies or Science. The passages will basically be like two normal passages cut in half, each coming in at about 350 words. There will be some significant connection between the two passages. They might deal with the same topic from different perspectives. One passage may build upon the ideas presented in the other one, or it may present different examples and findings. The passages may agree with each other, or they may form an argument when placed one after the other.

The questions that accompany paired passages will have three different focuses:
1. Questions about Passage 1 only
2. Questions about Passage 2 only
3. Questions about both Passage 1 and Passage 2

While paired passages will still feature the same Information and Ideas, Words in Context, Command of Evidence, and Rhetoric questions that accompany all SAT® Reading Test passages, they will also include **Synthesis** questions. These questions test your ability to understand the differences and similarities and analyze the connections between the two passages in a paired passage set.

NOTE: Synthesis questions are exclusive to paired passages and passages that include informational graphics.

Informational graphics are tables, charts, graphs, diagrams, and maps. Some of these graphics might seem like the kinds of things you'd be more likely to encounter on a math test than a reading test, but they won't be used to test complex math skills. Instead, you will use them just as you will use the two passages in the paired passage set: to understand the differences and similarities and analyze the connections between the passages and its accompanying informational graphic. One History/Social Studies passage and one Science passage on the SAT® Reading Test will include informational graphics.

The questions that accompany passages with informational graphics will generally ask you to answer questions about the passage only or both the passage and the graphic. There won't really be questions about the graphic alone.

Read the following paired physics passage set, which includes an informational graphic. Try reading it actively since you will be using this paired passage set and its graphic to answer some sample questions a bit later in this chapter.

Passage 1

This passage is excerpted from Letters on Astronomy *by Denison Olmsted.*

Indeed, what is more admirable, than that astronomers should be able to tell us, years beforehand, the exact instant of the commencement and termination of an eclipse, and describe all the attendant circumstances with the greatest fidelity.
Line You have doubtless, my dear friend, participated in this admiration, and felt a
5 strong desire to learn how it is that astronomers are able to look so far into futurity. I will endeavor, in this Letter, to explain to you the leading principles of the calculation of eclipses, with as much plainness as possible.

An *eclipse of the moon* happens when the moon, in its revolution around the earth, falls into the earth's shadow. An *eclipse of the sun* happens when the moon,
10 coming between the earth and the sun, covers either a part or the whole of the solar disk.

The earth and the moon being both opaque, globular bodies, exposed to the sun's light, they cast shadows opposite to the sun, like any other bodies on which the sun shines. Were the sun of the same size with the earth and the moon, then
15 the lines drawn touching the surface of the sun and the surface of the earth or moon (which lines form the boundaries of the shadow) would be parallel to each other, and the shadow would be a cylinder infinite in length; and were the sun less than the earth or the moon, the shadow would be an increasing cone, its narrower end resting on the earth; but as the sun is vastly greater than either of these bodies,
20 the shadow of each is a cone whose base rests on the body itself, and which comes to a point, or vertex, at a certain distance behind the body.

Passage 2

This passage is adapted from The Story of Eclipses *by George F. Chambers.*

To bring about an eclipse of the Sun, two things must combine: the Moon must be at or near one of its Nodes; and, this must be at a time when the Moon is also in "Conjunction" with the Sun. Now the Moon is in Conjunction with the
25 Sun (= "New Moon") 12 or 13 times in a year, but the Sun only passes through the Nodes of the Moon's orbit twice a year. Hence an eclipse of the Sun does not and cannot occur at every New Moon, but only occasionally. An *exact* coincidence of Earth, Moon, and Sun, in a straight line at a Node is not necessary to ensure an eclipse of the Sun. So long as the Moon is within about 18½° of its Node, with a
30 latitude of not more than 1° 34′, an eclipse *may* take place. If, however, the distance is less than 15¼° and the latitude less than 1° 23′ an eclipse *must* take place, though between these limit the occurrence of an eclipse is uncertain and depends on what are called the "horizontal parallaxes" and the "apparent semi-diameters" of the two bodies at the moment of conjunction, in other words, on the nearness or "far-
35 offness" of the bodies in question. Another complication is introduced into these matters by reason of the fact that the Nodes of the Moon's orbit do not occupy a fixed position, but have an annual retrograde motion of about 19¼°, in virtue of which a complete revolution of the Nodes round the ecliptic is accomplished in 18 years 218⅞ days (= 18.5997 years).

40   The backward movement of the Moon's Nodes combined with the apparent motion of the Sun in the ecliptic causes the Moon in its monthly course round the Earth to complete a revolution with respect to its Nodes in a less time (27.2 days) than it takes to get back to Conjunction with the Sun[20] (29.5 days); and a curious consequence, as we shall see directly, flows from these facts and from one other
45 fact. The other fact is to the Sun starting coincident with one of the Moon's Nodes, returns on the Ecliptic to the same Node in 346.6 days. The first named period of 27.2 days is called the "*Nodical* Revolution of the Moon" or "Draconic Month," the other period of 29.5 days is called the "*Synodical* Revolution of the Moon." Now the curious consequence of these figures being what they are is that 242 Draconic
50 Months, 223 Lunations, and 19 Returns of the Sun to one and the same Node of the Moon's orbit, are all accomplished in the same time within 11 hours. Thus (ignoring refinements of decimals):—

		DAYS	DAYS	YEARS	DAYS	HOURS
242	×	27.2	6,585.36	18	10	8.5
223	×	29.5	6,585.32	18	10	7.75
19	×	346.6	6,585.78	18	10	18.75

SAT® READING QUESTION TYPES: A CLOSER LOOK

Let's now look in more detail at the five different kinds of multiple-choice questions that make up the SAT® Reading Test. As you take your practice tests, and then the actual SAT® exam, it will help to know every type of question you might face. If you know what's coming, you can read every passage with these following questions in your mind—chances are, you will have to address all of them after you finish reading.

> **1. Information and Ideas questions:** What are the main ideas and important details of the passage, and what can you infer about them?

> **2. Rhetoric questions:** How does the writer use language to convey important ideas and be persuasive?

> **3. Words in Context questions:** What is the meaning of a word based on the way it is used in the passage?

> **4. Synthesis questions:** What are the similarities, differences, and connections between passages or passages and informational graphics?

> **5. Command of Evidence questions:** Which specific lines in the passage best support the answers to other questions?

Now let's take a little more detailed look at each type to see how they are asked on the SAT® Reading Test and try some sample questions.

INFORMATION AND IDEAS QUESTIONS

Information and Ideas questions have a deceptively simple name. In fact, they test quite a number of detailed things and can be asked in a number of ways. There are four essential kinds of Information and Ideas questions: Reading Closely, Determining Central Ideas and Themes, Understanding Relationships, and Citing Textual Evidence.

NOTE: Questions that ask you to find the "best" or "most likely" answer are most likely to have incorrect answer choices that really do seem correct and might technically be correct if there wasn't a better or likelier answer.

Reading Closely Questions

These questions ask you about the information that is stated and implied in the passage and then what you can infer from this information. To answer these questions correctly, you'll need to pay attention to *what* details the author includes and *why*. Details are not there for any old reason—the SAT® exam tests your ability to recognize them and then use them to draw inferences, or predictions, about what is happening or will happen in the future.

Examples:

- *It can reasonably be inferred that the main character appeared "old and tired" (line 15) because...*

- *The narrator indicates that the main character is not from the same country as her roommates because...*

- *The main character's predicament is most likely related to what event in her past?*

Determining Central Ideas and Themes

These questions want you to look at larger sections of the passage to determine the author's purpose. What are the main idea, claims, and themes of individual paragraphs of the passage or the passage as a whole?

Examples:

- *The main idea of the first paragraph is that...*

- *The main purpose of the passage is to...*

- *What is the author's central claim in the passage?*

Understanding Relationships

How do ideas within the passage connect? How do characters relate to one another? What are the cause and effect, comparison-contrast, and sequential relationships present within a passage?

Examples:

- *According to the passage, the main character leaves because...*

- *The author of the passage suggests that the main character is less admirable than her sister because...*

- *After the main character leaves, it is likely she is going to go...*

Citing Textual Evidence

These questions ask you to think critically about writing and why an author makes certain decisions. You'll have to answer questions about why the author includes particular information and details in the passage, and how this information (either the language used or the information given) affects how the passage comes across.

Example:

- *In line 1 ("Once upon ... time"), what is the most likely reason the author notes that the main character felt upset?*

Evidence questions can be asked in two ways on the SAT® Reading Test. Citing Textual Evidence questions ask why the writer included a particular line in the passage. Command of Evidence questions ask you to find the line or lines that support the answer to the previous question. You'll learn more about Command of Evidence questions a little later in this chapter.

INFORMATION AND IDEAS PRACTICE

It's almost time to answer a few Information and Ideas questions, but first let's look at that U.S. and World Literature passage again. You read it actively the first time. Now try reading it closely by checking out the questions that immediately follow before you read it very carefully. Remember—as you read closely, keep the questions you've read in mind, marking down where in the passage you will go to find the exact answer.

This passage is excerpted from Sense & Sensibility *by Jane Austen.*

The family of Dashwood had long been settled in Sussex. Their estate was large, and their residence was at Norland Park, in the centre of their property, where, for many generations, they had lived in so respectable a manner as to
Line engage the general good opinion of their surrounding acquaintance. The late
5 owner of this estate was a single man, who lived to a very advanced age, and who for many years of his life, had a constant companion and housekeeper in his sister. But her death, which happened ten years before his own, produced a great alteration in his home; for to supply her loss, he invited and received into his house the family of his nephew Mr. Henry Dashwood, the legal inheritor of the Norland
10 estate, and the person to whom he intended to bequeath it. In the society of his nephew and niece, and their children, the old Gentleman's days were comfortably spent. His attachment to them all increased. The constant attention of Mr. and Mrs. Henry Dashwood to his wishes, which proceeded not merely from interest, but from goodness of heart, gave him every degree of solid comfort which his age
15 could receive; and the cheerfulness of the children added a relish to his existence.

By a former marriage, Mr. Henry Dashwood had one son: by his present lady, three daughters. The son, a steady respectable young man, was amply provided for by the fortune of his mother, which had been large, and half of which devolved on him on his coming of age. By his own marriage, likewise, which happened soon
20 afterwards, he added to his wealth. To him therefore the succession to the Norland estate was not so really important as to his sisters; for their fortune, independent of what might arise to them from their father's inheriting that property, could be but small. Their mother had nothing, and their father only seven thousand pounds in his own disposal; for the remaining moiety of his first wife's fortune was also
25 secured to her child, and he had only a life-interest in it.

The old gentleman died: his will was read, and like almost every other will, gave as much disappointment as pleasure. He was neither so unjust, nor so ungrateful, as to leave his estate from his nephew; but he left it to him on such

terms as destroyed half the value of the bequest. Mr. Dashwood had wished for it
30 more for the sake of his wife and daughters than for himself or his son; but to his
son, and his son's son, a child of four years old, it was secured, in such a way, as to
leave to himself no power of providing for those who were most dear to him, and
who most needed a provision by any charge on the estate, or by any sale of its
valuable woods. The whole was tied up for the benefit of this child, who, in occa-
35 sional visits with his father and mother at Norland, had so far gained on the affec-
tions of his uncle, by such attractions as are by no means unusual in children of two
or three years old; an imperfect articulation, an earnest desire of having his own
way, many cunning tricks, and a great deal of noise, as to outweigh all the value of
all the attention which, for years, he had received from his niece and her daughters.
40 He meant not to be unkind, however, and, as a mark of his affection for the three
girls, he left them a thousand pounds a-piece.

Mr. Dashwood's disappointment was, at first, severe; but his temper was
cheerful and sanguine; and he might reasonably hope to live many years, and
by living economically, lay by a considerable sum from the produce of an estate
45 already large, and capable of almost immediate improvement. But the fortune,
which had been so tardy in coming, was his only one twelvemonth. He survived his
uncle no longer; and ten thousand pounds, including the late legacies, was all that
remained for his widow and daughters.

1 The main idea of the first paragraph is that

A. the Dashwood estate was a
large piece of property with
Norland Park in the center of it.

B. after the uncle's sister died, he
welcomed his nephew's family
into his estate.

C. Mr. Henry Dashwood had a son
who married into a wealthy
family, so the estate wasn't
important to him.

D. Mr. and Mrs. Henry Dashwood
took very good care of their
uncle, who owned the estate.

2 It can reasonably be inferred that
Mr. Dashwood is

A. mostly motivated by wealth
and bitterness.

B. disappointed that his son has
been so fortunate.

C. generally kindhearted and
good humored.

D. terrified that his daughters will
fall into poverty.

3 According to the passage, Mr. Dashwood was disappointed in his uncle's will because

A. the wealthiest people received the largest inheritance.

B. Mr. Dashwood was left nothing in the will.

C. it proved the uncle favored his great nephew over his grand nieces.

D. the boy who received most of the inheritance was cunning and noisy.

Answer Key and Explanations

1. **The correct answer is B.** All of the answer choices refer to information that appears in the passage, but only choice B sums up all the main details in the first paragraph. Choice A basically rewords the second sentence of the paragraph, which introduces the estate, while ignoring important details about the uncle and his nephew's family who came to live with him at the estate. Choice C mistakenly states the main idea of the second paragraph, not the first, as this question requires. Choice D is just one detail in the first paragraph, and it fails to explain how the Dashwoods came to live with their uncle.

2. **The correct answer is C.** Mr. Dashwood is disappointed by how the wealth is distributed in his uncle's will, but he still manages to remain "cheerful and sanguine" (line 43) and care for his uncle from "goodness of heart" before the old man died, which supports choice C. These facts also eliminate choice A, which suggests that Mr. Dashwood was motivated more by money and his feelings of disappointment than his naturally kindhearted and good-natured disposition. Choice B is tricky: Mr. Dashwood is disappointed that his son has received such a large inheritance from the uncle, but he is disappointed only in that specific situation and not disappointed that his son has been fortunate in general. Choice D is too extreme; Mr. Dashwood is disappointed that his less fortunate daughters did not receive larger inheritances, but there is no evidence that he is *terrified* that they are doomed to poverty because of that.

3. **The correct answer is A.** According to the passage, Mr. Dashwood wanted the will to give him the power to provide for his daughters, but his son and grandson received the most money, even though the son had married into a wealthy family, which is discussed in the second paragraph. Based on this information, it is reasonable to infer the conclusion in choice A. Choice B is untrue because Mr. Dashwood did receive the estate; he just did not have the power to decide who received the majority of the wealth. Choice C is not the best answer, because although it may be true that the will indicated that the uncle favored his great nephew, Mr.

Dashwood was more disappointed that his daughters received relatively small inheritances than *why* they received relatively small inheritances. The narrator does refer to the great nephew as "cunning" and a maker of "a great deal of noise" (line 38), but Mr. Dashwood thought the boy didn't deserve the money because he was already wealthy, not because of the boy's personality.

RHETORIC QUESTIONS

Rhetoric questions generally ask you to analyze how writers use words to convey ideas, persuade a reader, or create tone. As is the case with Information and Ideas questions, there are four kinds of Rhetoric questions: Analyzing Word Choice, Analyzing Text Structure, Analyzing Point of View, and Analyzing Arguments.

Analyzing Word Choice

Why does the author use particular words and phrases? What message does the author's language convey, and what does it tell you about the people, places, and things within a passage?

Examples:

- *The author uses the words "big problem" (line 1) mainly to emphasize that…*

- *The primary impression created by the author's description of the house as a "grinning monster" (lines 2–3) is that it is…*

Analyzing Text Structure

These questions ask you to look at the choices an author has made about the order and presentation of his or her words. Assume that no element of a passage was there "just because." If the SAT® Reading Test makers kept in a paragraph or a sentence, it serves a purpose. Their words are limited, so know that every one counts and helps you understand an author's intentions. How does the way the author structures sentences and paragraphs affect arguments, ideas, and tone?

Examples:

- *The primary function of the second paragraph (lines 10–12) is to…*

- *Over the course of the passage, the main focus shifts from a discussion of history to…*

Analyzing Point of View

These questions ask you to a) understand why the author wrote his or her piece and what stance he or she takes on the issues presented, and then b) take that understanding to help you realize why he or she included certain details. Do they help to strengthen the point of view? How does the author's position and attitude affect the topic of the passage and any arguments in it?

Examples:

- *The passage is written from the point of view of a...*
- *The passage most strongly suggests that the central message of the Bill of Rights is...*

Analyzing Arguments

If you are reading a persuasive piece, as you make your way through, ask yourself this: What claims, reasons, and evidence does the author supply to support an argument, and how strong are they?

Examples:

- *What is the author's central claim?*
- *The question that begins the first paragraph primarily serves to...*
- *Which of the following claims is supported by the second paragraph?*
- *As presented in the passage, the author's argument primarily relied on which type of evidence?*

 Watch out for extreme language in incorrect answer choices. For example, if a choice suggests that something is "the best" but it's actually merely good, then that answer choice is incorrect.

RHETORIC PRACTICE

Now let's look at some sample Rhetoric questions after rereading the Founding Document you already read actively earlier in this chapter. Be sure to read it closely this time by checking what the questions require you to know before reading the passage very carefully.

The following is Franklin Delano Roosevelt's Fourth Inaugural Address.

Mr. Chief Justice, Mr. Vice President, my friends, you will understand and, I believe, agree with my wish that the form of this inauguration be simple and its words brief.

Line
5
We Americans of today, together with our allies, are passing through a period of supreme test. It is a test of our courage—of our resolve—of our wisdom—our essential democracy.

If we meet that test—successfully and honorably—we shall perform a service of historic importance which men and women and children will honor throughout all time.

10
As I stand here today, having taken the solemn oath of office in the presence of my fellow countrymen—in the presence of our God—I know that it is America's purpose that we shall not fail.

In the days and in the years that are to come we shall work for a just and honorable peace, a durable peace, as today we work and fight for total victory in war.

15
We can and we will achieve such a peace.

We shall strive for perfection. We shall not achieve it immediately—but we still shall strive. We may make mistakes—but they must never be mistakes which result from faintness of heart or abandonment of moral principle.

20
I remember that my old schoolmaster, Dr. Peabody, said, in days that seemed to us then to be secure and untroubled: "Things in life will not always run smoothly. Sometimes we will be rising toward the heights—then all will seem to reverse itself and start downward. The great fact to remember is that the trend of civilization itself is forever upward; that a line drawn through the middle of the peaks and the valleys of the centuries always has an upward trend."

25
Our Constitution of 1787 was not a perfect instrument; it is not perfect yet. But it provided a firm base upon which all manner of men, of all races and colors and creeds, could build our solid structure of democracy.

And so today, in this year of war, 1945, we have learned lessons—at a fearful cost—and we shall profit by them.

30
We have learned that we cannot live alone, at peace; that our own well-being is dependent on the well-being of other nations far away. We have learned that we must live as men, not as ostriches, nor as dogs in the manger.

We have learned to be citizens of the world, members of the human community.

35   We have learned the simple truth, as Emerson said, that "The only way to have a friend is to be one."

We can gain no lasting peace if we approach it with suspicion and mistrust or with fear. We can gain it only if we proceed with the understanding, the confidence, and the courage which flow from conviction.

40   The Almighty God has blessed our land in many ways. He has given our people stout hearts and strong arms with which to strike mighty blows for freedom and truth. He has given to our country a faith which has become the hope of all peoples in an anguished world.

So we pray to Him now for the vision to see our way clearly—to see the
45 way that leads to a better life for ourselves and for all our fellow men—to the achievement of His will to peace on earth.

---

4 What is President Roosevelt's central claim?

- **A.** The United States is in the midst of a war that will have terrible consequences for all citizens of the world.
- **B.** The United States is in the midst of a war, but a just, honorable, and durable peace will be achieved very soon.
- **C.** The United States has been failing because of its Constitution, which requires major alterations to become perfect.
- **D.** The United States is in trouble because of the war, but Americans can help overcome that problem if they all work hard to adjust their attitudes.

5 President Roosevelt uses the words *courage, resolve,* and *wisdom* (line 5) mainly to emphasize that

- **A.** Americans are all naturally gifted.
- **B.** America cannot achieve anything without its allies.
- **C.** Americans should feel confident that they can overcome hard times.
- **D.** other nations should become democracies like America.

6 The primary function of the quote in the eighth paragraph (lines 19–24) is to

- **A.** suggest that challenging times are a simple fact of history.
- **B.** prove that President Roosevelt received a superior education.
- **C.** explain how America first became involved in the war.
- **D.** show that secure and untroubled times can be had again.

Answer Key and Explanations

4. D	5. C	6. A

4. **The correct answer is D.** In his fourth inaugural address, President Roosevelt mainly focuses on the hardships of the current war, but explains that those hardships and troubles can be overcome and peace can be achieved if all Americans adjust their attitudes by learning not to live alone and working to be more friendly and less suspicious and fearful (lines 30–39). Choice A focuses only on the war's hardships without the overall positive message about how all Americans can overcome that war's hardships. By focusing on one sentence in the passage (lines 13-14), choice B oversimplifies the problem of the war and all Americans' role in overcoming its hardships. Choice C makes the mistake of focusing on one particular detail and inflating its importance without taking into account all of the details that help form President Roosevelt's central claim about the war and how all Americans can overcome its hardships.

5. **The correct answer is C.** In the second paragraph, President Roosevelt uses strong and encouraging words to describe the American personality: *courage*, *resolve*, and *wisdom*. By getting Americans to think of themselves as courageous, resolute, and wise, the president is persuading them that they can deal with the hard times they are facing. Choice A is incorrect, because the president has a greater purpose than merely showing that Americans are naturally gifted; he is trying to persuade them to feel a certain way and achieve a particular goal. Choice B is incorrect because it focuses too much on the small detail about America's allies. President Roosevelt is addressing Americans directly in his speech, not America's allies or other nations, which is why choice D is incorrect, as well.

6. **The correct answer is A.** A schoolmaster teaches the essential lessons that all students need to get through life, and the fact that Roosevelt is quoting a schoolmaster rather than, for example, a head of state, implies that he is imparting basic, essential wisdom about history. Therefore, choice A is the best answer. Any student can have a schoolmaster, even those who did not necessarily receive a superior education, and the president is more concerned with imparting essential truths than showing off in this speech, so choice B is not the best answer. Choice C is incorrect; there is nothing in the schoolmaster's quote that explains anything about how America first became involved in the war. Choice D focuses too much on the introduction to the quote, which explains that it was given in "secure and untroubled times." The quote, itself, is about difficult times, not secure and untroubled ones.

Words in Context Questions

Words in Context questions are one of two question types on the SAT® Reading Test that always look the same. Here's an example of what this question will look like on the test:

As used in line 1, "*fire*" most nearly means

A. blaze.

B. dismiss.

C. shoot.

D. ash.

Words in Context questions are a bit different from standard vocabulary questions that simply require you to define words. On the SAT® Reading Test, you will have to find clues in the passage that tell you how words are used. While some of these words may be totally unfamiliar, most will be familiar words that have more than one meaning. Your job is to find the right meaning for the word's specific use in the passage.

 When answering Words in Context questions, always eliminate any answer choice that is a different part of speech from the word used in the passage.

When you see a question like this, you must slow down and make sure *not* to answer it right away based on the question by itself—on what you think is the correct definition. Some of the wrong answer choices will use a meaning that is correct ... but wrong for the particular context. Other answer choices will simply be wrong definitions in any context, such as *ash* (choice D) in the sample Words in Context question above.

 When answering Words in Context questions, try substituting each answer choice in place of the word as it is used in the context of the passage. The correct choice will be the one that makes the most sense in the passage.

Read the Social Science passage again, checking out the questions first, then reading the passage carefully for a close read. Then answer the sample Words in Context questions that follow.

WORDS IN CONTEXT PRACTICE

This passage is excerpted from The Battle of Gettysburg *by Samuel Adams Drake.*

Stripped of the glamour which has made its every stick and stone an object of eager curiosity or pious veneration, Gettysburg becomes a very plain, matter-of-fact Pennsylvania town, of no particular antiquity, with a very decided
Line Dutch flavor in the names and on the tongues of its citizens, where no great man
5 has ever flourished, or anything had happened to cause its own name to be noised abroad, until one day in the eventful year 1863—the battle year—fame was suddenly thrust upon it, as one might say, not for a day, but for all time. The dead who sleep in the National Cemetery here, or who lie in unknown graves about the fields and woods, and counting many times more than the living, help us to understand
10 how much greater was the battle of Gettysburg than the town which has given it its name.

Gettysburg is the market town—or borough, accurately speaking—of an exclusively farming population, planted in one of the most productive sections of the Keystone State. It is the seat of justice of the county. It has a seminary and
15 college of the German Lutheran Church, which give a certain tone and cast to its social life. In short, Gettysburg seems in all things so entirely devoted to the pursuits of peace, there is so little that is suggestive of war and bloodshed, even if time had not mostly effaced all traces of that gigantic struggle that, coming as we do with one absorbing idea in mind, we find it hard to reconcile the facts of history
20 with the facts as we find them.

There is another side to Gettysburg—a picturesque, a captivating side. One looks around upon the landscape with simple admiration. One's highest praise comes from the feeling of quiet satisfaction with which the harmony of nature reveals the harmony of God. You are among the subsiding swells that the South
25 Mountain has sent rippling off to the east. So completely is the village hid away among these green swells that neither spire nor steeple is seen until, upon turning one of the numerous low ridges by which the face of the country is so cut up, you enter a valley, not deep, but well defined by two opposite ranges of heights, and Gettysburg lies gleaming in the declining sun before you—a picture to be long
30 remembered.

Its situation is charming. Here and there a bald ridge or wooded hill, the name of which you do not yet know, is pushed or bristles up above the undulating prairie-land, but there is not one really harsh feature in the landscape. In full view off to the northwest, but softened by the gauzy haze of a midsummer's afternoon,
35 the towering bulk of the South Mountain, vanguard of the serried chain behind it, looms imposingly up between Gettysburg and the Cumberland Valley, still beyond, in the west, as landmark for all the country round, as well as for the great battlefield now spreading out its long leagues before you; a monument more aged than the Pyramids, which Napoleon, a supremely imaginative and magnetic man himself,

40 sought to invest with a human quality in the minds of his veterans, when he said
to them, "Soldiers! from the summits of yonder Pyramids forty ages behold you." In
short, the whole scene is one of such quiet pastoral beauty, the village itself with
its circlet of fields and farms so free from every hint of strife and carnage, that again
and again we ask ourselves if it can be true that one of the greatest conflicts of
45 modern times was lost and won here.

Yet this, and this alone, is what has caused Gettysburg, the obscure country
village, to be inscribed on the same scroll with Blenheim, and Waterloo, and
Saratoga, as a decisive factor in the history of the nations. Great deeds have lifted
it to monumental proportions. As Abraham Lincoln so beautifully said when dedi-
50 cating the National Cemetery here, "The brave men, living and dead, who struggled
here have consecrated it far above our power to add or detract. The world will little
note, nor long remember, what we say here, but it can never forget what they did
here."

---

7 As used in line 4, "flavor" most
nearly means

A. season.

B. essence.

C. idea.

D. savor.

---

8 As used in line 14, "seat" most
nearly means

A. bottom.

B. sit.

C. base.

D. bench.

---

9 As used in line 32, "bristles" most
nearly means

A. brims.

B. stands.

C. teems.

D. angers.

ANSWER KEY AND EXPLANATIONS

7. B	8. C	9. B

7. **The correct answer is B.** In this line, the author is explaining that the essence of Gettysburg's Dutch heritage can be detected in the names and speaking manners of its citizens. Choice A is a definition of *flavor*, but it is a totally different part of speech; *season* is a verb, while the author uses *flavor* as a noun. Choice C is not the most sensible answer because an idea would not really be detected in someone's name or way of speaking. Choice D is not the best answer because it would apply to the taste of food rather than the flavor, or essence, of a name or way of speaking.

8. **The correct answer is C.** In this line, the author is using *seat* to describe Gettysburg's position in terms of the country's justice system. If this warrants mention, then that position must be important, such as the base position, making choice C the best answer. The bottom position would be the least important, so choice A

is incorrect even though *bottom* could be used as a synonym for *seat* or even *base* in a different context. Choice B is the wrong part of speech; the author uses *seat* as a noun but *sit* is always a verb. Choice D is a noun, but it mistakes *seat* for a piece of furniture for sitting, which is not how the author is using the word in this particular context.

9. **The correct answer is B.** Once again, the author is using a multiple-meaning word to describe a position, and as he precedes *bristles* by stating that a bald ridge is "pushed" up over the landscape, you can conclude that the correct answer similarly describes something that stands up or out. Choice B is the best answer. Choices A and C are less appropriate because *brims* and *teems* are more often used to describe a liquid, not a solid object such as a ridge. Choice D can be used as a synonym for *bristles*, but it makes no sense to suggest that a ridge gets angry.

Synthesis Questions

Synthesis questions require you to read two different pieces and find the similarities, differences, and/or connections between them. These two pieces could be the two passages in a paired passage set (**Analyzing Multiple Texts** questions) or a passage and its accompanying informational graphic (**Analyzing Quantitative Information** questions). The questions that ask you about both the passages in a paired passage set or the passage and the graphic in a passage/informational graphic set are Synthesis questions.

 Although all questions that require you to synthesize information between a passage and an informational graphic are called Analyzing Quantitative Information questions, you won't always be dealing with numbers in these questions. Some will ask you about text captions that accompany the graphic.

Synthesis questions may ask you how two pieces are similar or different. They may ask you about how one piece builds upon or contradicts the information in the other piece. They may even ask more speculative questions, such as what the author of one passage or graphic might likely think about details in the other passage. Synthesis questions will often have something in common with Information and Ideas or Rhetoric questions, requiring you to make inferences or analyze language, but they will always refer to more than a single passage.

Here are some sample Analyzing Multiple Texts questions:

- *Based on both passages, both authors would agree with which of the following claims?*
- *Which choice best states the relationship between the two passages?*
- *The primary purpose of each passage is to...*
- *The author of Passage 1 would most likely have reacted to lines 1–3 of Passage 2 with...*
- *Based on the passages, the author of Passage 2 would most likely describe the attitude of the author of Passage 1 as...*

Here are some sample Analyzing Quantitative Information questions:

- *Which of the following claims is supported by the diagram?*
- *Data presented in the table most directly support which idea from the passage?*

Synthesis Practice

Read the physics paired passages closely this time. See what the questions are asking you, read the passages carefully, and answer the two synthesis questions that follow.

Passage 1

This passage is excerpted from Letters on Astronomy *by Denison Olmsted.*

Indeed, what is more admirable, than that astronomers should be able to tell us, years beforehand, the exact instant of the commencement and termination of an eclipse, and describe all the attendant circumstances with the greatest fidelity.
Line You have doubtless, my dear friend, participated in this admiration, and felt a
5 strong desire to learn how it is that astronomers are able to look so far into futurity. I will endeavor, in this Letter, to explain to you the leading principles of the calculation of eclipses, with as much plainness as possible.

An *eclipse of the moon* happens when the moon, in its revolution around the earth, falls into the earth's shadow. An *eclipse of the sun* happens when the moon,
10 coming between the earth and the sun, covers either a part or the whole of the solar disk.

The earth and the moon being both opaque, globular bodies, exposed to the sun's light, they cast shadows opposite to the sun, like any other bodies on which the sun shines. Were the sun of the same size with the earth and the moon, then
15 the lines drawn touching the surface of the sun and the surface of the earth or moon (which lines form the boundaries of the shadow) would be parallel to each other, and the shadow would be a cylinder infinite in length; and were the sun less than the earth or the moon, the shadow would be an increasing cone, its narrower end resting on the earth; but as the sun is vastly greater than either of these bodies,
20 the shadow of each is a cone whose base rests on the body itself, and which comes to a point, or vertex, at a certain distance behind the body.

Passage 2

This passage is adapted from The Story of Eclipses *by George F. Chambers.*

To bring about an eclipse of the Sun, two things must combine: the Moon must be at or near one of its Nodes; and, this must be at a time when the Moon is also in "Conjunction" with the Sun. Now the Moon is in Conjunction with the
25 Sun (= "New Moon") 12 or 13 times in a year, but the Sun only passes through the Nodes of the Moon's orbit twice a year. Hence an eclipse of the Sun does not and cannot occur at every New Moon, but only occasionally. An *exact* coincidence of Earth, Moon, and Sun, in a straight line at a Node is not necessary to ensure an eclipse of the Sun. So long as the Moon is within about 18½° of its Node, with a
30 latitude of not more than 1° 34', an eclipse *may* take place. If, however, the distance is less than 15¼° and the latitude less than 1° 23' an eclipse *must* take place, though between these limit the occurrence of an eclipse is uncertain and depends on what are called the "horizontal parallaxes" and the "apparent semi-diameters" of the two bodies at the moment of conjunction, in other words, on the nearness or "far-
35 offness" of the bodies in question. Another complication is introduced into these matters by reason of the fact that the Nodes of the Moon's orbit do not occupy a fixed position, but have an annual retrograde motion of about 19¼°, in virtue of

which a complete revolution of the Nodes round the ecliptic is accomplished in 18 years 218 7/8 days (= 18.5997 years).

40   The backward movement of the Moon's Nodes combined with the apparent motion of the Sun in the ecliptic causes the Moon in its monthly course round the Earth to complete a revolution with respect to its Nodes in a less time (27.2 days) than it takes to get back to Conjunction with the Sun (29.5 days); and a curious consequence, as we shall see directly, flows from these facts and from one other
45   fact. The other fact is to the Sun starting coincident with one of the Moon's Nodes, returns on the Ecliptic to the same Node in 346.6 days. The first named period of 27.2 days is called the "*Nodical* Revolution of the Moon" or "Draconic Month," the other period of 29.5 days is called the "*Synodical* Revolution of the Moon." Now the curious consequence of these figures being what they are is that 242 Draconic
50   Months, 223 Lunations, and 19 Returns of the Sun to one and the same Node of the Moon's orbit, are all accomplished in the same time within 11 hours. Thus (ignoring refinements of decimals):—

		DAYS	DAYS	YEARS	DAYS	HOURS
242	×	27.2	6,585.36	18	10	8.5
223	×	29.5	6,585.32	18	10	7.75
19	×	346.6	6,585.78	18	10	18.75

10 Which choice best states the relationship between the two passages?

A. Passage 1 describes the composition of celestial bodies, and Passage 2 explains how those bodies move.

B. Passage 2 is a very general description of a phenomenon, and Passage 1 is a more technical description of the same phenomenon.

C. Both passages make judgments about the characters of astronomers.

D. Passage 1 explains how a phenomenon affects two bodies, and Passage 2 develops on one of those explanations.

11 The data presented in the table most directly supports which idea from Passage 2?

A. There are 242 Nodical revolutions in 18 years, 10 days, and 8½ hours.

B. There are 223 Lunations every 29.5 days.

C. The Synodical Revolution of the Moon occurs once every 18 years.

D. The Draconic Month is longer than the time it takes for there to be 19 Returns of the Sun.

ANSWER KEY AND EXPLANATIONS

10. D	**11.** A

10. **The correct answer is D.** Passage 1 presents a general description of eclipses of the sun and moon, while Passage 2 develops on the first passage description of eclipses of the sun with much deeper, technical details. Therefore, choice D is the best answer, and choice B can be eliminated because it confuses the two passages. Although Passage 1 does describe the composition of both the moon and Earth as "globular" and "opaque," these descriptions are not the passage's main purpose, so choice A is a weak description of the relationship between the two passages. Choice C is incorrect because only the first passage describes astronomers' intentions as "admirable," and it is not a very important detail in the passage. Choice C is an answer that would be chosen by someone who did not read more than the first line of Passage 1.

11. **The correct answer is A.** Although the table does not give the name of which event occurs 242 times in 18 years, 10 days, and 8 ½ hours, the passage explains that this is the *Nodical* Revolution of the moon, so choice A is correct. Choice B is incorrect; according to information in the passage and the graphic, there are actually 223 lunations every 18 years, 10 days, and 7 ¾ hours. Choice C is incorrect because the passage indicates that the Synodical Revolution of the moon is a lunation, which means it also occurs 223 times every 18 years, 10 days, and 7 ¾ hours. Choice D is incorrect because information in the passage and graphic show that it takes 11 hours longer for there to be 19 returns of the sun than a complete Draconic month.

COMMAND OF EVIDENCE QUESTIONS

Command of Evidence questions require you to find the information directly stated in the passage that supports the correct answer to the previous question. This is a unique question type because it is the only one that depends on other questions in the test. Command of Evidence questions always follow Information and Ideas, Rhetoric, or Synthesis questions and ask you to find the lines in the passage that support your answers to those Information and Ideas, Rhetoric, or Synthesis questions.

Here's an example of how a Command of Evidence question would follow an Information and Ideas question you answered earlier in this chapter:

According to the passage, Mr. Dashwood was disappointed in his uncle's will because

A. the wealthiest people received the largest inheritance.

B. Mr. Dashwood was left nothing in the will.

C. it proved the uncle favored his great nephew over his grand nieces.

D. the boy who received most of the inheritance was cunning and noisy.

Which choice provides the best evidence for the answer to the previous question?

A. Lines 12–13 ("The constant . . . interest")

B. Lines 16–17 ("By a former . . . daughters.")

C. Lines 17–18 ("The son . . . mother")

D. Lines 20–21 ("To him . . . sisters")

 Command of Evidence questions always follow the same format. The question always reads: "Which choice provides the best evidence for the answer to the previous question?" The answer choices always provide the line numbers and the first and final words of the lines in parentheses.

The cool thing about Command of Evidence questions is that they can actually help you answer other questions on the SAT® Reading Test. After examining a Command of Evidence question, you may find that there is no evidence to support your previous answer and decide to choose a better one. However, this means that choosing the right answer to a Command of Evidence question also depends on answering the previous question correctly.

 Some incorrect answer choices in Command of Evidence questions can be very tricky because they may seem to support incorrect answers to the previous question.

Be sure to always choose the very best piece of evidence. One answer choice may seem correct, but you may find that another one provides much more specific evidence to support your previous answer. The *most specific* answer is the best one.

COMMAND OF EVIDENCE PRACTICE

Command of Evidence questions are unique because they depend so much on other questions, so your final selection of sample questions is a bit different from the others. Instead of answering only one question type, you will answer three. Once again you will read a passage you've already read actively, and you will read it closely by reading the questions before rereading the passage very carefully. Here's that Science passage again:

This passage is excerpted from How Snakes Eat *by Catherine C. Hopley.*

The Hamadryad's appointed diet is one ring-snake per week; but "Ophi," as we now call him, is occasionally required—and with no sacrifice of his principles either—to eat an extra snake to satisfy the curiosity of some distinguished visitor.
Line Sometimes, too, colubers are plentiful, and two small ones are not too much for his
5 ten or twelve feet of appetite. This splendid serpent has rewarded care by remaining in perfect health, and growing several feet. He was between eight and nine feet long when he came, and is now not far short of twelve and proportionately larger in circumference. Sometimes during winter, when ring-snakes are scarce, "Ophi" is compelled to fast; for he is not then to be tempted with other food. During the
10 first year of his residence in the Gardens, the supply was good, and he ate no less than eighty-two fellow-creatures before the winter was well over. Towards spring, however, the supply ran short, and only two more remained for him. He had now fasted two entire weeks, and looked hungry and eager. The keeper offered him a guinea-pig, at which he took great offence, raising his hood and hissing angrily for
15 a long while. Eggs he declined, also a lizard and a rat, in great disgust. In India the Ophiophagi are said to feed on lizards and fish occasionally, but our Ophiophagus preferred to fast. At last one of the two ring-snakes was produced, and Ophio was to be regaled. It was the 31st of March, 1876, and he had been a denizen of the Gardens just one year. My note-book informs me that it was a lovely, soft spring day,
20 and that Ophio was quite lively. He had rejected frogs on his own account, but in the uncertainty of more ring-snakes arriving, he was now decoyed into eating half a dozen. Holland contrived that the snake destined for his dinner should answer the purpose of a feast, and had allowed it to eat as many frogs as it chose. Like the poor wretch who, doomed to the gallows, is permitted to fare sumptuously the
25 last morning of his life, the ring-snake ate three frogs, by which the Ophiophagus was to derive chief benefit; he, all unconscious of the cause of his victim's unusual plumpness, swallowed him speedily.

Soon after this Ophio doffed his winter coat entire, and having again fasted for ten days, was at once rewarded by the last remaining ring-snake in a similarly ple-
30 thoric condition, namely, with three more frogs inside him. Now and then during the winter months the scarcity of ring-snakes has compelled the sacrifice of some

far rarer colubers to Ophio's cannibal tastes. And yet each year we hear of hundreds of ring-snakes being ruthlessly killed in country districts, while at great cost and trouble others are purchased or brought from the Continent for the Hamadryad's
35 sustenance. Lord Lilford, one of the Ophidarium's best patrons, sometimes sends presents of game in the shape of ring-snakes to the Hamadryad.

Diet of a Garter Snake	
Frogs	85%
Invertebrates	11%
Mammals	4%

12 The passage is written from the point of view of someone who

A. sees human characteristics in snakes.

B. believes all snakes to be splendid.

C. overemphasizes the effect of the seasons on snakes.

D. finds nature to be fascinating and confusing.

13 Which choice provides the best evidence for the answer to the previous question?

A. Lines 5–6 ("This splendid . . . feet.")

B. Lines 10–12 ("he ate . . . ran short,")

C. Lines 13–15 ("The keeper . . . while.")

D. Line 15 ("Eggs he . . . rat,")

14 Which of the following claims is supported by the table?

A. The garter snake will eat frogs but the Ophio will not.

B. The garter snake will never fast but the Ophio fasts regularly.

C. The garter snake and the Ophio will both eat other kinds of snakes.

D. The garter snake has a different staple food than the Ophio.

15 Which choice provides the best evidence for the answer to the previous question?

A. Lines 20–22 ("He had . . . dozen.")

B. Lines 22–23 ("Holland . . . feast,")

C. Lines 25–26 ("the ring-snake . . . benefit;")

D. Lines 28–29 ("Soon after . . . ten days,")

ANSWER KEY AND EXPLANATIONS

12. A	13. C	14. D	15. A

12. **The correct answer is A.** The author makes several comparisons between the reactions of the snakes she observes and human emotions, so choice A is the best answer. Choice B is an overstatement; that the author describes one particular kind of snake as "splendid" does not mean she believes all snakes to be splendid. The author makes a few mentions of weather and season in the passage, but she never really overemphasizes the effects weather and seasons have on snakes, so choice C is not the best answer. Choice D is only partially correct; the author does seem to find nature fascinating, but she never seems particularly confused by it in the passage. An answer cannot be partially correct; it must be completely correct.

13. **The correct answer is C.** Lines 13–15 describe the snake as taking offense at something, and taking offense is a distinctly human trait, so choice C is the best support for the previous answer. Animals can be splendid, so choice A is not the best answer, as it implies that choice B was the correct answer to the previous question. Choice B implies that choice C was the correct answer to the previous question since it refers to seasons, and lines 10–12 discuss snake behavior in winter and spring. Choice D is a bit tricky since it describes a snake rejecting food, which is something a human might do, but it is also something many animals would do, so rejecting food is not exclusive to humans as the taking of offense is.

14. **The correct answer is D.** According to the table, the garter snake's staple food is frogs, but the Ophio prefers to eat other snakes and eats frogs only under duress. Therefore, choice D is the most sensible conclusion. Although the Orphio does eat frogs under duress, it eats frogs nevertheless, so choice A is not the best answer. The passage indicates that the Orphio can fast, but there is no evidence of whether or not the garter snake also fasts in the table, so choice B is incorrect. There is no evidence in the table that the garter snake will eat other snakes, so choice C is incorrect.

15. **The correct answer is A.** Lines 20–22 show that the Orphio prefers eating ring-snakes over eating frogs and actually refuses frogs for a long time before eating them, which indicates that frogs are not the Orphio's staple food. The informational graphic, however, shows that frogs are the garter snake's staple food, which means that choice A is the best answer. Choice B refers to Orphio eating, but it does not indicate what it eats. Choice C seems to contradict the correct answer to the previous question since it describes the Orphio eating frogs without also indicating that Orphio ate the frogs only under duress. Choice D implies that choice B is the correct answer to the previous question, since both refer to how the Orphio fasts.

Bring Your Best Test-Taking Tools!

We can't say this enough: The tools in your test-taking arsenal that have served you well thus far in your academic career will be among your *best* tools on test day. The *key* is to practice before test day, to make sure you're comfortable using your test-taking skills within the format and timing of the official exam.

Some skills are transferrable for any test—some aren't. We recommend you work on combining your existing skills with the strategies provided in this book, and with careful practice, you'll have an effective mix of tools in your corner on test day!

SUMMING IT UP

- The SAT® Reading Test is a 65-minute test consisting of 52 multiple choice questions and six passages (four standalone and one paired passage). You will see three different kinds of passages you'll read on the SAT® Reading Test: **U.S. and World Literature, History/Social Studies,** and **Science.**

- Two passages on the SAT® Reading Test will also include an **informational graphic** in the form of a chart, table, diagram, graph, or map.

- When you face a new passage, first practice **active reading** and then **close reading**. In active reading, you quickly read a passage to get the main idea and thesis and to note where in the passage to return for relevant details. In close reading, you go back after seeing the question stems to read again carefully for the finer details.

- All the information you need to answer SAT® Reading questions is contained in the passages given to you—you do not need to bring in any outside knowledge.

- Do *not* memorize vocabulary lists—in order to answer **Words in Context** questions correctly, all you'll need to do is understand the definition of a word as it appears in a passage. Use the words around it to help determine the answer. Don't work too quickly and answer with what you think is the correct definition. Double-check back in the passage to make sure your answer makes sense in context.

- U.S. World and Literature passages are short excerpts from literary works. They aim to give an impression of a character or place, and they sometimes introduce a conflict.

- You will see two History/Social Studies passages: one social science passage on a topic like economics, politics, or sociology; and one "founding document," like an important political speech or text from the Constitution.

- Science passages on the SAT® Reading Test can cover Earth science, biology, chemistry, or physics. You do *not* have to study science before taking the exam—all the information you need to know for the test is contained within the given passage.

- You will see one **paired passage**—a set of History/Social Studies passages or a set of Science passages. You will have to answer questions about each passage individually and questions on how the passages relate to one another. These are called **Synthesis** questions.
    - When reading paired passages, keep in the back of your mind that you will see Synthesis questions. As you read, take notes about how the passages differ and how they are similar.

- **Information and Ideas** questions ask you to read the passage closely to pick out relevant details. You will have to identify a passage's main idea and theme and draw inferences and conclusions about why the author included specific information. No information in a passage is random—if you read details about a person, place, or thing, take note. Either you will see a question asking about it, or you can use it to find out more about the subjects of your passage and their actions.

- **Rhetoric** questions ask you about the author's style of writing—how did he or she convey information, and why did he or she make certain stylistic choices? If an argument is made, ask yourself how the author's point of view came across, whether or not a strong argument was made, and why or why not.

- When reading a passage accompanied by a **informational graphic,** take a mental note of how the graphic supports the text—does it add additional information that helps you better understand the passage? Does it reiterate with a visual what the passage already states? What are you learning from the graphic, and how does it strengthen the piece as a whole?

- **Command of Evidence** questions ask you to find the proof for your answer to a previous question. You will choose the quoted line from the passage that best supports, or gives evidence, that the previous question is correct. Always pick the most specific answer—the one that offers the most precise evidence of the four provided.

CHAPTER 4: THE SAT® MATH TEST

OVERVIEW

- A Brief Introduction to the SAT® Math Test
- The Heart of Algebra
- Problem Solving and Data Analysis
- Passport to Advanced Math
- Additional Topics in Math
- Summing it Up

The SAT® Math Test is used to simply assess a student's shallow understanding of a broad swath of math topics. But since the test changed in 2016, it now tests your ability to apply problem solving and mathematical modeling to a refined body of the most critical math skills. You will be tested on the mathematical concepts that you are most likely to come across in your personal life, your work world, and your college courses in the fields of math, science, and social science.

We've designed this chapter to power you through an explanation of every single math topic tested on the SAT®. You'll get a taste of each question type you will see in addition to the math fundamentals you'll need to know to do well on test day.

Let's get started!

NOTE: For comprehensive information regarding the Math Test, visit the College Board's official website: ***https://collegereadiness.collegeboard.org/sat/inside-the-test/math***.

A BRIEF INTRODUCTION TO THE SAT® MATH TEST

There are two math sections on the redesigned SAT® Math Test:
1. The No Calculator Section prohibits the use of a calculator. It contains 20 questions and is 25 minutes long.
2. The Calculator Section permits the use of a calculator. It contains 38 questions and is 55 minutes long.

About 90 percent of questions you will see on test day will fall into three main content areas:
1. **The Heart of Algebra:** These questions concentrate on creating, solving, and interpreting linear equations and systems of linear equations.
2. **Problem Solving and Data Analysis:** These questions will focus on applying percentages, ratios, proportions, and unit of measurement conversions to real-world situations.
3. **Passport to Advanced Math:** These questions will test your mastery with more advanced functions and equations that are the foundation for college-level courses in math, science, engineering, and technology.

About 10 percent of questions will fall into the **Additional Topics in Math** category, which includes geometry, trigonometry, and complex numbers.

NOTE: If you don't use it, you'll lose it! You will have to do calculations by hand with fractions, decimals, and percentages in the No Calculator section, so don't forget to review these important foundational skills.

Almost 80 percent of the questions on the exam will be multiple-choice questions for which you select your answer from four given choices. Approximately 20 percent of the questions will be grid-in questions for which you must come up with your own answer—no choices are provided to you.

Don't be intimidated by grid-in questions—they are sometimes more straightforward than the multiple-choice questions! Just make sure to double-check your work before you enter your answer into the grid.

The questions you will see on the Math Test are not often just straightforward math problems to solve with no context around them. Most are applied problems, where you will need to use your math skills to answer questions that relate to science as well as historical or social science contexts. These questions may be in the form of information presented graphically or in a word problem. So, you'll need to sharpen your comprehension skills as well as your math skills.

There is no penalty for incorrect answer selections, so it is in your best interest to not leave any answers blank.

This chapter is broken into four sections:
1. The Heart of Algebra
2. Problem Solving and Data Analysis
3. Passport to Advanced Math
4. Additional Topics in Math

We will discuss the most important skills you must know for success in each of these sections. You will notice that there are many sample questions to give you a feel of what to expect on test day. Although these sample questions may not be accompanied by multiple answer options (just like grid-in questions), the explanations provided will walk you through the most efficient ways to crack the trickiest aspects of these problems.

THE HEART OF ALGEBRA

Approximately 33 percent of the questions on the SAT® Math Test will test skills in The Heart of Algebra subsection, which covers linear equations and systems. Heart of Algebra questions will be in both the Calculator and the No Calculator sections.

SOLVING LINEAR EQUATIONS AND INEQUALITIES ALGEBRAICALLY

One of the most straightforward questions you could see on the SAT® Math Test might be a question that tests your fluency in solving linear equations and inequalities. Here, we'll focus on three different pitfalls to watch out for in these types of questions.

Sometimes you'll be able to use mathematical reasoning to make the task of solving a question much easier! Don't rush when reading questions—look for patterns and similarities that can help you solve. Consider the following question:

Example:

$$\frac{1}{2}(x^2 - 8x + 15) = \frac{2}{5}(x^2 - 8x + 15)$$

Solution:

If you were to rush into this question before using any mathematical reasoning, you would distribute the fractions on both sides and end up with a mess of a quadratic equation. Instead, use mathematical reasoning to see that both of the quadratic expressions in parentheses, $(x^2 - 8x + 15)$, are equal. The only time that $ac = bc$ is when $c = 0$; therefore, it must be true that $(x^2 - 8x + 15) = 0$. Solving this quadratic equation with factoring would give you $(x - 3)(x - 5) = 0$, so $x = 3$ and 5.

Working Quickly With Fractions and Decimals

When answering questions in the No Calculator section of the test, you must have fluency working with fractions and decimals. In order to save time, it's important that you know how to convert fractions and decimals into whole numbers before solving linear equations:

To convert decimals into whole numbers: Multiply both sides of the equation by the smallest power of 10 that will eliminate all decimals. For example, look at how the following equation can be simplified by multiplying both sides by 100:

$$0.8x + 0.24 = 1.2 - 0.74x$$
$$100(0.8x + 0.24) = 100(1.2 - 0.74x)$$
$$80x + 24 = 120 - 74x$$

 **CAUTION** Don't get bogged down working with time-consuming fractions or decimals. Be smarter than the question by converting decimals or fractions to whole numbers using the tips illustrated in this section.

To convert fractions into whole numbers: Multiply both sides of the equation by the least common multiple of all fractions in an equation. For example, the following equation would take a lot of time if you worked it out using fractions. Look at how it can be simplified by multiplying both sides by 12:

$$\frac{3}{4}v + \frac{2}{3} = \frac{11}{12}v - \frac{5}{6}$$

$$12\left(\frac{3}{4}v + \frac{2}{3}\right) = 12\left(\frac{11}{12}v - \frac{5}{6}\right)$$

$$9v + 8 = 11v - 10$$

Inequalities

You likely remember that you solve linear inequalities with the same rules that you use to solve linear equations. The trickiest aspect about inequalities is remembering to switch the direction of the inequality symbol when dividing or multiplying by a negative number. It's likely that an inequality question on the SAT® Math Test will test this skill, so remember that if $-5x > 20$, then $x < -4$.

 *Always* switch the direction of the inequality symbol only when **dividing** or **multiplying**—not adding or subtracting—by a negative number.

WRITING AND SOLVING LINEAR EQUATIONS AND INEQUALITIES FROM A GIVEN CONTEXT

The SAT® Math Test emphasizes *creating* and *interpreting* linear equations and inequalities that model real-life situations, so your math skills, even if strong, will need to be kicked up a notch. Sometimes you will just need to write a single equation or inequality that represents a situation, but other times you might be asked to interpret the real-world meaning of the parts of a given equation.

Writing Equations and Finding Equivalent Expressions

Writing a linear equation can be a straightforward task, but what if the equation you construct doesn't match any of the given answer choices? In that case, you will need to identify an equivalent form of the equation, as illustrated in the following example:

Example:

> Gina is shopping for a sofa online. Shipping will cost a flat fee of $80, and a tax of 6% will apply to the cost of the sofa, but not to the shipping fee. Which model represents the total cost, $f(s)$, of a sofa that costs s dollars and has an $80 shipping fee?

Solution:

> First, write out the relationship of the information you are given (*cost*, *tax*, and *shipping*) and the information you are asked to find (*total price*):
>
> $$total\ price = sofa\ cost + tax + shipping$$
>
> The *sofa cost* of the sofa is s dollars. The *tax* on this sofa will be 6% of s, which is 0.06s. The *shipping* is $80 and the *total price* will be represented by $f(s)$. Input these values to get:

$$f(s) = s + 0.06s + 80$$

So what happens when you're so excited at how easy this question was, but your equation wasn't among the answer choices given? It happens all the time. In this situation, the correct answer choice will likely represent this equation as:

$$f(s) = 1.06s + 80$$

Before panicking, always take a second to see if you can simplify the answer you came up with to match one of the given choices.

 TIP Don't panic if your solution is not one of the answer choices given. Instead, determine which answer choice is an equivalent expression or equation to your answer.

If you first tried to solve this question through a "working backward" approach of scanning the answers to start, the 1.06 might have thrown you off. If you construct your own equation and then simplify it, you'll arrive at the correct answer.

 **CAUTION** When increasing a value v by a percentage, remember that you'll need to add the percentage increase to the original value. For example, a 20% increase of v is written as $0.20v$, but when added to the original value v, this yields $1.20v$. Don't make the mistake of representing a 20% increase of v as just $0.20v$!

Interpreting Equations and Inequalities

On the exam you may be given a context along with an equation (in the form of a word problem), and you will need to interpret the real-world meaning of the coefficients, constants, and/or variables represented.

Take a look at the following question.

Example:

Wyeth works at a car dealership that pays him a weekly salary in addition to a commission for each car he sells. If the relationship $P = 300c + 400$ represents his total pay, P, for the week after selling c cars, what do the coefficient 300 and the constant 400 represent?

Solution:

We love these questions where you don't have to compute any math! Instead, you just need to interpret the context. For this question, it's first important to understand that commission is money a salesperson earns based on his or her sales; it is an additional bonus on top of a steady salary that doesn't depend on sales. In this example, since the 300 is being multiplied by c, it must represent the *commission* Wyeth earns for each car he sells. The constant 400 does not change when c changes, so this is his *weekly salary*.

Writing and Solving Equations and Inequalities

When you see the words *at least* or *at most*, you know that you need to construct and/or solve an inequality. It's important to decide if the inequality will be a **less than** or **greater than** ($<$ or $>$) or if it will have an **or equal to** in the symbol ($\leq$ or $\geq$).

Let's look at our next sample question.

Example:

Liv has knitted 2 feet of a scarf. She can knit $\frac{2}{5}$ of a foot per hour. If she wants the scarf to be at least 6 feet long before she can give it as a birthday gift, which inequality represents the number of hours she must knit?

Solution:

First, we need to define a variable to represent the number of hours that Liv will knit: let h be hours. Then realize that after h hours, the scarf will be the existing 2 feet plus $\frac{2}{5}h$: $2 + \frac{2}{5}h$. Since she wants it to be *at least* 6 feet long, we know that $2 + \frac{2}{5}h$ must be greater than *or equal to* 6: $2 + \frac{2}{5}h \geq 6$.

In the previous example, you were given the rate of change, which was $\frac{2}{5}$ *of a foot per hour*. On the Math Test you might get a question that gives you enough information to determine the rate of change but does not give you the rate outright. In this case, you will need to organize the information in the question into coordinate pairs [in the (x, y) format] that match the independent variables with their corresponding dependent variables. Once you have two coordinate pairs, you can find the rate of change by using the slope formula, $m = \dfrac{\text{rise}}{\text{run}} = \dfrac{y_2 - y_1}{x_2 - x_1}$, which we'll discuss in a little more in depth later on in this chapter.

Tricky Rounding

Sometimes when solving a real-world math problem, you will end up with a decimal answer that needs to be rounded to the nearest whole number. When this happens, you need to think carefully about how the context of the question will influence the rounding and make an informed decision about whether you should round up or down.

Let's see how this situation applies in the next sample question.

Example:

Izzy is painting the interior of an office building. He has determined that the total area of the rooms he will paint is 12,550 square feet. If he is buying paint that covers 400 square feet for each gallon, how many gallons of paint does he need to purchase to complete this job?

Solution:

The solution of this is easy, but the rounding must be carefully considered. Dividing 12,550 by 400 shows that Izzy will need 31.375 gallons of paint. Standard rounding rules would indicate that 31.375 rounds to 31; however, since Izzy needs an extra 0.375 gallons, 31 gallons would not leave him with enough paint. Therefore, this answer must get rounded to 32 gallons.

 Sometimes rounding decimals in the real world goes against the rounding taught in classrooms. If a solution shows that a budget has enough money left over to purchase 5.9 packages of tile, this must be rounded down to 5 packages, since there is not enough money for the entire sixth package.

SOLVING SYSTEMS OF LINEAR EQUATIONS

All linear equations have infinite solutions of (x, y) coordinate pairs that satisfy the given relationship. A **system of linear equations** is two equations considered together. Systems of equations can have three different solution sets:

1. If the linear equations have **different slopes**, there will be just one coordinate pair (x, y) that satisfies both equations.

2. If the linear equations have the **same slopes and different y-intercepts**, they will be parallel lines and there will be no (x, y) coordinate pair that works simultaneously in both equations (because the lines will never cross).

3. If the linear equations have the **same slopes and the same y-intercepts**, the two lines are equivalent and there will be infinite (x, y) coordinate pair solutions to the system.

First, let's focus on solving systems of equations that have one solution. The two most useful methods are substitution and elimination.

Using Substitution to Solve a System of Equations

It's important to recognize which method of solving systems of equations would be easiest to use. When one of the equations has a single variable isolated and set equal to an expression in terms of the other variable, the best approach is to use substitution. Take a look at how a substitution system of equations question may be asked on test day:

If $3w + 6v = 9$ and $w = -7v + 13$, what is the value of $\dfrac{v}{w}$?

In this case, since w is isolated in the second equation and set equal to the expression $-7v + 13$, replace the w in the first equation with the expression $-7v + 13$ so you can solve a linear equation with just one variable:

$$3w + 6v = 9 \text{ and } w = -7v + 13$$

so

$$3(-7v + 13) + 6v = 9$$
$$-21v + 39 + 6v = 9$$
$$-15v + 39 = 9$$

$$-15v = -30, \text{ so } v = 2$$

After determining the value of one of the variables, plug it back into the equation to find the value of the other variable. Plug $v = 2$ into $w = -7v + 13$:

$$w = -7(2) + 13 = -1$$

You're not done yet! $v = 2$ and $w = -1$, so plug these values into the quotient

$$\frac{v}{w} : \frac{2}{-1} = -2$$

NOTE: Be prepared to see system of equations questions presented in new ways on the SAT® Math Test. In order to keep students from working backward by just plugging the given answers into the given equations, the exam questions may require you to determine the value of an expression like $x + y$ or xy.

Using Elimination to Solve a System of Equations

Now let's review how to use elimination to solve a system of equations. Remember, sometimes you need to multiply both equations by different factors in order to create opposite coefficients that will cancel out one of the variables. The following example could be a question you'd find in the No Calculator grid-in section.

Example:

What is the value of $p - q$ if it is given that $3p - 5q = 14$ and $4p - 3q = 4$?

Solution:

Neither equation has a variable that is isolated and defined in terms of the other variable. Quick inspection reveals that isolating a variable in either equation would create an equivalent expression with fractions, making this question more difficult than it needs to be. Therefore, you can most efficiently solve this problem using elimination. First, line up the two equations vertically:

$$3p - 5q = 14$$
$$4p - 3q = 4$$

It doesn't matter if we cancel out the p terms or the q terms to start, but we will begin with the p terms. The lowest common multiple of the coefficients of p is 12, so select factors that change one of the p coefficients to 12 and the other p coefficient to -12:

Multiply by 4: **4**$(3p - 5q) = $ **4**$(14) \rightarrow 12p - 20q = 56$

Multiply by -3: **-3**$(4p - 3q) = $ **-3**$(4) \rightarrow -12p + 9q = -12$

Adding these two equations together will cancel out the p terms and leave $-11q = 44$, so $q = -4$. Substitute this back into one of the first equations to determine the value of p:

$$3p - 5q = 14$$
$$3p - 5(-4) = 14$$
$$3p + 20 = 14$$

$$3p = -6, \text{ so } p = -2$$

Since the question asked for the value of $p - q$, perform $(-2) - (-4) = -2 + 4 = 2$, which is the final answer.

Systems of Linear Equations with No Solutions

Next let's investigate systems of equations that have no solutions. There are three ways to determine that a system of equations has no solution:

1. *Observe the graph:* The equations will form two parallel lines in the coordinate plane that will never intersect.

2. *Observe their slope-intercept equations:* When both equations are in $y = mx + b$ form, they will have the same slopes (m), but different y-intercepts (b).

3. *Solve the system algebraically:* When a system of equations is solved algebraically, all the variables cancel out and only a false numerical equation remains (like $6 = 7$).

Systems of Linear Equations with Infinite Solutions

A system of equations will have infinite solutions if both of the equations are identical and represent the same line. There are three ways to determine that a system of equations has infinite solutions:

1. *Observe the graph:* The two lines will fall on top of each other, as they are the same line.

2. *Observe the equations:* The equations are equivalent.

3. *Solve the system algebraically:* When a system of equations is solved algebraically, all the variables cancel out and only a true numerical equation remains (like $3 = 3$).

Quite often, a question will require you to determine the value of an unknown variable that would produce infinite solutions for a system of equations. As you work through the practice question below, remember that a system of equations will have infinite solutions if the equations are equivalent. This is the type of question you can expect to see in the grid-in section.

The system of equations $0.5x - 4y = s$ and $4x - ty = 7$ has infinitely many solutions. If s and t are non-zero integers, what is the value of s?

In order for this system to have infinite solutions, the equations must be equivalent. Multiply the first equation by 8 in order to get both of the x coefficients to be 4:

$$8(0.5x - 4y) = (s)(8) \rightarrow 4x - 32y = 8s$$

$$4x - ty = 7 \rightarrow 4x - ty = 7$$

In order for this system to have infinite solutions, it is clear that $t = 32$. It is also true that $8s$ must equal 7, so solve $8s = 7$ to get $s = \dfrac{7}{8}$.

WRITING AND SOLVING SYSTEMS OF LINEAR EQUATIONS AND INEQUALITIES FROM A GIVEN CONTEXT

On the SAT® Math Test, you may not be asked to just *solve* a system of given linear equations, but instead you may need to create the system of equations or inequalities from a given real-world context. Sometimes you will need to take this one step further and also solve the system of equations. Let's look at both skills.

When writing a system of equations from a real-world context, you will need to first identify what the unknown pieces of information are and assign variables to represent

---

each one. Next, you must determine how these unknowns relate to each other, and use the other given information to represent these relationships with equations or inequalities.

Sometimes a question will require you only to select the models that could be used to solve the equation, but other times you will need to solve the system of equations as well, and analyze the meaning of the solution in order to come up with the correct answer to the question. Let's look at an example.

Example:

Willamette Middle School is having a talent show. The auditorium holds 500 people, and they are hoping to sell tickets for all available seats. Student tickets cost $2 and adult tickets cost $8. If their goal is to have a sold-out performance and earn revenue of at least $2,500, what system of equations could be used to solve for the fewest number of adults that need to attend the talent show to meet the school's goal?

Solution:

First, identify the two unknowns in this question and assign them variables: the number of student tickets sold will be s and the number of adult tickets sold will be a. The first piece of information given is that there are 500 seats and the school wants to sell tickets for all seats. This means that the student and adult tickets must sum to 500: $s + a = 500$. Next you are given information about the ticket prices. Since the student tickets cost $2 each and s tickets will be sold, the revenue from student ticket sales will be $2s$. Similarly, the revenue for adult ticket sales will be $8a$. Since the school hopes to bring in at least $2,500, determine that $2s + 8a \geq 2,500$. Therefore, the system of equations that could be used to find the least number of adults required to make their sales goal is $s + a = 500$ and $2s + 8a \geq 2,500$.

INTERPRETING GRAPHS OF LINEAR EQUATIONS IN THE COORDINATE PLANE

It is critical that you have a deep understanding of how linear equations and their graphs in the coordinate plane relate to one another. For example, if a slope of a line is increased, you must know that this will make the line steeper. Also, you must have a solid understanding of what to look for with the slopes of parallel and perpendicular lines.

Linear Equations in $y = mx + b$

All linear equations can be written in **slope-intercept form** by isolating y and setting y equal to an x term plus a constant. The m term is the coefficient of x and represents the **slope**, or rate of change, of the line. The constant, b, represents the **y-intercept**, which is also referred to as the starting point. The slope of a line is the ratio of the *rise* (difference in y-coordinates) compared to its *run* (difference in x-coordinates) between any two coordinate pairs (x_1, y_1) and (x_2, y_2). You should remember that $m = \dfrac{\text{rise}}{\text{run}} = \dfrac{y_2 - y_1}{x_2 - x_1}$. You can find the slope between any two points by using this equation.

Here are a few tasks you must know how to handle on test day:

- Given an equation, you will need to select the graph that correctly represents it.

- Given a line graphed in the coordinate plane, you will need to select the equation that represents it.

- You should understand how the appearance of a graph will change according to alterations in the slope, intercepts, or a transformation applied either to the equation or directly to the graph.

Parallel and Perpendicular Lines

It's important to remember that parallel lines have the same slope. They move at the same rate of change and will never intersect. Perpendicular lines have slopes that are opposite reciprocals, like $\dfrac{2}{3}$ and $-\dfrac{3}{2}$. (The product of the slopes of perpendicular lines will always be -1.)

- If you are asked to find the equation of a line that is parallel to a given line, first identify the slope of the given line. Any line with the same slope and a different y-intercept will be parallel to it.

- If you are asked to find the equation of a line that is perpendicular to a given line, first identify the slope of the given line. Any line with the opposite reciprocal slope will be perpendicular to it. (The y-intercepts may be the same, but they do not have to be.)

Let's use this information to work through a sample problem.

Example:

Line *j* is graphed in the coordinate plane below. Which of the equations that follows will make a line that is perpendicular to line *j*?

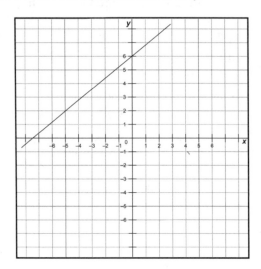

Solution:

Once you determine the slope of the given line in the coordinate plane, you will know that any line with an opposite reciprocal slope will be perpendicular to it. First, note that the coordinate pairs (0, 6) and (–5, 2) sit on the line. Next, use the slope formula to determine the slope of the line: $m = \dfrac{y_2 - y_1}{x_2 - x_1} = \dfrac{2 - 6}{-5 - 0} = \dfrac{-4}{-5} = \dfrac{4}{5}$. Since the slope of this line is $\dfrac{4}{5}$, all lines with a slope of $-\dfrac{5}{4}$ will be perpendicular to it.

Heart of Algebra Practice

1 What is the solution to the equation $\dfrac{3}{5}\left(-\dfrac{2}{5}x + 3\right) = -0.6$?

SHOW YOUR WORK HERE

A. 5

B. –5

C. 10

D. –10

2 The rainy season has arrived to the Pacific Northwest, and Rian is earning some money for school by cleaning gutters. She charges $20 per hour for the first three hours, and then her rate drops to $14 for every additional hour. Which expression could be used to determine the total amount she would earn for a gutter job that takes h hours if $h > 3$?

A. $14(h - 3) + 20$

B. $14h + 60$

C. $14h + 18$

D. $14(h - 3) - 60$

SHOW YOUR WORK HERE

3 Dessie knows that the local shipping center charges a flat rate plus a per-pound fee for all boxes shipped from Los Angeles to Portland. The first box she brought in weighed 60 pounds and cost her $33. The next day she paid $26 for a box that weighed 40 pounds. What is the flat rate that the local shipping center charges? (Enter your answer in the grid below.)

4 If $c \neq 0$, then how many solutions (x, y) exist for the following system of equations? (Enter your answer in the grid below.)

$$3x - 12y = c$$
$$x - 4y = c$$

5 Alpine Crest and Butternut Falls are two neighboring cities. Together, their populations totaled 26,000 people in the year 2000. By 2010, the population of Alpine Crest had fallen 20% while the population of Butternut Falls had increased by 20%. Their new combined population was just 400 people greater than what it had been in the year 2000. What was the difference in their populations by the year 2010?

A. 7,200

B. 9,600

C. 12,000

D. 14,000

ANSWER KEY AND EXPLANATIONS

1. C	2. C	3. 12	4. 0	5. A

1. **The correct answer is C.** Notice that $\frac{3}{5}$ and -0.6 are equivalent, but opposite, expressions. Therefore the expression within the parentheses, $\left(-\frac{2}{5}x+3\right)$, must be equal to -1:

$$-\frac{2}{5}x+3=-1$$
$$-\frac{2}{5}x=-4$$
$$x=-4\cdot\frac{-5}{2}=10$$

Choice A is incorrect because when subtracting 3 from both sides, you found an incorrect sum of -2 on the right-hand side. Choice B is incorrect because when subtracting 3 from both sides, you found an incorrect sum of -2 on the right-hand side, and then made a negative sign error when dividing by $-\frac{2}{5}$. Choice D is the result of dropping a negative sign during the solution, and is also incorrect.

2. **The correct answer is C.** First, identify that Rian will make $60 for her first three hours of work at $20 an hour. Then for every hour *after* three hours, she will earn $14 per hour. This can be represented as $14(h-3)$. Therefore if $h > 3$, then her total earnings would be $60 + 14(h-3)$. This equation simplifies to $14h + 18$. Choice A is

incorrect because she will earn $60, not $20, for her first three hours. Choice B is incorrect because it doesn't take into account that she will earn $14/hour *after* her first three hours. Choice D is wrong because the $60 should be *added* to the $14(h-3)$ and not subtracted.

3. **The correct answer is 12.** This question is asking you to determine the flat rate, or starting point, that the shipping center uses. This will be the y-intercept in a linear equation in the form $y = mx + b$. The rate of change, m, will represent the cost per pound of the packages. First, you must organize the given information into two coordinate pairs. Since the weight is influencing the cost, organize the given information into the pairs (60, 33) and (40, 26). Next find the rate of change by using the slope formula:
$m = \frac{y_2 - y_1}{x_2 - x_1} = \frac{33 - 26}{60 - 40} = 0.35$. Plug (60, 33) and $m = 0.35$ into $y = mx + b$ to solve for the b, which represents the flat rate:

$$33 = 0.35(60) + b$$
$$33 = 21 + b$$
$$b = 12$$

The flat rate for shipping a package is $12, and the cost per pound is $0.35.

4. **The correct answer is 0.** Solve this system by multiplying the second equation by –3 and then combining the two equations to get the x terms to cancel out:

$$3x - 12y = c \rightarrow 3x - 12y = c$$

$$-3(x - 4y) = (c)(-3) \rightarrow$$
$$-3x + 12y = -3c$$

Adding these two equations together yields $0x + 0y = -2c$, which is equivalent to $0 = -2c$. This is true only when $c = 0$, but based on the information given in the question, we know that $c \neq 0$, so for any possible value of c this would be a false statement. Therefore, this system of equations has no solutions.

5. **The correct answer is A.** First, define the starting populations of Alpine Crest and Butternut Falls as a and b respectively. Since their populations summed to 26,000, express this as $a + b = 26,000$. Next express the 20% decrease in the Alpine Crest population in 2010 as being 80% of its population in 2000: $0.80a$. Similarly, the 20% increased population of Butternut Falls in 2010 will be 120% of the 2000 population: $1.20b$. Since the combined population of these two cities in 2010 was just 400 greater than their combined populations in 2000, the second equation will be $0.80a + 1.20b = 26,400$.

Multiply the first equation by –0.8 so that both a terms cancel out when the new equations are combined:

$$a + b = 26,000 \rightarrow -0.8a + (-0.8b)$$
$$= -20,800$$

Adding this equation to $0.80a + 1.20b = -26,400$ yields $0.4b = 5,600$, so $b = 14,000$.

Put 14,000 into the first equation, $a + b = 26,000$ to see that $a = 12,000$. Lastly, we need to use this information to answer the question accurately. It asks for the difference in the cities' populations in the year 2010. Since Alpine Crest had 12,000 people in 2000, it will have 9,600 people in 2010 after a 20% decrease. Since Butternut Falls had 14,000 people in 2000, it will have 16,800 people in 2010 after a 20% increase. The difference between 16,800 and 9,600 is 7,200. Choice B is incorrect because 9,600 is the population of Alpine Crest in the year 2010, but it is not difference in the populations. Choice C is incorrect because 12,000 is the population of Alpine Crest in the year 2000. Choice D is wrong because 14,000 is the population of Butternut Falls in the year 2000.

While working out a multi-step problem, you must be careful to not prematurely select an answer from the list of choices just because you have arrived at that number in your process. Reread the question and make sure you are clear about *what* you have to solve for.

PROBLEM SOLVING AND DATA ANALYSIS

Approximately 29 percent of the questions on the SAT® Math Test will cover skills in the Problem Solving and Data Analysis subsection. All of these questions will be in the Calculator section. Pay attention: the topics covered in this section of the test will be the most practical and widely used skills you'll encounter in your personal life as well as in a variety of different careers.

PROPORTIONS, PERCENTAGES, AND UNIT CONVERSIONS

Using ratios to set up and solve proportions is a skill you might find yourself using long after mastering the SAT® exam. A **ratio** is a comparison of two different quantities. If your high school has a policy that on all field trips there are 2 chaperones for every 7 students, this could be written as the ratio 2:7. If you're going to use a ratio to solve a math problem, it is better to write the ratio as a fraction: $\frac{2}{7}$.

A **proportion** is any equation that sets two ratios equal to one another. Proportions are a convenient way to solve for a missing piece of information. For example, if your high school is planning a field trip with 100 students, how many chaperones would they need?

In order to solve problems like this, first write a fraction with words to represent which information will go in the numerator and which will go in the denominator: $\frac{\text{chaperones}}{\text{students}}$. Then fill in the complete pair of given information: $\frac{\text{chaperones}}{\text{students}} = \frac{2}{7}$. Finally, set that equal to another ratio with the last piece of information, and a variable representing the unknown:

$$\frac{\text{chaperones}}{\text{students}} = \frac{2}{7} = \frac{c}{100}$$

It doesn't matter if the chaperones are in the numerator or denominator, but it is very important that the given information is in the same relative position in *both* ratios! Notice that the c is in the same relative position as the 2, which represents the chaperones. Solve this equation by using cross multiplication:

$$\frac{2}{7} = \frac{c}{100}$$
$$7c = 2(100)$$
$$7c = 200$$
$$c = 28.6$$

This is one of those answers that *mathematically* rounds up to 29, and it makes practical sense because the additional 0.6 chaperones must be rounded to another (whole) chaperone to provide adequate coverage. **The correct answer is 29.**

Percentages

A percentage is a ratio that is literally *per cent* or "out of 100." Therefore, if a shipment of light bulbs arrive and 10% of them are broken, this means that 10 out of every 100 are broken. This ratio $\frac{10}{100}$ can of course be reduced to $\frac{1}{10}$, or one out of every 10. Here are a few quick tips along with examples of how to work efficiently with percentages:

- The general proportion $\frac{\text{part}}{\text{whole}} = \frac{\%}{100}$ can be used to work through many percentage questions. For example, if 68 students in 8th grade got food poisoning and that represents 34% of the 8th grade enrollment, you could find the total number of students in that grade by using: $\frac{68}{\text{whole 8th grade}} = \frac{34}{100}$.

- To calculate percent increase or decrease, use the formula $\frac{\text{amount of change}}{\text{original amount}} \times 100$. If the voter registration increased from 560 people per day to 690 people per day, then % increase $= \frac{690 - 560}{560} \times 100$. (Make sure you compare the difference of 130 to the original amount of 560, and not to the new amount of voters, 690.)

- When increasing a number by a percentage (like the cost of an item after tax) multiply the original number by (1 + percentage increase). For example, the final price of a $60 coat that has 8% tax would be found by multiplying $60(1.08).

- When decreasing a number by a percentage (like the cost of an item that is on sale) multiply the original number by (1 − percentage decrease). For example, the final price of a $60 coat that is 25% off would be found by multiplying $60(0.75).

 It is critical to remember that if a number n is increased by 20% and then decreased by 20%, it will NOT be back at the original number n! Instead, the 20% decrease will be represented by finding 80% of $1.20n$, which does not bring the price back to n: 80% of $120\%(n) = 0.80(1.20n) = 0.96n$, which is 96% of n.

Another percentage concept that can be conceptually tricky is when there is a **compounding percentage** increase or decrease. For example, if a population drops by 10% four years in a row, one might initially think it will experience a 40% decrease. However, this is not the case. Instead, a 10% decrease every year to a population of p people will be 90% of the previous year's population. The expression that would represent the population each successive year would look like this:

Years	Population after 10% decrease
0	p
1	$0.90p$
2	$0.90(0.90p) = 0.81p$
3	$0.90(0.81p) = 0.729p$
4	$0.90(0.729p) = 0.6561p$

So after 4 years, the population is 65.6% of the starting population—not just 60% of the initial population.

Unit Conversions

Similar to percentages, unit conversions are useful for comparing information presented in different units—like miles per hour versus feet per second. Observe how a conversion ratio is used to solve the following model question, which you might find in the grid-in section:

Example:

The sun is 152 million kilometers away from planet Earth. If light travels at an approximate speed of 300,000,000 meters per second, how many minutes does it take a sunbeam to reach Earth? Round your answer to the nearest tenth.

Solution:

This question is presenting kilometers, meters, seconds, and minutes, so there are several different conversions that need to happen. First, we'll use a conversion ratio to turn 300,000,000 meters per second into kilometers per second. To set up a conversion ratio, use equivalent measures on the top and bottom of your ratio, but in different units. For example, a conversion ratio for kilometers and meters is $\frac{1\ kilometer}{1,000\ meters}$. Multiply this ratio by a ratio representing 300,000,000 meters per second: $\frac{300,000,000\ meters}{1\ second}$. (When you multiply a ratio by a conversion ratio, put like units diagonal from each other so they will cancel out.)

$$\frac{300,000,000\ meters}{1\ second} \times \frac{1\ kilometer}{1,000\ meters} = \frac{300,000\ kilometers}{1\ second}$$

Since the sun is 152 million kilometers away, we now need to figure out how many seconds it takes sunlight to reach Earth. Set up a proportion to solve:

$$\frac{distance}{time} = \frac{300,000\ kilometers}{1\ second} = \frac{152,000,000\ kilometers}{s\ seconds}$$

$$300,000s = 152,000,000$$

$$s = 506.67$$

It takes sunlight 507 *seconds* to reach Earth, so dividing this by 60 shows that it takes approximately 8.4 minutes for a sunbeam to reach Earth.

The SAT® Math Test will assess your ability to apply unit conversions to the concept of area. For example, in the following question, notice the dimensions of the room are given in feet but the carpet is sold in square yards:

Example:

The living room in Tabitha's home is 18 feet long by 14 feet wide. The carpet she will install is $16 per square yard. What will be the total price of the carpeting for Tabitha's living room?

Solution:

First conclude that the area of Tabitha's living room is $(18)(14) = 252$ square feet. Since the carpet is sold only by the square yard, it is important to determine how many square feet are in a square yard. Remember that a yard is 3 feet long, so a square yard will be 3 feet by 3 feet. Therefore, a square yard is equivalent to 9 square feet, which can be used to make the conversion ratio $\frac{1\ square\ yard}{9\ square\ feet}$. Multiply the area of 252 square feet by the conversion ratio to change the square footage into square yards:

$$\frac{252\ square\ feet}{1} \times \frac{1\ square\ yard}{9\ square\ feet} = 28\ square\ yards$$

At $16 per square yard, 28 square yards of carpeting will cost Tabitha $448.

EXPONENTIAL MODELS, GRAPHS, SCATTERPLOTS, AND WORKING WITH INTEREST

Your knowledge of graphs and models must extend past linear equations. It will be important to be able to discern when a quadratic or exponential model is a better fit for a graph or real-world situation. You will also need to understand the difference between simple interest and compound interest in addition to knowing the formulas for both of these. In addition, a fluency in reading and interpreting bivariate data displayed in scatterplots will likely be key to answering some problems.

Exponential Models

In linear models, as x changes at a constant rate, there is a constant *difference* between the y-values. In exponential models, as x changes at a constant rate, instead of there being a constant difference, there is a constant *quotient* between the y-values, which is referred to as the **ratio**. In the following tables, a look at the linear equation $y = 2x + 3$ shows that as x changes by 1, there is a common difference of 2 between the successive y-values. The right side shows the exponential equation $y = 3(2^x)$. Notice that as x changes by 1, y increases by a common *ratio* of 2.

$$\boxed{y = 2x + 3}$$

x	y
0	3
1	5
2	7
3	9

$5 - 3 = 2$
$7 - 5 = 2$ } Common Difference
$9 - 7 = 2$

$$\boxed{y = 3 \times 2^x}$$

x	y
0	3
1	6
2	12
3	24

$6 \div 3 = 2$
$12 \div 6 = 2$ } Common Quotient
$24 \div 12 = 2$

If given a table of coordinate pairs where the x-values are changing at a constant rate and the successive y-values have a common ratio, you can be certain the function is exponential. The general form for an exponential function is $y = a(r^x)$, where r is the common ratio and a is the starting point when $x = 0$ (a is therefore the y-intercept). Notice that x is an exponent in exponential models. Use this information to come up with an equation for the model illustrated in the next example question.

Example:

Rabbits have been brought to an island in the South Pacific where there is no natural predator. Their growth over four months is illustrated in the table below. What function is an accurate model for the number of rabbits, $R(m)$, after m months?

Months	Population
0	6
1	18
2	54
3	162
4	486

Solution:

There would typically be a list of functions for you to choose from. Some of them would be linear, but you could immediately rule those out because it's apparent that the rate of change is dramatically increasing as time goes by, rather than increasing at a constant rate. Investigate the ratios of the successive pairs to find that:

$$\frac{18}{6} = \frac{54}{18} = \frac{162}{54} = \frac{486}{162} = 3 = r$$

The common ratio is 3. We can see that the starting point was 6, so using the general formula, $y = a(r^x)$, we can determine that the rabbit population can be modeled using $R(m) = 6(3^x)$.

We'll discuss quadratic models in depth in the Passport to Advanced Math section, but these models are easy to recognize in a graph since they have a parabolic shape that is either upward facing and has a minimum or downward facing and has a maximum.

Two real-world contexts that would be modeled with quadratic functions are the trajectory of an object that has been thrown up into the air or dropped from a point above ground. Quadratic functions are also used to create models that maximize profit or that minimize expenses in financial models. You will review them more thoroughly later in this chapter.

Interpreting Line Graphs

You are probably familiar with the expression "a picture is worth a thousand words." This is totally true for graphs too—a graph provides lots of useful information, and the SAT® Math Test assesses your ability to read a graph.

When looking at a line graph, it's critical you know that the steeper the slope, the faster the growth or decline. It's also important to remember that a section of horizontal line indicates that growth has stagnated: the independent variable is still increasing; however, the dependent variable is remaining constant.

Let's look at an example.

Example:

The following line graph shows the number of pencils sold, in millions, by an office supply store from 2006 to 2011. During which single year did the sale of pencils experience the largest increase?

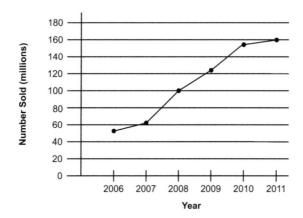

Solution:

Since you are looking for the largest increase in a single year, you must find the portion of the graph that has the steepest slope. This section occurs from the year 2007 to 2008, so the year 2007 is when the sale of pencils experienced the largest increase.

Interpreting Scatterplots

When working with a large data set, it is possible to create a scatterplot in order to determine how one variable influences another variable. For example, a survey might ask students to disclose how many hours they studied for the Math section of the SAT®, exam along with their top math score. All of the coordinate pairs could be plotted on a graph where *Hours Studied* is on the *x*-axis and *Highest Score* is on the *y*-axis. Once all the points are plotted, a **line of best fit** can be drawn through the data to best model the relationship between the variables. The line of best fit gives lots of information:

- If the data points are clustered close to the line of best fit, then there is a strong correlation between the independent and the dependent variable, meaning that the independent variable has a strong influence on the dependent variable.

- If the data points are spread out and many are far from the line of best fit, then there is a weak correlation between the independent and the dependent variable, meaning that the independent variable doesn't have a strong influence over the dependent variable.

- If the line of best fit has a positive slope, then the date has a positive correlation. Conversely, a line of best fit with a negative slope indicates a negative correlation.

The following two graphs illustrate a weak negative correlation and a strong positive correlation:

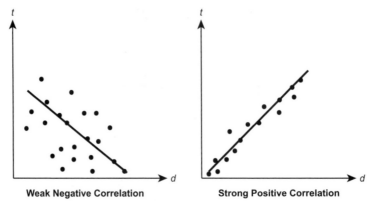

Weak Negative Correlation   **Strong Positive Correlation**

- If a data point is above (or below), the line of best fit, this means that the *y*-coordinate was higher (or lower), than its predicted value.

- The slope of the line of best fit shows the predicted rate of change in the dependent variable as the independent variable changes. For example, if the line of best fit modeling number of hours studied and highest score on the SAT® exam is $\frac{10}{7}$, that would indicate that for every 7 hours studied, a student should expect to score 10 points higher.

Let's test your comfort with reading scatterplots with the following graph and a series of brief questions.

The following scatterplot shows the results of a study on divorced men. It compares the relationship between the Age at Which a Man Met His First Spouse/Partner and the Number of Years of Marriage.

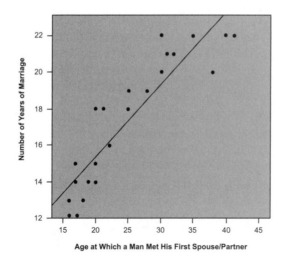

Age at Which a Man Met His First Spouse/Partner

1. **What describes the correlation?** This is a weak positive correlation since the points are not clustered tightly around the line of best fit, but the line has a positive slope.

2. **Interpret the slope of the line of best fit if the slope is** $\frac{1}{3}$. A slope of $\frac{1}{3}$ would indicate that for every 3 extra years of age upon meeting his partner, a man's marriage is predicted to last for an additional year.

3. **According to the line of best fit, at what age would it be predicted that a man met his partner if his marriage lasted for 17 years?** Locate 17 on the y-axis. Move horizontally over until you hit the line of best fit, and then move vertically down to the x-axis to determine that the predicted age would be 25.

4. **Comparing the two points in the scatterplot, (30, 22) and (38, 19), which coordinate pair illustrates a longer marriage?** Since the y-coordinate represents the length of the marriage, the point (30, 22) represents a longer marriage.

Working with Interest

Interest is the money earned on an investment or paid on a loan. It's an important concept to understand not only for the SAT® exam, but also in your personal life! There are two types of interest you are responsible for knowing on the exam: simple interest and compound interest.

Simple interest is a type of interest that adds a percentage of a fixed investment (or loan) every year. Simple interest is calculated with the linear model $A = P(1 + rt)$, where P is the principal (money initially invested), r is the annual interest rate expressed as a decimal, t is the time in years, and A is the final investment value, after interest.

Let's see how this works.

Example:

Suppose that Trek invests $6,000 into a bond that makes 5% simple interest. She doesn't want to withdraw the money until she has at least $7,000 to purchase her first car. How long will she need to wait for her investment to have a final value of $7,000?

Solution:

In this problem, we know that $A = 7,000$, $P = 6,000$, and $r = 0.05$, and will need to solve for t:

$$7,000 = 6,000(1 + 0.05t)$$
$$7,000 = 6,000 + 300t$$
$$1,000 = 300t$$
$$t = 3.33$$

So after $3\frac{1}{3}$ years, Trek will have enough money to buy her first car. (Note that on the exam, $3\frac{1}{3}$ years would most likely be listed as 3 years and 4 months if it were a multiple-choice question.)

Compound interest is a method of calculating interest not only on the original principal, but also on the accumulated interest from earlier periods of an investment or loan. Since the interest is being taken of the previous interest, it is **compounding**. Compound interest is not linear, but is actually exponential. It is calculated with the exponential model $A = P\left(1 + \dfrac{r}{n}\right)^{nt}$, where P is the principal (money initially invested), r is the annual interest rate expressed as a decimal, t is the time in years, n is the number of times per year interest is compounded, and A is the final investment value, after interest. Typically, interest is compounded annually ($n = 1$), semi-annually ($n = 2$), monthly ($n = 12$), or daily ($n = 365$).

Example:

Suppose that Trek invests $6,000 into a bond that makes 5% compound interest. It is compounded daily. She hopes that after 3 years, she'll have at least $7,000 to purchase her first car. Will she make her goal after 3 years?

Solution:

In this problem, we know $P = 6,000$, $r = 0.05$, $n = 365$, and $t=3$. Put these into the compound interest formula and solve for A:

$$A = 6{,}000\left(1 + \frac{.05}{365}\right)^{365 \cdot 3}$$

$$A = 6{,}970.93$$

So after three years, Trek will be $30 short of the savings goal for her car.

Statistics: Measures of Central Tendency, Two-Way Tables, and Margin of Error

The concepts in this section are incredibly important to know in real life, as well as for the SAT® exam, since they are used to analyze real-world statistics. It is important to be able to understand causality, know how reliable data is, and make predictions for future trends when analyzing data.

First, a brief review of **measures of central tendency** using the following data set:

$$\{1, 2, 7, 3, 6, 7, 20, 2\}$$

- **Mode:** the most frequently occurring number in a data set. There can be more than two modes in a data set. For example, the modes of the data set above are 2 and 7.

- **Median:** the center-most number in a data set after the numbers have been put in order from smallest to greatest. If there is an even number of entries, you must take the average of the two center terms. The data set above should be rearranged as $\{1, 2, 2, 3, 6, 7, 7, 20\}$, and the average of 3 and 6 is 4.5.

- **Mean:** the arithmetic average found by dividing the sum of the numbers by the quantity of numbers in the set: $\dfrac{1 + 2 + 7 + 3 + 6 + 7 + 20 + 2}{8} = 6$

- **Range:** the spread of the data set found by subtracting the smallest number from the largest number: $20 - 1 = 19$.

Be prepared for questions that you ask you to compare two different values, like the median and mean of a data set. You might also be asked which measures of central tendency will change if a single data point is changed.

 In general, change to a data point will alter the mean but will not necessarily influence the median, unless it impacts the central (or two central) numbers in an ordered list.

Finding the **weighted average** is necessary when not all quantities occur in equal amounts. For example, if Max bought a pound of peanuts for $3, a pound of almonds for $8, and a pound of roasted cashews for $10, you could easily find the average price per pound of these three different nuts by dividing their sum by 3. But let's take a look at how a question like this might appear on the SAT® Math Test:

Example:

Max is making a nut mix to have on hand for the holidays. She purchases 5 pounds of peanuts at $3 per pound, 2 pounds of almonds at $8 per pound, 3 pounds of dried cranberries at $4 per pound, and 1 pound of roasted cashews at $10 per pound. What will be the cost per pound of her nut mix if she combines all her ingredients together?

Solution:

In this case, since there are different amounts of each ingredient, the average cannot simply be found by dividing the per-pound price of each of the ingredients by 4. Instead, we must calculate the total amount spent on all the nuts and fruit, and divide that by the total number of pounds purchased. For example, 5 pounds of peanuts at $3 per pound cost 5($3) = $15. Finding each of the products shows that Max spent $16 on almonds, $12 on cranberries, and $10 on roasted cashews. In total, she spent $53 on 11 pounds of nuts and fruit, so the average price per pound is $\frac{53}{11} = \$4.82$.

Another context where you may need to find a weighted average is with a frequency **histogram,** on which the data is charted along the x-axis and the frequency of each data point is charted along the y-axis. The following histogram represents the number of cousins all students in a class reported having. Notice that the number of cousins students reported is on the x-axis, and goes from 3 to 9. The y-axis indicates how many students have that number of cousins. For example, the bar on the left side indicates that 2 students reported having 3 cousins.

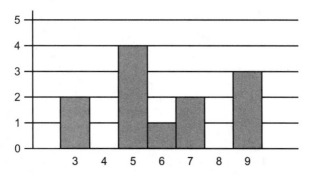

If you were asked to find the mean of this data set, you cannot simply find the average of all the numbers along the x-axis! You would need to determine the *total number of cousins reported* and divide that by the *total number of students*. Looking at the height of all the columns, you can see that the number of students is 2 + 0 + 4 + 1 + 2 + 0 + 3 = 12 students. Multiplying the *frequency of students* by the *number of cousins* in each column, and then adding those products together, will yield the total number of cousins:

$$3(2) + 4(0) + 5(4) + 6(1) + 7(2) + 8(0) + 9(3) = 73 \text{ cousins}$$

The weighted average will be 73 cousins divided by 12 students, which is 6.1 cousins. If this method is not clear to you, first think of the histogram above representing the data set 3, 3, 5, 5, 5, 5, 6, 7, 7, 9, 9, 9. Next, notice how this list of numbers relates to the products in the equation above: $3(2) + 5(4) + 6(1) + 7(2) + 9(3)$.

 When working with a frequency histogram, do not try to find the average by using just the numbers on the x-axis, or by using just the heights of the bars. Instead, you must multiply the data on the x-axis by the frequency represented by its height to find the quantities represented by each bar. Then add those products together and divide them by the total quantity of data, which will be the sum of the heights of the bars.

What if you were asked to find the median in the histogram shown? It is incorrect to simply pick the middle number along the x-axis. Instead, count the heights of the different bars to conclude there are 12 students being represented. The median of a data set consisting of 12 items will be the average of the sixth and seventh entry. You can either make an ordered list of the data points like we did above, or you can count up the columns from left to right. Either way, the sixth and seventh entries are 5 and 6, so the median is 5.5.

Another important measure of a data set is its **standard deviation**. Standard deviation is a type of score that indicates how close all the data points are to the mean. The larger the standard deviation is, the more spread out your data points are. Conversely, a smaller standard deviation indicates that the points are closer to the mean. You will not be tested on calculating the standard deviation, but you should be able to make inferences about how the standard deviations of different data sets compare to one another. To compare the standard deviations of two data sets, estimate the averages of each data set, and then determine which data set has points that sit closer to the mean of that set.

It is likely that you will be asked to answer percentage and probability questions using a **two-way frequency table**. A two-way frequency table is a table that presents data according to two different variables. The probability of an Event A happening is always between 0 and 1 and is calculated with the following formula:

$$\text{Probability of Event A} = \frac{\text{number of ways A can occur}}{\text{total number of possible outcomes}}$$

Let's look at the following example, where a group of high school males and females were asked which math course they enjoyed the most, and their responses were put into the following two-way frequency table:

		Course			
		Algebra I	Geometry	Algebra II	Total
Gender	Female	35	53	62	150
	Male	44	59	57	160
	Total	79	112	119	310

Note that the numbers along the bottom row represent the subtotals for each math subject, the numbers along the right column represent the subtotals for each gender, and the 310 in the bottom right corner represents the total number of students surveyed.

When using a two-way frequency table, you need to select the desired data entry from the correct box, and you must be certain you are comparing it to the correct subtotal. Here are common questions you would see on the exam when faced with this type of table:

- **What percentage of females enjoyed Algebra II the most?** Use 62 as the "part" and the total number of females, 150, as the "whole": $\frac{62}{150} = 41.3\%$.

- **What percentage of students enjoyed Algebra II the most?** Use 119 as the "part" and the total number of students, 310, as the "whole": $\frac{119}{310} = 38.4\%$.

- **What is the probability that a student chosen at random had chosen Geometry as their most-enjoyed math class?** Since this question is not taking gender into consideration, use the 112 subtotal at the bottom of the Geometry column as your "number of ways A can occur" and use 310 as the "total number of possible outcomes": $\frac{112}{310} = 0.36$.

- **What is the probability that if a female student is selected at random, she had chosen Algebra I as her most-enjoyed math class?** Since the student chosen was female, that narrows the "total number of possible outcomes" to 150. Since 35 females chose Algebra I, the correct answer to this question is $\frac{35}{150} = 0.23$.

Collecting and Analyzing Data

One nice thing about the redesigned SAT® exam is that many of the questions will not require you to do math, but instead will ask you to make conclusions about how reliable a pool of data is or what kind of conclusions can be drawn from data. This is a really important skill for you to have in your personal life, since claims are always being made about data, and it's useful to know when those claims are reliable and when they are not. First, let's look at how to randomly collect data:

It is of utmost importance for sample populations to be selected **at random**. This could be through a variety of different methods, but often many flawed methods are presented. For example, if trying to determine what the average GPA is at a school, it wouldn't make sense to sample 50 students studying in the cafeteria before school starts, because it's likely that you'd be speaking only to students who are more academically ambitious. Similarly, it wouldn't be reliable to sample 50 students at a basketball game, because those students might be more interested in sports and make less time for studying.

The best way to pick 50 students would be to go through the student roster and select every tenth name in the roster (depending on the total number of students). Or, you could ask the main office to use a computer to randomly generate names of students. Most important, a random sampling of data needs to be selected in a manner that doesn't create bias.

There might be a study that shows that "people who eat oatmeal for breakfast daily have a largely reduced chance of having a heart attack." While this may be true, this doesn't mean that this statistic alone supports a **cause-and-effect** conclusion. If you think about it, people who eat oatmeal for breakfast (instead of consuming donuts or fried sausages on a daily basis) are maybe doing other healthy things in their lives as well. Someone who takes the time to prepare oatmeal might be more conscientious about all of their other eating or exercise habits. There are likely other factors in that person's life that are decreasing the risk of heart attack, so it is misleading to assume a cause-and-effect relationship exists between oatmeal and decreased heart attacks.

You have to be very careful of questions that ask about cause and effect. There are two specific requirements before cause and effect can be concluded:

1. The data must come from subjects that were selected randomly from the general population.
2. Any treatments given to the selected subjects must be randomly assigned as well.

Margin of error is a recent addition to the exam. It is an indication of how accurate a statistic might be, and it can be used to create a reasonable range for the statistic. If a survey shows that 10% of sports fans wanted the Cleveland Indians to win the 2016 World Series, with a margin of error of ±4 points, it could be concluded that the *actual* percentage of people supporting the Cleveland Indians was as low as 6% (10% − 4%) or as high as 14% (10% + 4%).

Margin of error is often used in conjunction with a 95% **confidence interval**. You will not have to do any math when given the confidence interval (and in fact it's probably best to cross it out and ignore it on your test), but it is important to know what it means. If a newspaper reports that there is a 95% confidence interval that only 10% of sports fans wanted the Cleveland Indians to win the World Series, this means that the newspaper was 95% certain that the actual percentage of people supporting the Cleveland Indians was somewhere between 6% to 14%.

There are two important factors that affect margin of error:

1. The larger the sample size, the smaller the margin of error. Conversely, a small sample size will result in a larger margin of error.

2. The more randomization in the selection of a sample data pool, the smaller the margin of error. Conversely, if the data is not selected randomly, the margin of error will increase.

Use the following information to answer the questions below:

On the morning of election day, November 8, 2016, a survey of 10,000 people randomly selected in Philadelphia, PA, indicated that Hillary Clinton's support was 46.8%, and Donald Trump's support was 44.3%, with a confidence interval of 95% and a margin of error of ± 3.5 percentage points.

1. **According to this survey, what is the range of votes that Hillary Clinton should have received?** Since the margin of error is ± 3.5 percentage points, add 3.5% to 46.8% to find the upper limit of votes she should expect, and subtract 3.5% from 46.8% to find the lower limit: She should have received between 43.3% and 50.3%.

2. **According to this survey, what is the range of votes that Donald Trump should have received?** Since the margin of error is ± 3.5 percentage points, add 3.5% to 44.3% to find the upper limit of votes he should expect, and subtract 3.5% from 43.3% to find the lower limit: He should have received between 40.8% and 47.8%.

3. **A second survey conducted on the same day questioned 800 people in Pennsylvania. What can be expected about its margin of error?** Since 800 is a much smaller sample size than 10,000, the margin of error will be larger than ± 3.5 percentage points.

4. **A second survey conducted on the same day questioned 10,000 people randomly selected in 10 different cities across the country (1,000 per city). What can be expected about the margin of error of this survey?** Since selecting a sample population from 10 different cities is more random than just selecting people in Philadelphia, the margin of error of this survey should be lower than ± 3.5 percentage points.

PROBLEM SOLVING AND DATA ANALYSIS PRACTICE

1 Luke is making lemonade to share with his class. He's picked all the lemons off the tree in his backyard and squeezed $5\frac{1}{2}$ cups of lemon juice. The recipe he found online calls for 8 cups of water, $1\frac{1}{2}$ cups of lemon juice, and $1\frac{3}{4}$ cups of sugar. If Luke wants to use all of the lemon juice he squeezed, how many cups of sugar will he need? (Enter your answer to the nearest half cup in the grid below.)

2 Beam & Anchor sells furniture at a retail price that is 80% higher than the wholesale cost for which they buy the furniture. If they put a wardrobe that costs w wholesale dollars on sale at a 30% discount, which expression illustrates the sale price of the wardrobe?

A. $0.50w$

B. $0.54w$

C. $1.50w$

D. $1.26w$

3 The following two stem-and-leaf plots show the miles biked or driven one way to work by employees selected at random from two separate businesses. What is an accurate statement about how the standard deviations for each data set compare?

Business A

stem	leaf
0	2 2 4 8
1	3 5 6
2	2 5
3	1 7 7
4	6 8 9 9

Business B

stem	leaf
0	9
1	4 4 7 9
2	2 4 6 8 8
3	0 2 2 5
4	0

A. The standard deviation of the data of Business A is larger than the standard deviation of the data of Business B.

B. The standard deviation of the data of Business B is larger than the standard deviation of the data of Business A.

C. Businesses A and B have equal standard deviations.

D. There is not enough information provided to make any comparison about the standard deviations of these data sets.

4 Chucklitis is a rare condition characterized by a person's inability to stop laughing. There is a directory of 102,560 people in the world with chucklitis. In a recent experiment, a group of scientists assigned each person on the list a number, and then used a number generator to select 1,000 participants for their study. The scientists think they have found a natural drug, unfunnigus, that suppresses the symptoms of chucklitis when taken daily. Out of the 1,000 participants chosen for the study, 560 are female and 440 are male. The scientists prescribe unfunnigus to the 560 females and prescribe a placebo sugar pill to the 440 males. At the end of a six-month trial, 100% of the women have experienced a complete suppression of chucklitis symptoms, but only 5% of the men have reported a mild suppression of their symptoms.

Which of the following statements is a reasonable conclusion about the cause-and-effect relationship of unfunnigus on the suppression of chucklitis symptoms?

A. Taking unfunnigus daily for six months will lead to suppression in chucklitis symptoms for anyone with this condition.

B. Taking unfunnigus daily for six months will lead to suppression in chucklitis symptoms for women with this condition.

C. Taking a sugar pill daily for six months will lead to a mild suppression in chucklitis symptoms for 5% of people with this condition.

D. No conclusion can be made about the cause-and-effect relationship of taking six months of unfunnigus.

1. 6.5	2. D	3. A	4. D

1. **The correct answer is 6.5.** First, rule out the additional information that is not needed: the 8 cups of water. This question is asking about the relationship between lemon juice and sugar, so set up your proportion using the information from the recipe, along with the lemon juice:

$$\frac{\text{lemon juice}}{\text{sugar}} = \frac{1\frac{1}{2}}{1\frac{3}{4}} = \frac{5\frac{1}{2}}{s}$$

Don't be intimidated that there are mixed numbers within this proportion—perform cross multiplication as usual to solve for s:

$$1\frac{1}{2}s = \left(1\frac{3}{4}\right)\left(5\frac{1}{2}\right)$$

$$\frac{3}{2}s = \left(\frac{7}{4}\right)\left(\frac{11}{2}\right) = \frac{77}{8}$$

$$s = \frac{77}{8} \cdot \frac{2}{3} = \frac{77}{12} = 6\frac{5}{12}$$

So Luke will need just a touch less than $6\frac{1}{2}$ cups of sugar to make delicious lemonade!

2. **The correct answer is D.** After an 80% increase in the wholesale cost of w, the wardrobe will normally be sold for a retail price of 1.80w. When the wardrobe is marked at 30% off, it is being offered at 70% of the retail price of 1.80w: 0.70(1.80w) = 1.26w. Choice A is incorrect because it is simply the difference between 80% and 30%, but it does not make sense for the sale price to be just 50% of the wholesale cost for which the store buys the wardrobe. Choice B is incorrect because 0.54w represents just 30% of the 1.80w retail price. Instead, after a 30% discount, the sale price will be 70% of the retail price. Choice C is incorrect because this expression was found by just subtracting 30% from the 180% retail price, but percentage discounts are calculated with multiplication, not subtraction.

3. **The correct answer is A.** Notice that both data sets contain 16 entries. Although you could calculate the average of each data set, this is not necessary and would waste valuable time. Based on how the numbers are spread out in the stem-and -leaf plots, you can estimate that the average of both sets will be in the 20s. Looking at Business A, you see that there are four entries less than 10 and four entries greater than 40. Looking at Business B, there are only two entries that are either less than 10 or greater than 40. The shape of the stem-and-leaf plot of Business B shows that the data is more tightly clustered around the estimated mean, so it has a smaller standard deviation. Choice B is incorrect because standard deviation is not a measure of if the data is equally distributed, but rather, if it is clustered around the mean. Choice C is incorrect because the plots clearly show that the standard deviation will be smaller for Business B because the data points are closer together. Choice D is incorrect because there is enough information to make comparisons between the standard deviations.

4. **The correct answer is D.** Since the subjects were not chosen at random (all drug recipients were women), there is no cause-and-effect relationship that can be determined. Choice A is incorrect because the findings do not support a cause-and-effect relationship since the treatment population was just women and was not chosen at random. Choice B is incorrect because the findings do not support a cause-and-effect relationship since the treatment population was just women and there was no control population of women receiving placebo pills. Choice C is incorrect because a cause-and-effect relationship cannot be applied since the sugar pill treatment was given only to men and the treatment popu-lation was not selected at random.

PASSPORT TO ADVANCED MATH

Approximately 28 percent of the questions on the SAT® Math Test will cover skills in the Passport to Advanced Math subsection. These questions will ask you to work with more complex equations and expressions—writing, recognizing, and manipulating them. You will find these questions in both the Calculator and No Calculator sections.

The Passport to Advanced Math questions will assess your ability to perform all operations with polynomials: addition, subtraction, multiplication, and division.

MULTIPLYING POLYNOMIALS

Be careful with negative signs and exponents when performing multiplication with polynomials:

Example:

If $a = (x - 3)$ and $b = (x + 4)$, what is the value of ab^2?

Solution:

First, perform b^2 using FOIL: $(x + 4)^2 = (x + 4)(x + 4) = x^2 + 8x + 16$.

Now multiply that trinomial by $(x - 3)$:

$$(x - 3)(x^2 + 8x + 16) = x^3 + 8x^2 + 16x - 3x^2 - 24x - 48$$

$$ab^2 = x^3 + 5x^2 - 8x - 48$$

 **CAUTION** Do not make the careless error of distributing an exponent outside a sum or difference to the individual terms inside a set of parentheses. Remember that $(x + y)^2 \neq x^2 + y^2$. Instead, $(x + y)^2 = x^2 + 2xy + y^2$ and $(x - y)^2 = x^2 - 2xy + y^2$.

FACTORING BY GROUPING WITH POLYNOMIALS

You may be asked to use grouping to factor a polynomial with four terms:

Example:

If $x^3 - 4x^2 + 5x - 20 = 0$, then what is the only real number solution for x?

Solution:

Since there are four terms in this polynomial, begin by factoring out the greatest common factor (GCF) of the first two terms, as well as for the last two terms. The GCF of the first two terms is x^2 and the GCF of the second two terms is 5, so rewrite the equation as such: $x^2(x - 4) + 5(x - 4) = 0$. Now factor out the $x - 4$ from both terms and rewrite the equation as $(x^2 + 5)(x - 4) = 0$. The expression on the left will equal zero when either $(x^2 + 5) = 0$ or $(x - 4) = 0$. The second equation yields the only real number solution, $x = 4$.

DIFFERENCE OF PERFECT SQUARES

Another important factoring skill to keep in mind is the difference of perfect squares: $x^2 - y^2 = (x - y)(x + y)$. If you are given a difference of two terms and asked to factor it, you will need to use this formula, as in the next example.

Example:

What is an equivalent expression to the binomial $16w^4 - v^8$?

Solution:

Notice that both terms are perfect squares: $\sqrt{16w^4} = 4w^2$ and $\sqrt{v^8} = v^4$. Therefore, $16w^4 - v^8 = (4w^2 + v^4)(4w^2 - v^4)$. Notice that the second term, $(4w^2 - v^4)$, can be written as $(2w - v^2)(2w + v^2)$. Therefore, the complete factorization is $16w^4 - v^8 = (4w^2 + v^4)(2w - v^2)(2w + v^2)$.

DIVIDING POLYNOMIALS

Sometimes you will be required to divide a polynomial by a binomial. This is most easily done with the shortcut called **synthetic division**. (If you do not remember synthetic division and cannot follow the steps in this section, you may want to review it outside of this text.)

Here's an example:

Example:

If the polynomial $2x^4 + 10x^3 + 4x^2 + 14x + 2d$ is divisible by $x + 5$, what is the value of d?

Solution:

Since this polynomial is divisible by $x + 5$, it stands that -5 is a zero, or x-intercept, of the polynomial. This means that when performing synthetic division by -5, the remainder (the final carry-down term) will be zero. Set up and carry out synthetic division as follows:

$$-5 \,|\, \begin{array}{ccccc} 2 & 10 & 4 & 14 & 2d \\ & -10 & 0 & -20 & 30 \\ \hline 2 & 0 & 4 & -6 & 0 \end{array}$$

This must be zero

Once you get to the final carry-down step, you know that $2d + 30$ must equal zero. Therefore, set $2d = -30$ to determine that $d = -15$.

> **CAUTION**
>
> How would you use synthetic division if a polynomial were to be divided by a binomial such as $(2x + 5)$? Would you use -5 or -2 in your synthetic division? No! Instead, set $2x + 5 = 0$, and solve for x to use in your synthetic division. ($x = -2.5$.)

WORKING WITH QUADRATIC EQUATIONS

A quadratic is an equation that can be written in the form $y = ax^2 + bx + c$, such that $a \neq 0$. You will need to be able to match quadratic equations to graphs (and vice-versa), solve for the roots (or x-intercepts) of quadratics, and use quadratic equations to model real-world situations.

Solving Quadratic Equations Through Factoring

Quadratics are easy to solve if there is *only* one squared variable. Simply isolate the squared variable and take the square root of both sides:

$$4k^2 - 10 = 15$$
$$4k^2 = 25$$
$$k^2 = \frac{25}{4}$$
$$k = \sqrt{\frac{25}{4}} = \pm\frac{5}{2}$$

However, most quadratic equations will also have an x term, which will make them much more involved to solve. Most quadratics on the Math Test can be solved by factoring, after all the terms have been moved to one side and the equation has been set equal to zero.

Solving a quadratic that is in the form $ax^2 + bx + c = 0$ can be straightforward when $a = 1$. The two constants in each factor must *multiply* to c and must *add* to b.

For all real numbers b and c, it stands that $1x^2 + bx + c = (x + m)(x + n)$ when $mn = c$ and $m + n = b$.

Once you have the equation in the form $(x + m)(x + n) = 0$, simply set each factor equal to zero to solve for x: $(x + m) = 0$ and $(x + n) = 0$.

Sometimes the trickiest thing about a quadratic question will be recognizing that you can solve it through factoring.

Solving Quadratic Equations Using the Quadratic Formula

If a quadratic equation has a leading coefficient other than 1, it may not be easy to factor. In fact, some quadratic equations cannot be factored at all. In cases like this, solve a quadratic using the quadratic formula. The quadratic formula gives the x solutions to a quadratic equation that has been set equal to zero:

$$\text{If } ax^2 + bx + c = 0, \text{ then } x = \frac{-b \pm \sqrt{b^2 - 4ac}}{2a}$$

You can try factoring the following equation, but it might be faster to solve using the quadratic formula:

Example:

What is the sum of all the values that satisfy the equation $12x^2 - 24 = 23x$?

Solution:

First, recognize that this equation needs to be rearranged so all the terms are on one side and set equal to zero: $12x^2 - 23x - 24 = 0$. Now it is easy to see that $a = 12$, $b = -23$, and $c = -24$. We are not going to walk through all of the steps of evaluating these numbers in the quadratic formula, but the two solutions you should get when working this out on your own are $x = -\frac{3}{4}$ and $\frac{8}{3}$. These two solutions sum to $\frac{23}{12}$.

Quadratic Equations in the Coordinate Plane

When a quadratic equation $y = ax^2 + bx + c$ is graphed in the coordinate plane, it forms a parabola. You will see quadratic equations in two different forms on the Math Test. First, we will discuss standard form.

The **standard form** of a parabola is $y = ax^2 + bx + c$. Here are a few key facts to know about how the different parts of this form relate to a parabola's appearance in the coordinate plane:

- When the leading coefficient, a, is **positive**, the parabola will be an **upward curve** and will have a turning point, or **vertex**, that is a **minimum**.
- When the leading coefficient, a, is **negative**, the parabola will be a **downward curve** and will have a turning point, or **vertex**, that is a **maximum**.
- The larger the leading coefficient a, the steeper the walls of the parabola get and the narrower the shape. Conversely, if a is a non-zero fraction between 1 and −1, then the walls of the parabola will be less steep and the parabola will be wider.
- The constant, c, is always the **y-intercept**.
- The **x-intercepts** will occur at the values of x that make the quadratic equation equal to zero (when $ax^2 + bx + c = 0$).

Working With the Line of Symmetry

Aside from being familiar with these connections between a quadratic's equation and its graph, it's critical for you to know how to find the vertex of the parabola, which is the turning point that marks its minimum or maximum. The vertex always sits on the **line of symmetry**, which splits the parabola perfectly in half. To find the line of symmetry, use this equation:

$$\text{Line of Symmetry: } x = \frac{-b}{2a}$$

Since the line of symmetry goes *through* the vertex, you can find the vertex by plugging that x value back into the quadratic equation to solve for the y-coordinate of the vertex. For example, if the line of symmetry works out to $x = 5$, then plug $x = 5$ into the quadratic equation and solve for the y-coordinate of the vertex.

Sometimes you will be asked to work backward. If you are given the factors of a quadratic, you can easily determine the x-intercepts and the direction of parabola just by looking at the factors. The line of symmetry will always be halfway between the two x-intercepts. You can also easily find the y-intercept by multiplying the two constants together.

For example, given the factors $(x + 4)$ and $(x − 2)$, it should be clear to you that this is an upward parabola with x-intercepts at −4 and +2. Multiplying the two constants together makes it evident that the y-intercept is at −8. The axis of symmetry that divides the parabola symmetrically down the middle is halfway between the x-intercepts, so it will be at $x = −1$. Put all of this information together, and you should be able to sketch a parabola that looks like this:

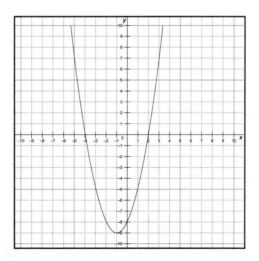

 Be sure that when you are given the factors of a parabola $(x + m)(x + n)$, you don't mistakenly conclude that the x-intercepts are m and n. Remember, they will be $-m$ and $-n$. This is an easy point to forget when working quickly!

Understanding Vertex Form

The vertex form of the equation of any parabola is $y = a(x - h)^2 + k$. The vertex is at (h, k). The leading coefficient a still has the same impact on the shape of the parabola in terms of it being upward, downward, steep, or narrow. It's also important to know that you may be presented with equations in this equivalent vertex form: $y - k = a(x - h)^2$.

Modeling with Quadratic Equations

Quadratic equations are commonly used to model the trajectory of an object that is thrown up in the air. The graph of this trajectory will be a downward-facing parabola with a vertex as a maximum. In this case, the vertex represents the greatest height of the object. The vertex also represents the moment at which the object is no longer going up and is not yet coming down—it is stopped for the briefest moment. The value at which the parabola crosses the positive x-axis represents the time at which the object hits the ground.

Be prepared to apply all this information to a type of question like this:

> Leaf stands at the top of a building and fires an arrow up into the sky at a speed of 10 meters per second. Use the graph shown that models its trajectory to answer the following questions.

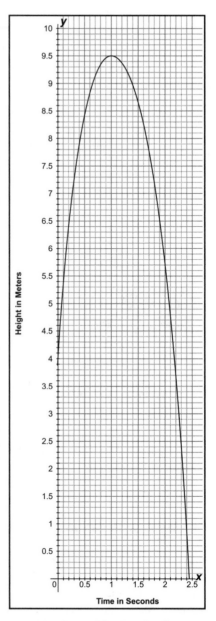

- **From what height did Leaf fire the arrow?** The y-intercept shows that when time was equal to 0, the height of the arrow was 5 meters, so Leaf fired the arrow from 5 meters off the ground.

- **After how many seconds will the arrow hit the ground?** The x-intercept shows that when height was equal to 0, the time in seconds was a little under 2.5 seconds, indicating the arrow hit the ground around 2.4 seconds.

- **What was the maximum height of the arrow and after how many seconds did it reach this maximum height?** The maximum point of this curve occurs around (1, 9.5), so at approximately 1 second, the arrow reached its maximum of 9.5 meters.

Sometimes you will have to *create* a quadratic model from the context of a word problem. In order to do this, you need to carefully dissect the parts of the question to determine how they can be used together in an algebraic relationship, as in the next example.

Example:

Ani has started a successful business designing cashmere fingerless gloves and sells them at the local Sunday market every weekend. She priced them low at first and has been increasing the price as the demand for them has been increasing. The relationship between the price she charges for the gloves, p, and the number of pairs she sells, g, is represented by the equation $p = -5g + 90$. To make the gloves each week, Ani pays \$5 per pair plus a \$20 flat fee for the label maker she rents for a few hours. If her profit is equal to her sales earnings minus her costs, which equation below could be used to find the maximum profit, $M(g)$, for g gloves sold?

Solution:

This question has a lot going on! First, use words to build an equation that can be used to find the profit:

$$\text{Profit} = \text{Revenue} - \text{Cost to make gloves}$$

Figure out how to represent revenue algebraically: sales revenue will be the product of (the price of each pair of gloves) times (the number of gloves she sells), so add that into the equation:

$$\text{Profit} = (\text{Price per pair of gloves})(\text{\# of gloves}) - \text{Cost to make gloves}$$

The cost to make g gloves is \$5 per pair plus a \$20 flat fee, so that is $5g + 20$. The price per pair of gloves is equal to p, which is equivalent to $(-5g + 90)$, and the number of gloves is g. Put all these parts into the formula:

$$\text{Profit} = (-5g + 90)(g) - (5g + 20)$$
$$\text{Profit} = -5g^2 + 90g - 5g - 20$$
$$\text{Profit} = -5g^2 + 85g - 20$$

EXPONENTIAL GROWTH AND DECAY

In the Problem Solving and Data Analysis section, we reviewed the general form for an exponential function, which is $y = a(r^x)$. Here, r is the common ratio and a is the starting point when $x = 0$ (the y-intercept). Exponential growth and decay are models that are used to fit real-world situations that have a percentage of growth or decay. Exponential growth models growing populations, while exponential decay is used to find the age of artifacts through carbon dating. Here are the formulas:

- **Exponential Growth:** $y = a(1 + r)^x$, where r is the percentage increase, a is the starting point, and x is the units of time.

- **Exponential Decay:** $y = a(1 - r)^x$, where r is the percentage decrease, a is the starting point, and x is the units of time.

SIMPLIFYING RATIONAL EXPRESSIONS AND SOLVING RATIONAL EQUATIONS

A rational expression is a fraction with an algebraic expression in the numerator, denominator, or both. In order to simplify rational expressions, you will need to use your factoring skills. You may need to factor a quadratic into two binomials or factor a greatest common factor out of two terms. Once your numerator and denominator have been fully factored, it is likely that some of the factors in the numerator and denominator will cancel each other out.

See how this works:

Example:

For all values of x in the domain of the function, $f(x) = \dfrac{8x^2 + 16x}{x^2 - 3x - 10}$, find an equivalent function.

Solution:

Factor the numerator and denominator, and the $(x + 2)$ factors cancel out:

$$\frac{8x^2 + 16x}{x^2 - 3x - 10} = \frac{8x(x+2)}{(x+2)(x-5)}$$
$$= \frac{8x}{(x-5)}$$

 **CAUTION** When simplifying rational expressions, remember that you may not cancel out individual *terms*. You can only cancel out *factors*. For example, in $\dfrac{8x+5}{24x+5}$, you may not reduce the coefficients 8 and 24. Similarly, you cannot cancel out the 5 constants that are the in the numerator and denominator. $\dfrac{8x+5}{24x+5} \neq \dfrac{8x}{24x}$

Sometimes you will see rational expressions in an equation that must be solved. In this case, first factor all of the polynomials in each expression. Then, identify the lowest common factor (LCF) and multiply every term in the equation by the LCF. This will cancel out the fractions and leave you with a linear or quadratic equation to solve.

Watch how this is done in the following sample question:

Example:

What values of x make the following equation true?

$$\frac{6}{x-2} + \frac{x}{x+2} = \frac{4x+37}{x^2-4}$$

Solution:

Multiply each term by the LCD $(x - 2)(x + 2)$:

$$\frac{(x-2)(x+2)}{1} \cdot \frac{6}{x-2} + \frac{(x-2)(x+2)}{1} \cdot \frac{x}{x+2} = \frac{(x-2)(x+2)}{1} \cdot \frac{(4x+37)}{(x-2)(x+2)}$$

Now all the denominators will cancel out:

$$(x+2)(6)+(x-2)(x)=4x+37$$
$$6x+12+x^2-2x=4x+37$$
$$x^2=25$$
$$x=\pm5$$

Systems of Non-Linear Equations

Earlier we reviewed solving systems of linear equations by substitution or elimination. A system of nonlinear equations includes at least one equation that is not linear and can be solved sometimes with elimination and often by substitution. (On a graph, the points at which the two equations intersect mark the solutions.) Remember that a question might ask you to perform an operation (such as addition or multiplication) on your answer.

Example:

Suppose that (x, y) satisfies the equations $x^2 + y^2 = 20$ and $y - 2 = -1(x + 4)$. If $y < 0$, what is the value of $x + y$?

Solution:

Notice that using elimination would be incredibly messy here since both x and y are squared in the first equation, but neither are squared in the second equation. The best approach is to use substitution. Isolate y in the linear equation to get $y = -x - 2$. Now sub $-x - 2$ in for y and solve the equation:

$$x^2+y^2=20$$
$$x^2+(-x-2)^2=20$$
$$x^2+x^2+4x+4=20$$
$$2x^2+4x-16=0$$
$$2(x^2+2x-8)=0$$
$$2(x+4)(x-2)=0$$
$$x=-4, x=2$$

When subbed back into either equation, we get the two coordinate pair answers $(-4, 2)$ and $(2, -4)$. Since the question stated that $y < 0$, we must use the point $(2, -4)$ to determine that $x + y = -2$.

COMPOUND FUNCTIONS

Function notation uses $f(x)$ (read "f of x") to indicate "the value of y at x." Therefore, if you are given a function $f(x) = x + 2$, the notation $f(6)$ means "the value of y when $x = 6$." In this case, $f(x) = 8$. Sometimes you will be given two different functions and asked to make a compound function, which is when one function is substituted into the other. You might be asked to find the algebraic expression of a compound function, or the value of a compound function for a particular value of x, as in this example:

Example:

If $f(x) = 8 - x$ and $g(x) = x^2 + 2x + 10$, which is an equivalent expression to $g(f(p + 3))$?

Solution:

This question is first asking for the expression $p + 3$ to be put into the $f(x)$ function. This will create $f(p + 3) = 8 - (p + 3)$, so $f(p + 3) = 5 - p$. Next input the expression for $f(p + 3)$ into all of the x terms in the $g(x)$ function:

$$g(x) = x^2 + 2x + 10 \text{ and } f(p + 3) = 5 - p$$

$$g(f(p + 3)) = (5 - p)^2 + 2(5 - p) + 10$$

Now expand and simplify like terms:

$$g(f(p + 3)) = 25 - 10p + p^2 + 10 - 2p + 10$$

$$g(f(p + 3)) = p^2 - 12p + 45$$

KEY FEATURES OF FUNCTIONS AND GRAPHS

It will be important for you to be able to identify key features of functions from both their algebraic representations as well as their graphical representations. We have already discussed some of these important features such as the direction and steepness of slope, x- and y-intercepts, and maximums and minimums. The next important features critical for you to know are domain and range.

Domain

The **domain** is the set of all x-values for which a function $f(x)$ is defined. Look for these two cases when finding the domain from an equation:
1. Any x-value for which the denominator of a function would equal zero will not be in the domain.
2. In functions with radicals, all x-values for which the radicand would equal a negative number are not in the domain. (Note that this is true only for even roots: square root, 4th root, 6th root, etc.)

All other x-values will be in the domain. Here are a few examples:

- $f(x)=\dfrac{x}{3}+7$: The domain is all real numbers since there is no value for x for which this $f(x)$ is undefined.

- $g(x)=\dfrac{3}{x+5}$: The domain is all real numbers other than –5, since when $x=-5$, the denominator would be equal to zero.

- $h(x)=\sqrt{18-6x}$: Since this has a radical, set the radicand to be non-negative and solve for x: $18 - 6x \geq 0$, so $x \leq 3$ is the domain of $h(x)$.

When looking at a graph, the domain can be identified as all of the x-values that are defined on the graph. Look for open dots on the graph, which represent points for which x is not in the domain. Also look for asymptotes, which will be discussed shortly.

Range

The **range** is the set of all y-values that are produced from the x-values in the domain. The range can be found by looking at the set of y-coordinates that are defined on the graph.

Vertical Asymptotes

Asymptotes are invisible vertical lines that a function will approach but never reach. Instead, the function will extend to either positive or negative infinity as the x-values get closer and closer to the x-value of the asymptote. There will be a vertical asymptote with the equation $x = k$ for any number k that causes the denominator to equal zero. For example, for the function $g(x)=\dfrac{3}{x+5}$, the vertical line $x = -5$ will be an asymptote.

Transformations

A transformation is a vertical or horizontal shift of the graph of a function:

1. **Vertical shifts** occur when a constant is added or subtracted to the entire function. $f(x) + k$ will shift the graph of $f(x)$ up k units if $k > 0$ and will shift a graph down if $k < 0$. For example, given an original function $g(x)=\dfrac{3}{x+5}$, we could determine that $g(x)+k=\dfrac{3}{x+5}+k$ will shift the graph vertically by k.

2. **Horizontal shifts** occur when a constant is added or subtracted into the fiber of a function. Notice that the direction of the shift is a little counter-intuitive: $f(x + k)$ will shift the graph of $f(x)$ *left* k units if $k > 0$ and will shift a graph *right* if $k < 0$. For example, given an original function $h(x)=\sqrt{18-6x}$, we could determine that $h(x+k)=\sqrt{18-6(x+k)}$ will shift the graph to the left by k units when $k > 0$ and to the right by k units when $k < 0$.

To see how asymptotes undergo transformations and recognize how transformations affect domains and ranges, let's look at these three graphs:

Observe the graph $f(x)=\dfrac{1}{|x|}$. You should be able to see that the domain is all real numbers except for 0, and the range is $y > 0$:

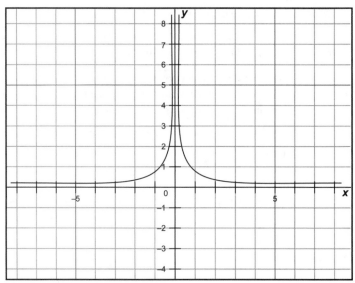

Next, observe the vertical transformation of the graph of $f(x)=\dfrac{1}{|x|}$ when we subtract 2: $f(x) - 2 = \dfrac{1}{|x|} - 2$. We can see that the domain is still all real numbers except for 0, but the range has shifted to $y > -2$:

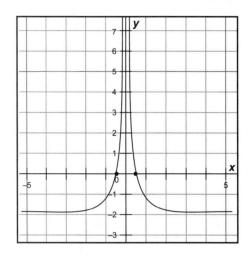

Now, let's add a horizontal transformation to the above graph by adding 3 within the absolute value brackets: $f(x + 3) - 2 = \dfrac{1}{|x+3|} - 2.$ Now the domain will shift to be all real numbers except for –3, and the range is still $y > -2$:

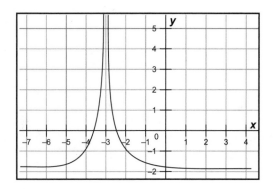

Passport to Advanced Math Practice

1 When the third-degree polynomial $3p^3 + 13p^2 - 22p + 50$ is divided by $(p + 6)$, the result is

$3p^2 - 5p + 8 + \dfrac{Q}{(p+6)}$, where Q is a real number. Determine the value of Q. (Enter your answer in the grid below.)

SHOW YOUR WORK HERE

2 What is the sum of the solutions to the equation $\sqrt{-5x-6} = x+4$?

A. −2

B. 13

C. −13

D. 22

 When working with quadratics, read the question carefully to see what is asked of you. Quite often you will be asked for the larger or smaller solution, or for the sum or product of the solutions. The SAT® Math Test cleverly does this in order to keep students from simply working backward by plugging the given answer choices into the equation.

3 Which is the graph of the equation $y = (x + 3)^2 + 4$?

A.

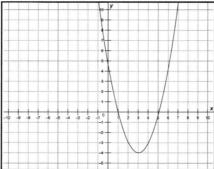

B.

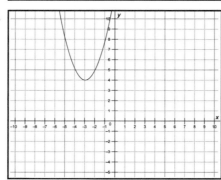

C.

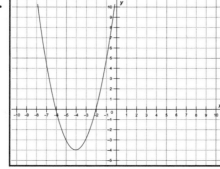

D.

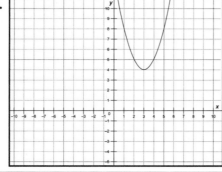

4 The gross domestic product (GDP) of the United States was approximately $12.96 trillion at the start of 2003. By the start of 2004, the GDP had grown to $13.53 trillion. An economist is creating a formula to model what the GDP would have been each year after 2004 if it had continued to grow at the same percentage rate. Which model accurately represents the GDP in trillions of dollars, $f(t)$, where t is the number of years after 2003?

A. $f(t) = 12.96(0.956)^t$

B. $f(t) = 12.96(1.044)^t$

C. $f(t) = 12.96 + (0.956t)^t$

D. $f(t) = 12.96 + 1.044t$

Answer Key and Explanations

1. 2	**2.** A	**3.** B	**4.** B

1. **The correct answer is 2.** This question might look impossible to solve at first, but this is easily conquered with synthetic division:

$$
\begin{array}{r|rrrr}
-6 & 3 & 13 & -22 & 50 \\
   &   & -18 & 30 & -48 \\
\hline
   & 3 & -5 & 8 & \boxed{2}
\end{array}
$$

This shows that when $3p^3 + 13p^2 - 22p + 50$ is divided by $(p + 6)$, the result will have the carry-down numbers 3, –5, and +8 as coefficients to variables p—each to one less power than the original dividend plus the remainder of 2 over the divisor, $(p + 6)$:

$$(3p^3 + 13p^2 - 22p + 50) \div (p+6) =$$
$$3p^2 - 5p - 8 + \frac{2}{(p+6)}$$

Therefore, the value of Q is 2.

2. **The correct answer is A.** The equation must be squared on both sides to get rid of the radical:

$$\left(\sqrt{-5x-6}\,\right)^2 = (x+4)^2$$
$$-5x - 6 = x^2 + 8x + 16$$

Then move all the terms to one side, factor, and solve for x:

$$0 = x^2 + 13x + 22$$
$$0 = (x+11)(x+2)$$
$$x = -2, -11$$

Both answers must be plugged back into the original equation to see if either or both are extraneous. Only –2 works; –11 does not, so the sum of the solutions is –2. Choice B is incorrect because this is the opposite of the sum of –2 and –11, but –11 was an extraneous solution to begin with. Choice C is incorrect because this is the sum of –2 and –11, but –11 is an extraneous solution. Choice D is incorrect because this is the product of –2 and –11, but –11 is an extraneous solution.

3. **The correct answer is B.** The vertex form of the equation of any parabola is $y = a(x - h)^2 + k$. The vertex is at (h, k). Given the equation $y = (x + 3)^2 + 4$, the vertex is at $(-3, 4)$ and it opens upward. Only the graph shown in choice B has a vertex at this point. Choice A is incorrect because the vertex of the given equation is at $(-3, 4)$, however the vertex in this graph is at $(3, -4)$. Choice C is incorrect because the vertex in this graph is at $(-4, -4)$. Choice D is incorrect because the vertex in this graph is at $(3, 4)$.

4. **The correct answer is B.** Since the GDP is expected to grow at the same percentage rate each year, it must be represented by an exponential growth equation, $y = a(1 + r)^x$. We know that a will be 12.96 since that is the starting point. Find the percentage of change as follows: $(13.53 - 12.96) \div 12.96 = 0.044$. So $r = 0.044$ and the correct equation is $f(t) = 12.96(1.044)^t$. Choice A is incorrect because this would be the model of exponential decay, since the percentage of change, 4.4%, was *subtracted* from 1 instead of added. Choice C cannot be correct because it is set up as an exponential decay instead of exponential growth. Choice D is incorrect because this is a linear model and not an exponential model.

Remember that there are two different ways that a parabola can be expressed in vertex form: $y = a(x - h)^2 + k$ and $y - k = a(x - h)^2$. It is important that you are careful with the positive and negative signs when determining (h, k)!

ADDITIONAL TOPICS IN MATH

Approximately 10 percent of the questions on the SAT® Math Test will cover skills in the Additional Topics in Math subsection. You will find these questions, which span skills including geometry, trigonometry, and complex numbers, in both the Calculator and Non-Calculator sections.

Volume & Surface Area

On the Math Test, you will be asked to solve real-world problems concerning volume and surface area for three-dimensional shapes. These questions will demand more critical thinking and less formulaic number crunching. You'll have some help, though: you will be provided a formula sheet with the basic volume formulas, and for questions that have more complex shapes, the formula will be given within the context of the question. Nonetheless, it is still valuable for you to be familiar with all the formulas below so that you are not working to figure them out on test day. You should understand what each variable stands for and how to identify it from an illustration.

Surface area of a cube: $SA = 6s^2$, where s is side length.

Surface area of a rectangular prism: $SA = 2lw + 2lh + 2wh$, with length l, width w, and height h.

Surface area of a cylinder: $SA = 2\pi rh + 2\pi r^2$, with radius r and height h.

Volume of a cube: $V = s^3$, where s is side length.

Volume of a rectangular box: $V = l \times w \times h$, with length l, width w, and height h.

Volume of a cylinder: $V = \pi r^2 h$, with radius r and height h.

Often you will be asked to work backward—using one unit of measurement like volume or surface area to find the dimensions of an object, only to use those dimensions in another formula. Also, be prepared to define different variables in terms of each other to solve for missing dimensions.

You will be challenged to do both these tasks in the next example.

Example:

At a pharmaceutical production plant, a cylindrical steel mixing tank is 4 times as wide as it is tall. When the tank is $\frac{3}{4}$ full, its volume is $6{,}591\pi$. If the circumference of the tank is $k\pi$, what is the value of k?

Solution:

The volume formula for cylinders is $V = \pi r^2 h$. First, you need to define the radius and height in terms of each other. If the height of this tank is h units, then the diameter will be $4h$. Cutting the diameter in half results in the expression $2h$ for the radius.

Next, put this information into the formula for $\dfrac{3}{4}$ of the volume. Since the volume at $\dfrac{3}{4}$ full is $6,591\pi$, we can write $6,591\pi = \dfrac{3}{4}(\pi r^2 h)$. Next plug in h for height and $2h$ for radius and solve the equation:

$$6,591\pi = \frac{3}{4}(\pi(2h)^2 h)$$

$$6,591 = \frac{3}{4}(4h^2 h)$$

$$6,591 = 3h^3$$

$$2,197 = h^3$$

$$h = 13$$

This means that the radius is 26. Since the formula for circumference is $C = \pi d$, the circumference of the tank is 52π, and $k = 52$.

THE PYTHAGOREAN THEOREM

The Pythagorean theorem can be used in right triangles to solve for missing side lengths. The two shorter sides of right triangles that form the right angle are the **legs** of the triangle, and the **hypotenuse** is always the longest side that sits opposite the right angle. The Pythagorean theorem states that the sum of the squares of the legs is equal to the square of the hypotenuse:

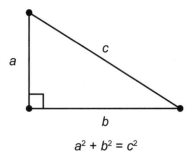

$$a^2 + b^2 = c^2$$

Most likely, you will not encounter a straightforward equation that simply applies the Pythagorean theorem to a right triangle, but you might find triangles embedded in composite shapes where you should use the Pythagorean theorem to solve for a missing piece of information required to solve the problem.

CAUTION When using the Pythagorean theorem, don't assume you will always be solving for the hypotenuse, which is the isolated c^2. And remember to always take the square root of both sides of the equation as your final step.

Right Triangle Trigonometry

The Pythagorean theorem is used to find a single missing side length in a right triangle when two sides are known, but it cannot be used to reveal any information about angle measures within the triangle. Right triangle trigonometry can use the side lengths of a right triangle to solve for the measures of the missing angle. It can also be used to solve for missing sides when only the measure of one angle and one side is given.

Observe how the following side ratios summed up by the mnemonic SOH-CAH-TOA, relate to the angle θ and the side lengths a, b, and c in the figure:

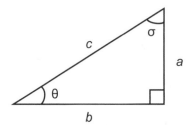

- SOH represents $\sin\theta = \dfrac{\text{opposite}}{\text{hypotenuse}}$, so $\sin\theta = \dfrac{a}{c}$

- CAH represents $\cos\theta = \dfrac{\text{adjacent}}{\text{hypotenuse}}$, so $\cos\theta = \dfrac{b}{c}$

- TOA represents $\tan\theta = \dfrac{\text{opposite}}{\text{adjacent}}$, so $\tan\theta = \dfrac{a}{b}$

Now let's take a look at the side ratios for angle σ:

- $\sin\sigma = \dfrac{\text{opposite}}{\text{hypotenuse}}$, so $\sin\sigma = \dfrac{b}{c}$

- $\cos\sigma = \dfrac{\text{adjacent}}{\text{hypotenuse}}$, so $\cos\sigma = \dfrac{a}{c}$

- $\tan\sigma = \dfrac{\text{opposite}}{\text{adjacent}}$, so $\tan\sigma = \dfrac{b}{a}$

Now let's focus on the fact that $\sin\theta = \dfrac{a}{c}$, and $\cos\sigma = \dfrac{a}{c}$, since this illustrates that $\sin\theta = \cos\sigma$.

It is true in all right triangles that the sine of one of the acute angles will be equal to the cosine of the other acute angle. Because the two acute angles in a right triangle are supplementary, this brings us to the identity that $\cos\theta=\sin(90-\theta)$, and it also stands that $\sin\theta=\cos(90-\theta)$.

 **CAUTION** The following trig identities may be critical for solving some of the questions you see on test day: $\sin\theta=\cos(90-\theta)$ and $\cos\theta=\sin(90-\theta)$.

When at least two side lengths of a right triangle are given, inverse trig functions can be used to solve for the acute angles of the triangle. This is indicated either by putting the word *arc* in front of the sin, cos, or tan, or by using an exponent of –1 with the trig function. When you use the inverse trig function keys on your calculator with the associated side ratio, your answer will be the measure of the related angle.

The following **inverse trig ratios** can be used to solve for an acute angle θ in a right triangle:

$$\theta=\sin^{-1}\left(\frac{\text{opposite}}{\text{hypotenuse}}\right)$$

$$\theta=\cos^{-1}\left(\frac{\text{adjacent}}{\text{hypotenuse}}\right)$$

$$\theta=\tan^{-1}\left(\frac{\text{opposite}}{\text{adjacent}}\right)$$

Radian Measure

In addition to being measured in degrees, angles are also measured in radians, which use π to represent 180°. In order to convert an angle from radian measure into degrees, just replace π with 180° in the expression and evaluate it. If given an angle that is $\frac{7\pi}{3}$ in radian measure, it can be converted into degree measure as follows: $\frac{7\pi}{3}=\frac{7\times180}{3}=420°$. You might more commonly need to convert an angle from degrees to radian measure. In order do this conversion, multiply the angle by $\frac{\pi}{180}$, reduce the product to its lowest terms, and do not replace π with 180. Using this method, 240° can be converted into radians as follows:

$$240°\times\frac{\pi}{180}=\frac{240\pi}{180}=\frac{4\pi}{3}$$

Angles in the Coordinate Plane

An angle in standard position in the coordinate plane has its vertex at the origin $(0, 0)$, its initial side on the positive x-axis, and its terminal side in Quadrant I, II, III, or IV. Any point in the coordinate plane can be used to make an angle in standard position by connecting the point with a line segment to the origin. Notice how we do this with the point $(-\sqrt{3}, 1)$:

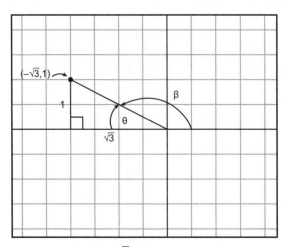

As you can see, the coordinate pair $(-\sqrt{3}, 1)$ was also used to make a right triangle using a portion of the x-axis as one of the legs. Now it is possible to use an inverse trig function to determine the measure of $\angle\theta$:

$$\theta = \tan^{-1}\left(\frac{1}{\sqrt{3}}\right)$$

$$\theta = 30°$$

Since $\angle\theta + \angle\beta$ make a straight angle, which measures 180°, it is now easy to determine that $m\angle\beta = 150°$.

Coterminal Angles

Now that you are comfortable with angles in standard position in the coordinate plane, let's discuss **coterminal angles**. Coterminal angles are two angles in standard position that share the same terminal side. Remember that an angle that opens counterclockwise from the x-axis is measured in positive degrees, whereas an angle that opens clockwise from the x-axis is measured in negative degrees. Notice how the angles 120° and –240° in the following figure share the same terminal side:

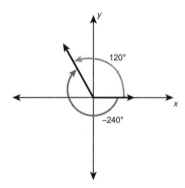

Coterminal angles can be calculated by adding or subtracting 360° or 2π to an angle (depending on if the original angle is in degrees or radians). Use $m\angle\theta\pm(360°)(n)$ or $m\angle\theta\pm(2\pi)(n)$ for any integer n to determine the terminal angles to $\angle\theta$. Therefore, we can see that another coterminal angle to 120° would be 120° + 360° = 480°.

Angles that are coterminal will have the same values for the sine and cosine functions. For example, sin(120) = sin(–240) = sin(480).

Let's work through the following exercise.

Example:

If $\cos\left(\dfrac{5\pi}{3}\right) = \cos\theta$, find the two smallest positive and the two smallest negative values for θ in radian measure.

Solution:

First, use $m\angle\theta\pm(2\pi)(1)$: $\dfrac{5\pi}{3}\pm 2\pi = \dfrac{5\pi}{3}\pm\dfrac{6\pi}{3} = \dfrac{11\pi}{3}$ and $-\dfrac{1\pi}{3}$

Next, use $m\angle\theta\pm(2\pi)(2)$: $\dfrac{5\pi}{3}\pm 4\pi = \dfrac{5\pi}{3}\pm\dfrac{12\pi}{3} = \dfrac{17\pi}{3}$ and $-\dfrac{7\pi}{3}$

CIRCLES, CHORDS, ARCS, AND SECTORS

In this section we'll discuss chords and angles within circles, as well as the lengths of arcs and sectors they create.

Inscribed and Central Angles

A **chord** is a line segment whose endpoints sit on the circumference of the circle. The longest possible chord in a circle is the diameter, which passes through the center of the circle. When two chords intersect, they form the vertex of an **inscribed angle**. The shortest distance along the circumference of the circle between the two endpoints of an angle within the circles is called the **intercepted arc**, and an inscribed angle has a measure that is half its intercepted arc. (Similarly, if given the arc length, the inscribed angle will be half of the arc length.)

The following illustration shows the relationship between an inscribed angle and the arc it creates. Specifically, $\angle ABC = 45°$ and $\overset{\frown}{AC} = 90°$.

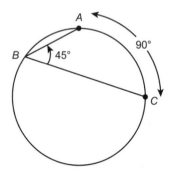

 An **inscribed angle** is made by two chords that intercept to form a vertex on the circumference of the circle. The measure of an inscribed angle is half of its intercepted arc.

When two radii intersect to create a vertex at the center of the circle, they form a **central angle**. A central angle has the same measure as the arc it intercepts. The following illustration shows a 70° central angle forming a 70° intercepted arc:

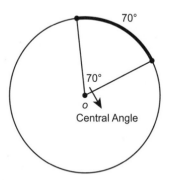

 A **central angle** is made by two radii that meet at the center of the circle. The measure of a central angle is equal to its intercepted arc.

Let's put our knowledge to work with the next sample question.

Example:

In circle D, chords AX, BX, and CX exist such that BX goes through the center, and $m\angle AXB = \frac{3}{2}m\angle BXC$. If $m\angle BXC = \frac{2\pi}{9}$, what is the measure of $\overset{\frown}{AX}$?

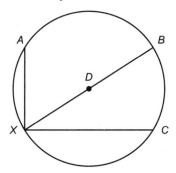

Solution:

First, solve for $m\angle AXB$ using the givens that $m\angle AXB = \frac{3}{2}m\angle BXC$ and $m\angle BXC = \frac{2\pi}{9}$: $m\angle AXB = \frac{3}{2}\left(\frac{2\pi}{9}\right) = \frac{\pi}{3} = 60°$. Convert the radian measure of $\frac{2\pi}{9}$ to 40°. Now label the measures of $\angle AXB$ and $\angle BXC$ as well as the lengths of their associated arcs:

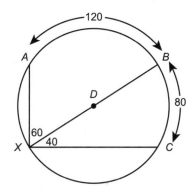

Notice that since chord XB passes through the center of the circle, its two arcs are both semicircles with measures of 180°. Since $\overset{\frown}{AB}$ is 120°, this determines that $\overset{\frown}{AX}$ must equal 60°.

Intersecting Chords in a Circle

When two chords intersect within a circle, the products of their segments will be equal. In the following circle, chords *BC* and *AD* intersect at point *P*, creating line segments *a*, *b*, *c*, and *d*. It stands that $a \times d = b \times c$:

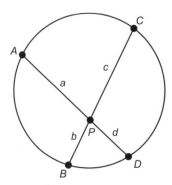

Be prepared to apply this information to an algebraic model, as illustrated in the next example.

Example:

In the circle in the illustration that follows, chords *AB* and *CD* intersect at point *P* such that $AP = x + 7$, $BP = x$, $CP = x + 2$, and $DP = x + 3$. Find the length of chord *AB*.

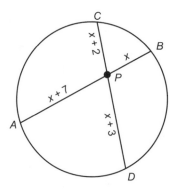

Since the products of the line segments of each chord are equal, write an equation and solve for x:

$$(x + 7)(x) = (x + 2)(x + 3)$$
$$x^2 + 7x = x^2 + 5x + 6$$
$$2x = 6$$
$$x = 3$$

Chord $AB = 2x + 7$, so since $x = 3$, $AB = 13$.

Unit Measurement of Arcs

In the earlier section on finding arc lengths, we measured the arc lengths in degrees. Arcs can also be measured in unit lengths like inches or centimeters when given a central angle and the length of the radius. Given a central angle θ, we can determine the ratio $\dfrac{\theta}{360}$ (or $\dfrac{\theta}{2\pi}$ if working in radians) would represent the portion of the circumference that the angle intercepts. For example, a 90° angle would intercept an arc that is $\dfrac{90}{360}$, or $\dfrac{1}{4}$ of the circle. Observe this in the following image:

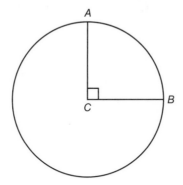

It follows that if the circumference of $C = 100$ inches, then arc AB would be one-quarter of that, which is 25 inches. Since the formula for the circumference is $C = 2\pi r$, we can generalize this process to the following relationship.

In a circle with radius r, the length of an arc formed by a central angle θ is $2\pi r \times \dfrac{\theta}{360}$.

Area of a Sector

The same exact line of reasoning applies to finding the area of a partial sector of a circle. Since the formula for the area of a circle is $A = \pi r^2$, the formula for the area of a sector is as follows:

> In a circle with radius r, the area of a sector formed by a central angle θ is $\pi r^2 \times \dfrac{\theta}{360}$.

Use the techniques for arc length and sector area to solve the following two-part practice question.

Example:

In a the circular garden illustrated below, Pauli is fencing off a part of it to plant native flowers. She will do this in the shaded region, labeled A. If $r = 12$ feet and $\theta = 120°$, determine the total length of fence she will need to enclose her native flower region. Also determine the square footage of her plot. Round these answers to the nearest tenth.

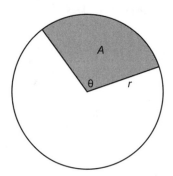

Solution:

First, find the length of fence needed along the circular edge of her plot:

$$\text{Arc Length: } 2\pi(12) \times \frac{120}{360} = 24\pi \times \frac{1}{3} = 8\pi = 25.1 \text{ feet}$$

Now this must be added to the two 12-foot sections she will need for each straight edge of her garden, so the total is 49.1 feet.

Next, find the area of her plot:

$$\text{Sector Area: } \pi(12)^2 \times \frac{120}{360} = 144\pi \times \frac{1}{3} = 150.8 \text{ ft}^2$$

PLANE GEOMETRY BASICS

Plane geometry is the collection of properties of two-dimensional shapes that exist in a plane, such as lines, angles, circles, and polygons.

Plane Geometry Definitions You Should Know

- **Straight Angle:** An angle that measures 180° that will have the appearance of a straight line.

- **Vertex:** The point at which two lines, line segments, or rays intersect to form an angle.

- **Right Angle:** An angle that measures 90°, formed by two perpendicular line segments or lines.

- **Obtuse Angle:** An angle that measures more than 90°, but less than 180°.

- **Acute Angle:** An angle that measures less than 90°, but more than 0°.

- **Congruent:** Two angles that have the same degree measure. Congruency is indicated with the symbol ≅, such as $\angle 1 \cong \angle 3$, or in an illustration, identical hash marking is used to indicate congruent angles.

- **Complementary Angles:** Two angles that have a sum of 90°. Adjacent complementary angles share a common side and form a right angle.

- **Supplementary Angles:** Two angles that have a sum of 180°. Adjacent supplementary angles shared a common side and form a straight angle.

- **Vertical angles:** The nonadjacent angles formed when two lines or line segments intersect. Vertical angles are always congruent. In the following figure, the vertical angle pairs are $\angle 1 \cong \angle 2$ and $\angle 4 \cong \angle 3$:

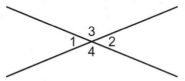

- **Bisect:** To cut a line segment or an angle in half (into two equal line segments or angles).

ANGLES FORMED BY PARALLEL LINES

As discussed earlier, parallel lines will never touch. A **transversal** is a line that intersects two or more lines. When a pair of parallel lines is intersected by a transversal, it forms several pairs of congruent angles and supplementary angles. Use the following illustration as a reference for the review of special angle pairs formed by parallel lines.

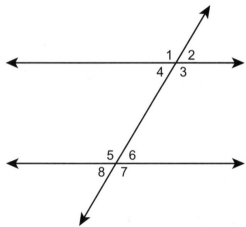

1. **All of the acute angles will be congruent and all of the obtuse angles will be congruent.** Unless the transversal intersects the parallel lines at a right angle, there will be four obtuse and four acute angles formed. Given the illustration, this guarantees the following congruencies:

   - Congruent Obtuse Angles: $\angle 1 \cong \angle 3 \cong \angle 5 \cong \angle 7$
   - Congruent Acute Angles: $\angle 2 \cong \angle 4 \cong \angle 6 \cong \angle 8$

NOTE: If the way an illustration is drawn makes it difficult to tell which angles are obtuse or acute, remember that the vertical angle pairs are all congruent. Unless the transversal intersects at a right angle, the congruent angles will not be adjacent.

---

2. **Any angle pair of an acute and obtuse angle will be complementary.** Notice that $\angle 1$ and $\angle 2$ form a straight angle and are complementary. Since all the acute angles are congruent and all the obtuse angles are congruent, any combination of acute and obtuse angles will sum to 180°.

3. **Alternate interior angles are congruent.** Alternate interior angles sit *inside* the parallel lines on opposite sides of the transversal, and they are congruent. $\angle 4$ and $\angle 6$ are an example of congruent alternate interior angles in the figure above.

4. **Alternate exterior angles are congruent.** Alternate exterior angles sit *outside* the parallel lines on opposite sides of the transversal, and they are congruent. $\angle 2$ and $\angle 8$ are an example of congruent alternate exterior angles in the figure above.

A little further on in this lesson, you will have an opportunity to apply algebraic equations to solving questions with these special angle relationships.

EVERYTHING YOU NEED TO KNOW ABOUT TRIANGLES

The following is a list of the most important facts on angle and side relationships in triangles that you should understand when you take the Math Test:

- **Interior Angles:** The interior angles of a triangle have a sum of 180°.

- **Remote Angles:** This fact relates an *exterior* angle of a triangle to its two *remote interior* angles. (The remote angles are the nonadjacent interior angles.) The measure of an exterior angle of a triangle is equal to the sum of its two remote interior angles. Looking at the following illustration, this means that $\angle z = \angle x + \angle y$:

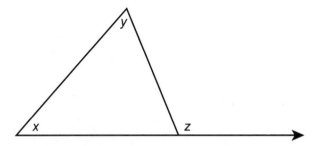

- **Side-Angle Relationships:** In all triangles, the shortest side is opposite the smallest angle, the longest side is opposite the largest angle, and the middle length side is opposite the middle angle.

- **The Sum of Any Two Sides:** The sum of any two sides of a triangle must be greater than the third side.

- **Right Triangle:** A triangle with one 90° angle is a right triangle.

- **Equilateral Triangle:** If it is given that a triangle has three equal sides or three equal angles, then it is an equilateral triangle and both of the side and angle equivalence relationships hold true.

- **Isosceles Triangle:** If it is given that a triangle has two congruent angles or two congruent sides, then it is an isosceles triangle and both of these equivalence relationships hold true.

Let's see how to apply these skills to a practice question.

Example:

Given the following triangle, what is the measure of ∠*REM*?

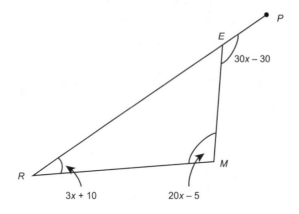

Solution:

The measure of exterior ∠ *MEP* will be equal to the sum of its two remote interior angles *R* and *M*:

$$30x - 30 = (3x + 10) + (20x - 5)$$
$$30x - 30 = 23x + 5$$
$$7x = 35$$
$$x = 5$$

Since $x = 5$, the exterior angle, $30x - 30$, will equal 120°. Since ∠*REM* and exterior angle ∠*PEM* form a 180° straight angle, it can be determined that ∠*REM* = 60°.

Similar Triangles

Similar triangles have the same exact shape, but are different sizes. It is important to know how to identify them and how to use proportional relationships to solve for missing sides. You may encounter a question on the exam that fits similar triangles into a pair of parallel lines, or you may see them in the context of a word problem.

Two triangles are **similar** if just one of the following holds true:
1.   Their corresponding angles are congruent.
2.   The ratios of their three corresponding side pairs are proportional.

TIP

If it is given that two triangles have two pairs of congruent corresponding angles, then they are similar. Remember that angle-angle congruency guarantees triangle similarity.

As soon as it has been determined that two triangles are similar, then you can be certain that both of the previous statements are true. It is important to know that if two pairs of corresponding angles are congruent, then this guarantees that the third corresponding angle pair is also congruent. Therefore, in order to prove triangle similarity, only two pairs of congruent angles are needed.

Let us consider the two triangles in the following illustration.

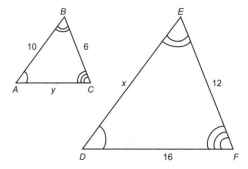

You should remember that the hash markings in each angle are used to indicate congruence. Since these two triangles have corresponding angles that are congruent, they are similar triangles. Similarity is shown with the symbol ~, and the similarity statement for these triangles is $\triangle ABC \sim \triangle DEF$. (Note: it is critical that the corresponding angles are written in the same order in each triangle. Since angle A was written first in the smaller triangle, corresponding angle D must be written first in the larger triangle.)

Now that similarity has been established, we know that all three of their corresponding side pairs are proportional. Use this knowledge to set up ratios that compare the sides of the smaller triangle to the sides of the larger triangle:

$$\frac{\text{side of smaller triangle}}{\text{side of larger triangle}} = \frac{6}{12} = \frac{10}{x} = \frac{y}{16}$$

You can break this down into two separate proportions to determine the values of x and y:

$$\frac{6}{12} = \frac{10}{x} \rightarrow x = 20 \text{ and } \frac{6}{12} = \frac{y}{16} \rightarrow y = 8$$

Midpoint and Distance Formulas

On the Math Test, you will likely come across a question where you will need to find the midpoint between any two coordinate pairs (x_1, y_1) and (x_2, y_2) in the coordinate plane. The midpoint is simply the average of the x-coordinates, followed by the average of the y-coordinates:

$$\text{Midpoint between } (x_1, y_1) \text{ and } (x_2, y_2) = \left(\frac{x_1 + x_2}{2}, \frac{y_1 + y_2}{2} \right)$$

In addition to finding the midpoint between two points, you will need to be able to find the distance between two points:

$$\text{Distance between } (x_1, y_1) \text{ and } (x_2, y_2) = \sqrt{(x_2 - x_1)^2 + (y_2 - y_1)^2}$$

You will get to apply these formulas to some questions further along in this lesson.

Circles in the Coordinate Plane

When graphed in the coordinate plane, a circle with a center at (h, k) with a radius of r can be represented by the general equation $(x - h)^2 + (y - k)^2 = r^2$. Let's look at a sample question that addresses this concept.

Example:

What is the equation for a circle that has a center at $(3, -2)$ and passes through the point $(7, 1)$?

Solution:

You are given the center point and a point on the circumference. Start by finding the radius by putting these two points into the distance formula:

$$d = \sqrt{(x_2 - x_1)^2 + (y_2 - y_1)^2} = \sqrt{(7-3)^2 + (1-(-2))^2} = \sqrt{25} = 5$$

The radius equals 5, so using the general form $(x - h)^2 + (y - k)^2 = r^2$ with center at (h, k), the equation for the circle is $(x - 3)^2 + (y + 2)^2 = 25$.

Putting Circles into Standard Form

Sometimes you may be given a circle that is not in standard form, and you will be asked to find the center, the radius, or the full equation written in standard form. This will require you to work through a series of steps, referred to as **completing the square**. For example, if given the formula $x^2 + y^2 - 4x - 14y + 17 = 0$, it will take several steps to get it into the form $(x - h)^2 + (y - k)^2 = r^2$:

First, get the x^2 term and the bx term grouped together on the same side of the equation as the y^2 and by terms. Move the constant term to the opposite side of the equation:

$$x^2 - 4x + y^2 - 14y = -17$$

Next, add spaces for the constants you will have to add in order to rewrite the x terms and the y terms as perfect squares. Whatever you add to the left side of the equation, you will also have to add to the right side of the equation, so make sure you also add two spaces on the right side of the equation:

$$x^2 - 4x + \underline{\quad} + y^2 - 14y + \underline{\quad} = -17 + \underline{\quad} + \underline{\quad}$$

Take half of each of the coefficients of the bx and by term and square them $\left(\dfrac{b}{2}\right)^2$. This will be what you will add to each side of the equation so that you can write the left side as the sum of two perfect squares. $\left(\dfrac{b}{2}\right)^2$ of $-4x$ is 4 and $\left(\dfrac{b}{2}\right)^2$ of $-14y$ is 49, so add 4 and 49 to both sides of the equation:

$$x^2 - 4x + \left(\frac{-4}{2}\right)^2 + y^2 - 14y + \left(\frac{-14}{2}\right)^2 = -17 + \left(\frac{4}{2}\right)^2 + \left(\frac{-14}{2}\right)^2$$

$$x^2 - 4x + 4 + y^2 - 14y + 49 = -17 + 4 + 49$$

Now rewrite $x^2 - 4x + 4$ as $(x - 2)^2$ and $x^2 - 14y + 49$ as $(y - 7)^2$ and sum the right side of the equation to 36:

$$(x - 2)^2 + (y - 7)^2 = 36$$

This shows us that the center is (2, 7) and the radius is 6.

Let's try another one.

Example:

What is the radius of the circle given in the equation $x^2 + y^2 + 6x = 16$?

Solution:

Only the $x^2 + 6x$ terms need to be rewritten as perfect squares since the y^2 term is already the perfect square:

$$x^2 + 6x + \underline{} + y^2 = 16 + \underline{}$$

$$x^2 + 6x + \left(\frac{6}{2}\right)^2 + y^2 = 16 + \left(\frac{6}{2}\right)^2$$

$$x^2 + 6x + 9 + y^2 = 16 + 9$$

$$(x+3)^2 + y^2 = 25$$

Since $r^2 = 25$, the radius equals 5.

COMPLEX NUMBERS

A complex number is an imaginary number that is the result of taking the square root of a negative number: $\sqrt{-1}$ is represented by the imaginary number i. Complex numbers have a standard form of $a + bi$, where a and b are real numbers and $i = \sqrt{-1}$. The first four powers of i are the most critical to know, since the values for i^n follow this pattern when $n > 4$:

- $i = \sqrt{-1}$
- $i^2 = -1$
- $i^3 = i^2 \times i = -i$
- $i^4 = i^2 \times i^2 = -1 \times -1 = 1$

Multiplying Complex Numbers

On the exam, you will be tested on performing operations with complex numbers. Commonly, you will be required to multiply complex numbers, as in the next example question.

Example:

What is an equivalent expression to $(4 - 3i)^2$?

Solution:

Do not make the mistake of distributing the exponent of 2 to the individual terms in the binomial. Instead, use FOIL to expand $(4 - 3i)^2$: $16 - 24i + i^2$.

Replacing i^2 with −1 will give the final answer:

$$16 - 24i + i^2 = 16 - 24i + (-1) = 15 - 24i$$

Rationalizing the Denominator in Complex Numbers

Division with complex numbers is another area that you may see on the Math Test, presented as a fraction that will need to be written in an equivalent form. The denominator of a fraction must always be a rational number. When a complex number is multiplied by its conjugate, the product will always be a real number. (The conjugate of a complex number $a + bi$ is $a - bi$.) In order to divide with complex numbers, multiply the numerator and denominator by the conjugate of the denominator.

Example:

What is an equivalent expression to the quotient $\dfrac{4+3i}{2-4i}$?

Solution:

In order to rationalize the denominator of $\dfrac{4+3i}{2-4i}$, multiply both numerator and denominator by the conjugate of the denominator, $2 + 4i$:

$$\frac{4+3i}{2-4i} = \frac{(4+3i)}{(2-4i)} \cdot \frac{(2+4i)}{(2+4i)}$$

$$= \frac{8+16i+6i+12i^2}{4+8i-8i-16i^2}$$

$$= \frac{8+22i-12}{4+16}$$

$$= \frac{-4+22i}{20}$$

1 Given the following right triangle, which of the following statements is true?

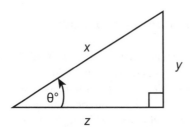

A. $\sin\theta = \dfrac{x}{y}$

B. $\sin\theta = \dfrac{y}{z}$

C. $\cos(90-\theta) = \dfrac{y}{x}$

D. $\tan(90-\theta) = \dfrac{y}{z}$

2 What is the measure of an angle in standard position with a terminal side that goes through the point $(-2, -4\sqrt{3})$? (Enter your answer in the grid below.)

3 Transversals *l* and *m* pass through a pair of parallel lines, intersecting at point *e*, as shown below. Find the length of *AB* if the following segments are defined as follows (Enter your answer in the grid below):

$AE = x + 2$

$BE = x + 6$

$CE = x + 4$

$DE = x + 1$

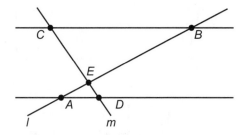

C   *B*

E

A   *D*

l   *m*

Answer Key and Explanations

1. C	2. 240	3. 12

1. **The correct answer is C.** Given the figure, conclude that $\sin\theta = \dfrac{\text{opposite}}{\text{hypotenuse}} = \dfrac{y}{x}$. Since $\sin\theta = \cos(90-\theta)$, it is possible to determine that $\cos(90-\theta) = \dfrac{y}{x}$.

    Choice A is incorrect because $\sin\theta = \dfrac{\text{opposite}}{\text{hypotenuse}} = \dfrac{y}{x}$. Choice B is incorrect because $\sin\theta = \dfrac{\text{opposite}}{\text{hypotenuse}} = \dfrac{y}{x}$. Choice D is incorrect because $\tan\theta = \dfrac{y}{z}$ and $\tan(90-\theta) = \dfrac{z}{y}$.

2. **The correct answer is 240.** First, sketch a coordinate plane with the point $(-2, -4\sqrt{3})$ and connect that point to the origin. Next, create and label the sides of the triangle with the appropriate coordinates of the point:

    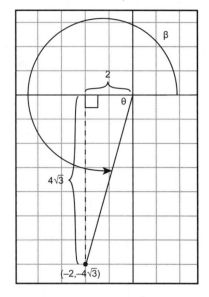

    Now you can use the dimensions of the given triangle to solve for the measure of $\angle\theta$. The inverse trig function for tangent should be used to solve for $\angle\theta$:

    $$\theta = \tan^{-1}\left(\frac{4\sqrt{3}}{2}\right)$$
    $$\theta = 60°$$

    Since the question asks for the measure of an angle in standard position, the positive x-axis must be its initial side, and therefore

$\angle\beta=180°+m\angle\theta$ is drawn in above. Notice that $\angle\beta=180°+m\angle\theta$ is composed of the 180° made by the straight angle of the x-axis, plus the measure of $\angle\theta$:

$$m\angle\beta=180°+m\angle\theta$$
$$m\angle\beta=180°+60°$$
$$m\angle\beta=240°$$

3.   **The correct answer is 12.** Since $\triangle AED$ and $\triangle BEC$ have two sets of congruent alternate side interior angles, it can be determined that they are similar. Make sure that the similarity statement keeps the corresponding congruent angles in the same order: $\triangle AED \sim \triangle BEC$. Now, redraw the triangles so that they are oriented in the same direction, label their sides with the given expression, set up a similarity proportion, and solve for x:

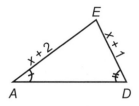

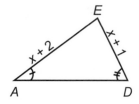

$$\frac{x+2}{x+6}=\frac{x+1}{x+4}$$
$$(x+2)(x+4) = (x+6)(x+1)$$
$$x^2+6x+8 = x^2+7x+6$$
$$2 = x$$

Now that $x = 2$, substitute that into the expressions for AE and BE to find that $AB = 12$ units.

SUMMING IT UP

- There are two math sections on the SAT® Math Test. The No Calculator section contains 20 questions and is 25 minutes long. The Calculator section contains 38 questions and is 55 minutes long.

- About 90 percent of SAT® Math Test questions fall into three main content areas: **The Heart of Algebra** (creating, solving, and interpreting linear equations and systems of linear equations), **Problem Solving and Data Analysis** (applying percentages, ratios, proportions, and unit-of-measurement conversions to real-world situations), and **Passport to Advanced Math** (more advanced functions and equations that are the foundation for college-level courses in math, science, engineering, and technology). About 10 percent of questions fall into the **Additional Topics in Math** category (geometry, trigonometry, and complex numbers).

- Don't rush when reading questions—look for patterns and similarities on both sides of equations and inequalities that can help you solve.

- **To convert decimals into whole numbers**, multiply both sides of the equation by the smallest power of 10 that will eliminate all decimals; **to convert fractions into whole numbers**, multiply both sides of the equation by the least common denominator of all fractions in an equation.

- Remember to switch the direction of the inequality symbol when dividing or multiplying by a negative number (but *not* when adding or subtracting).

- If an equation you construct doesn't match any of the given answer choices, you will need to identify an equivalent form of the equation. Look for ways to combine or simplify.

- When **increasing a value by a percentage**, remember to add the percentage increase to the *original* value. For example, a 40% increase of x is written as $0.40x$, but when added to the original value, x, the final value is $1.4x$.

- Pay close attention to whether an inequality should be a **less than** or **greater than** ($<$ or $>$) or if it will have an **or equal to** in the symbol ($\leq$ or $\geq$).

- The context of the question will matter when you decide whether you should round up or down. If you cannot break something into smaller portions and you absolutely need a decimal amount of it, you still need to round *up*—no matter how small the decimal.

- If linear equations have **different slopes,** there will be just one coordinate pair (x, y) that satisfies both equations; if they have the **same slopes and different y-intercepts**, then they will be parallel lines with no coordinate pair that works simultaneously in both equations; if they have the **same slopes and the same y-intercepts**, then the two lines are equivalent and there will be infinite coordinate pair solutions to the system.

- When solving a system of equations, sometimes you need to multiply both equations by different factors in order to create opposite coefficients that will cancel out one of the variables.

- When writing a system of equations from a real-world scenario, take it slowly. Identify the unknown pieces of information and assign variables to represent each one. Then determine how these unknowns relate to each other and represent the relationships with equations or inequalities.

- **Slope-intercept form** is $y = mx + b$. The m term is the coefficient of x, and represents the **slope** of the line. The b term represents the **y-intercept**.

- The **slope of a line** is the ratio of the *rise* (difference in y-coordinates) compared to its *run* (difference in x-coordinates) between any two coordinate pairs (x_1, y_1) and (x_2, y_2): $m = \dfrac{\text{rise}}{\text{run}} = \dfrac{y_2 - y_1}{x_2 - x_1}$. **Parallel lines** have the same slope; **perpendicular lines** have slopes that are opposite reciprocals.

- A **ratio** is a comparison of two different quantities. A **proportion** is any equation that sets two ratios equal to one another and can be used to solve for a missing piece of information.

- A **percentage** is a ratio that is literally *per cent* or "out of 100." The proportion $\dfrac{\text{part}}{\text{whole}} = \dfrac{\%}{100}$ can be used to work through many percentage questions.

- To calculate percent increase or decrease, use the formula $\dfrac{\text{amount of change}}{\text{original amount}} \times 100$. When increasing a number by a certain percentage, multiply the original number by (1 + percentage increase in decimal format). When decreasing a number by a percentage, multiply the original number by (1 − percentage decrease in decimal format).

- In **linear models**, as x changes at a constant rate, there is a constant *difference* between the y-values; in **exponential models**, as x changes at a constant rate there is a constant *quotient* (or ratio) between the y-values. The general form for an exponential function is $y = a(r^x)$, where r is the common ratio and a is the starting point when $x = 0$ (a is therefore the y-intercept).

- In a **line graph**, the steeper the slope, the faster the growth or decline.

- In a **scatterplot**, a **line of best fit** can be drawn through the data to best model the relationship between the variables. A strong or weak correlation between the dependent and independent variables can be determined by the proximity of the data points to the line of best fit.

- **Simple interest** is calculated with the linear model $A = P(1 + rt)$, where P is the principal (money initially invested), r is the annual interest rate expressed as a decimal, t is the time in years, and A is the final investment value after interest.

- **Compound interest** is exponential and is calculated with the exponential model $A = P\left(1 + \dfrac{r}{n}\right)^{nt}$, where P is the principal (money initially invested), r is the annual interest rate expressed as a decimal, t is the time in years, n is the number of times per year interest is compounded, and A is the final investment value after interest.

- The **mode** is the most frequently occurring number in a data set. The **median** is the center-most number in a data set after the numbers have been put in order from smallest to greatest. The **mean** is the arithmetic average found by dividing the sum of the number by the quantity of the number in the set. The **range** is the spread of the data set found by subtracting the smallest number from the largest number.

- **Standard deviation** indicates how close all the data points are to the mean: the larger the standard deviation, the more spread out the data points; a smaller standard deviation indicates that the points are closer to the mean.

- When drawing conclusions about the reliability of a pool of data or what kind of conclusions can be drawn from data, remember that sample populations *must* be selected **at random**. The data must come from subjects that were selected randomly from the general population, and any treatments given to the selected subjects must be randomly assigned.

- Be careful with negative signs and exponents when multiplying polynomials. When you FOIL, keep track of any negative signs inside and outside of the parentheses, and beware that you cannot distribute an exponent outside a sum or difference to the individual terms inside a set of parentheses.

- The **difference of perfect squares** is $x^2 - y^2 = (x - y)(x + y)$.

- A **quadratic** is an equation that can be written in the form $y = ax^2 + bx + c$, such that $a \neq 0$. Solving a quadratic in this form can be straightforward when $a = 1$. The two constants in each factor must *multiply* to c and must *add* to b.

- For real numbers b and c, $x^2 + bx + c = (x + m)(x + n)$ when $mn = c$ and $m + n = b$. Once the equation is in the form $(x + m)(x + n) = 0$, set each factor equal to zero to solve for x: $(x + m) = 0$ and $(x + n) = 0$.

- The quadratic formula gives the x solutions to a quadratic equation that has been set equal to zero:

$$\text{If } ax^2 + bx + c = 0, \text{ then } x = \frac{-b \pm \sqrt{b^2 - 4ac}}{2a}$$

- When a quadratic equation is graphed in the coordinate plane, it forms a parabola. The **standard form** of a parabola is $y = ax^2 + bx + c$. If a is **positive**, the parabola will be an **upward curve** and will have a **vertex** that is a **minimum**. If a is **negative**, the parabola will be a **downward curve** with a **vertex** that is a **maximum**.

- The constant, c, is always the **y-intercept**, and the **x-intercepts** will occur at the values of x that make the quadratic equation equal to zero.

- The vertex always sits on the **line of symmetry**: $x = \dfrac{-b}{2a}$.
- The **vertex form** of the equation of any parabola is $y = a(x - h)^2 + k$; the vertex is at (h, k).
- The formula for **exponential growth** is $y = a(1 + r)^x$, where r is the percentage increase, a is the starting point, and x is the units of time; the formula for **exponential decay** is $y = a(1 - r)^x$, where r is the percentage decrease and a is the starting point.
- In order to simplify **rational expressions**, you will probably need to factor a quadratic into two binomials or factor a greatest common factor out of two terms.
- **Function** notation uses $f(x)$ to indicate "the value of y at x." The **domain** is the set of all x values for which a function $f(x)$ is defined. The **range** is the set of all y values that are produced from the x values in the domain.
- A **transformation** is a vertical or horizontal shift of the graph of a function. **Vertical shifts** occur when a constant is added or subtracted to the entire function. **Horizontal shifts** occur when a constant is added or subtracted into the fiber of a function.
- Use the Pythagorean theorem ($a^2 + b^2 = c^2$) to solve for missing side lengths in right triangles. The two shorter sides that form the right angle are the **legs,** and the **hypotenuse** is always the longest side opposite the right angle.
- Find missing angle measures of triangles using right triangle trigonometry. Memorize the mnemonic SOH-CAH-TOA, which summarizes the following relationships:

  ○ SOH represents sin $= \dfrac{\text{opposite}}{\text{hypotenuse}}$

  ○ CAH represents cosine $= \dfrac{\text{adjacent}}{\text{hypotenuse}}$

  ○ TOA represents tangent $= \dfrac{\text{opposite}}{\text{adjacent}}$

- Memorize these trig identities, which may be critical for solving some of the questions you see on test day: $\sin\theta = \cos(90 - \theta)$ and $\cos\theta = \sin(90 - \theta)$.
- In order to convert an angle from radian measure into degrees, replace π with $180°$ in the expression and evaluate it. In order to convert an angle from degrees to radian measure, multiply the angle by $\dfrac{\pi}{180}$ and reduce the product to lowest terms.
- An angle in **standard position** has its vertex at the origin $(0, 0)$, its initial side on the positive x-axis, and its terminal side in Quadrant I, II, III, or IV.
- A **chord** is a line segment with endpoints on the circumference of the circle. The longest possible chord in a circle is the diameter, which passes through

the center of the circle. When two chords intersect, they form the vertex of an **inscribed angle**.

- Given a **central angle** θ, you can determine the ratio $\dfrac{\theta}{360}$ (or $\dfrac{\theta}{2\pi}$ in radians) would represent the portion of the circumference the angle intercepts.

- The **area of a sector (or portion) of a circle** = $\pi r^2 \times \dfrac{\theta}{360}$.

- A **straight angle** measures 180° and looks like a straight line. A **right angle** measures 90°. An **obtuse angle** measures more than 90°, but less than 180°. An **acute angle** measures less than 90°, but more than 0°.

- **Congruent angles** have the same degree measure. **Complementary angles** have a sum of 90°. **Supplementary angles** have a sum of 180°.

- **Vertical angles** form when two lines or line segments intersect. Vertical angles are always congruent.

- The **interior angles** of a triangle have a sum of 180°.

- The measure of an **exterior angle** of a triangle is equal to the sum of its two remote interior angles.

- In all triangles, the shortest side is opposite the smallest angle, the longest side is opposite the largest angle, and the middle length side is opposite the middle angle; also, the sum of any two sides of a triangle must be greater than the third side.

- A **right triangle** has one 90° angle; an **equilateral triangle** has three equal sides and three equal angles; an **isosceles triangle** has two congruent sides and two congruent angles.

- If two triangles are **similar**, their corresponding angles are congruent or the ratios of their three corresponding side-pairs are proportional.

- The **midpoint of a line** is the average of its x-coordinates followed by the average of its y-coordinates: midpoint between (x_1, y_1) and (x_2, y_2) = $\left(\dfrac{x_1 + x_2}{2}, \dfrac{y_1 + y_2}{2} \right)$.

- A circle with center (h, k) and radius r can be represented by the general equation $(x - h)^2 + (y - k)^2 = r^2$.

- A **complex number** is an imaginary number that is the result of taking the square root of a negative number. Complex numbers have a standard form of $a + bi$, where a and b are real numbers and $i = \sqrt{-1}$. The first 4 powers of i are as follows:
  - $i = \sqrt{-1}$
  - $i^2 = -1$
  - $i^3 = -i$
  - $i^4 = 1$

CHAPTER 5: THE SAT® WRITING AND LANGUAGE TEST

OVERVIEW

- A Brief Introduction to the SAT® Writing and Language Test
- Expression of Ideas: An Overview
- Organization Questions
- Development Questions
- Effective Language Use Questions
- Standard English Conventions: An Overview
- Sentence Structure Questions
- Conventions of Punctuation Questions
- Conventions of Usage Questions
- Attacking Writing and Language Passages and Questions
- Summing It Up

The purpose of the SAT® Writing and Language Test is to see how well you make key editorial decisions to improve writing passages given to you on the exam. We know you're short on time to prepare for the SAT® exam, and you need to make every available moment of study time between now and test day really count. This chapter is designed to help you get ready for all the information you will face on the SAT® Writing and Language Test—*fast*!

NOTE: For comprehensive information regarding the Writing and Language Test, visit the official website: ***https://collegereadiness.collegeboard.org/sat/ inside-the-test/writing-language***.

A BRIEF INTRODUCTION TO THE SAT® WRITING AND LANGUAGE TEST

The Writing and Language Test measures your abilities to read critically, recognize errors and weaknesses in writing, and make necessary fixes to improve the writing passages—valuable and practical skills that will serve you well throughout your academic career and into your professional life after school. On test day, you will have 35 minutes to answer 44 multiple-choice questions divided among four passages.

The Writing and Language Test is comprised of two major concepts, which we'll cover in detail throughout this chapter: Expression of Ideas and Standard English Conventions.

EXPRESSION OF IDEAS

These questions will test your ability to recognize and address structural issues that impact the overall effectiveness of a piece of writing, including **organization, development,** and **effective language use.**

> **Why is this important?** Your ability to *effectively* express your ideas, both in written and verbal communication, will seriously impact how your ideas are understood and received—both in the classroom and in the world of work.

STANDARD ENGLISH CONVENTIONS

Questions in this skill area will test your ability to recognize—and fix—issues involving **sentence structure, conventions of usage,** and **conventions of punctuation.**

> **Why is this important?** As you've probably learned, your ability to use good grammar, punctuation, and sentence structure can seriously impact your grades—on tests, reports, projects, and term papers, to name just a few.

Make the Most of Your Time!

You have only 35 minutes for this portion of the test so you'll need to work **quickly** in order to make efficient use of your time on test day.

The key is to establish a good test-taking pace *before* test day arrives. Use the practice in this book to establish a working pace that will help you achieve your test goals.

Students who show up on test day who *haven't* done this are at a real disadvantage!

Within *each* of the two core skills areas tested, questions on the Writing and Language Test will measure your skills in the following areas:

- **Words in Context:** These questions will measure your ability to recognize effective and appropriate word choice, based on context within the passages provided. Your vocabulary skills should be *razor sharp* for test day, and you'll need to be able to use available context clues to make decisions that impact **tone, style,** and **syntax,** with the goal of improving a given piece of writing.

- **Command of Evidence:** These questions are designed to test your ability to grasp how effectively a piece of writing conveys ideas and information and to make critical improvements in the following areas: to **enhance meaning, sharpen a claim or argument,** and **provide appropriate details and support.**

- **Analysis in History/Social Studies and in Science:** These questions will measure your ability to critically read, comprehend, and analyze passages based on these important topic areas—and to make key decisions on how best to improve them.

NOTE: Good news! You don't need to be an expert in *any* specific subject to do well on the SAT® Writing and Language Test! It will *not* test your knowledge of any specific subject. Everything you'll need to know about the topics covered in the writing passages is included in the test.

Let's review each of the two major concept areas on the Writing and Language Test and discover how to make the most of your time—however long that is—to achieve SAT® success.

EXPRESSION OF IDEAS: AN OVERVIEW

Questions that fall into the Expression of Ideas category on the SAT® Writing and Language Test measure your ability to analyze a written passage and make decisions regarding the author's use of **organization, development,** and **effective language choices.**

You'll be tasked with making decisions about adding, deleting, moving, and revising words, sentences, and phrases within the passage. Your ultimate goal is to improve the readability, appropriateness, and effectiveness of the author's work.

These questions focus on core **rhetorical skills,** including the overall clarity and effectiveness of a piece of writing. They also involve making sure that:

- The **tone** and **mood** of a piece of writing are consistent and appropriate
- Each writing passage reflects effective **organization**
- Each passage is free from **off-topic** and **redundant details**
- **Transitions** between ideas are strong
- **Wordiness** is avoided
- Each writing passage is in the best possible shape

So, what's your job on test day? Simply put: Your job is to determine whether the author of each passage made appropriate choices to express his or her ideas at various points in the writing and to decide if the alternative options provided in the answer choices for each question improve the passage and more effectively express the ideas contained within.

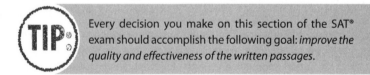

Every decision you make on this section of the SAT® exam should accomplish the following goal: *improve the quality and effectiveness of the written passages.*

EXPRESSION OF IDEAS QUESTIONS: THE BOTTOM LINE

Expression of Ideas questions can be a bit more challenging than questions involving Standard English Conventions, so proceed carefully.

Why?

Because the issues in these questions may not always be as immediately obvious as punctuation or spelling errors, for example. They are often more subtle and require a deeper level of analysis and comprehension. Factor in the pressure of the ticking clock on test day, and you'll quickly understand why it's in your best interest to come equipped with a proven set of test-taking strategies—and plenty of advanced practice—if you're going to succeed.

Hopefully, it's now clear why you should devote a portion of your SAT® study time to building and practicing your Expression of Ideas skills before tackling the official exam. It's up to you to determine how to best utilize the time you have between now and test day to achieve your SAT® goals.

We've condensed everything you need to know in this concise yet effective section and recommend that you make the most of the targeted practice and review to get ready for test day. We'll first take a brief look at each question type, and then move forward with helpful practice. So keep reading!

ORGANIZATION QUESTIONS

On the SAT® Writing and Language Test, you'll encounter a variety of organization questions, which are designed to assess how well you can make decisions about effective **grouping, distribution,** and **arrangement** of ideas at the word, phrase, sentence, and paragraph levels.

LOGICAL SEQUENCE QUESTIONS

Logical Sequence questions will test your ability to recognize if information provided in the passage—either a word, phrase, sentence, or paragraph—is in the **correct and most effective order**—and if it isn't, you'll be tasked with fixing it. A question can also introduce a new piece of text and ask you to determine where it best fits within the passage. This order can vary, depending on a given passage and its intended purpose.

Always keep in mind that the goal of logical sequence questions is to make the information in the passage as cohesive and logical as possible. Here's an example of a Logical Sequence question that you may encounter on the SAT® exam:

[1] You'll need a large container, some dry ice, and hot water. [2] Are you ready to discover how to make smoke? [3] For an adequate smoke effect, add approximately 4 gallons of hot water to 5 pounds of dry ice in a large enough container to hold both. [4] As the dry ice melts from the hot water, it will create a steady stream of smoke. [5] Smoke can really enhance a simulated volcano for a school project, and is an effective special effect for videos and movies.

To make this paragraph most logical, sentence 2 should be placed

A. NO CHANGE
B. before sentence 1.
C. after sentence 4.
D. after sentence 5.

This is a typical logical sequence question. You can see from this example how important organization is to ensure your ideas flow logically and that your audience can understand the thoughts you're trying to convey. Sentence 2 is an introductory sentence, designed to introduce the main topic of the paragraph—how to make smoke. Therefore, it belongs before sentence 1, so **the correct answer is B**.

 Some questions on the SAT® exam will focus on information in the passage that's correct as is. If the passage is correct as written, select "NO CHANGE" for that question.

INTRODUCTIONS, CONCLUSIONS, AND TRANSITIONS

These questions will test your ability to recognize the proper use and placement of information to introduce, conclude, and connect ideas within a passage and to effectively move between related ideas between paragraphs in a passage.

Once again, this type of question can include moving, revising, adding, or deleting an underlined word, phrase, sentence, or paragraph within the passage or can ask you to consider introducing new text to the existing passage.

As you probably know, solid introductions, conclusions, and transitions are essential tools for writing effective essays and papers. (In fact, these elements will be an essential part of your SAT® Essay if you choose to write one!) They help you engage with your audience, connect them with your ideas, and convince them that your thoughts and point of view are worth considering.

Here's an example of a question that falls under the Introductions, Conclusions, and Transitions category that you may encounter on the SAT® exam:

> Ant colonies are as organized as any manufacturing factory. Each worker ant has a specific job, knows what to do, and works hard to support the needs of the group. Some ants forage and gather food, some defend the nest, and others are tasked with building chores or caring for the queen.
>
> Which of the following sentences would make the most effective conclusion to this paragraph?
>
> **A.** Do you ever find ants crawling around your house?
> **B.** Spiders love capturing ants in their webs and eating them.
> **C.** Ants can vary greatly in size, depending on the type you encounter.
> **D.** Ants are an incredibly efficient and orderly species.

When determining an appropriate conclusion sentence for a paragraph or passage, a key strategy is to first determine the main idea of the piece. Here, the preceding sentences all relate to how organized and well-structured ant colonies are. Choices A, B, and C all relate to ants, but fail to adequately sum up this core message. However, choice D captures this notion appropriately. **The correct answer is D**.

Transition Word Clues

Keep an eye out for transition words in questions—they'll provide valuable context clues to help you arrive at the correct answers. For example, *in contrast*: If you see this phrase, you'll know that the information that follows should provide an opposing point of view from something the author said previously.

The chart under the Recognizing Effective Transition Words and Phrases section of this chapter provides details on the most common transition words and phrases. Use this information to your advantage on test day!

Beware of the Answer-as-You-Go Approach!

Often, students who are pressed for time and in a rush try to work as fast as possible on the SAT® Writing and Language Test and tackle each question as they encounter the relevant number or underlined portion while reading a passage for the first time.

This *can* be a good time-saving approach, but it's a strategy that's often more effective on Standard English Conventions questions, where context is usually less relevant.

On Expression of Ideas questions, the answer-as-you-go approach may *backfire*—particularly if there are carefully designed answer distractors that may *seem* correct until you've read and fully digested the passage and realize they were just cleverly designed traps. Proceed with caution!

Opening Sentences

Starting a piece of writing with a powerful and effective opening sentence is essential. The opening sentence sets the tone for the entire piece. It's also the sentence that can hook the reader's interest—or fail to do so. If you fail to capture a reader's attention early on, he or she may stop reading before reaching your key points.

On the Writing and Language Test, you may be tasked with identifying effective opening sentences for the writing passages provided. You'll typically be given a series of possible introductory sentences in a set of answer choices and will be asked to determine which is the most effective, given the context of the passage.

Effective opening sentences in Writing and Language passages will do the following:

- **Use engaging words to garner interest and capture attention.** (Example: *The sailfish, a brilliantly hued ocean dweller known for its distinctive sail-like dorsal fin, is the swiftest swimmer in the ocean.*)

- **State the topic of the piece succinctly, confidently, and clearly.** (Example: *The sailfish is without peer when it comes to speed in the ocean.*)

- **Ask an intriguing or provocative question.** (Example: *Do you know which ocean animal is the absolute fastest swimmer?*)

- **Deploy a point-counterpoint structure.** (Example: *The peregrine falcon may be the fastest animal in the air, but it wouldn't stand a chance against the sailfish in the water.*)

- **Use a surprising fact, theory, or bit of interesting trivia.** (Example: *Did you know that sailfish have been recorded at astounding speeds of nearly 70 mph in the water?*)

- **If appropriate, use a bit of humor.** (Example: *I consider myself a decent swimmer, but if I ever had to race a sailfish, I'd probably give up before even trying!*)

- **Start with a poignant quote.** (Example: *It has been said that "sailfish are as swift as hurricane wind while swimming."*)

Concluding Sentences

How you end a piece of writing is just as crucial as how you begin it. Remember, good writing should have two key impacts:

1. An engaging first impression

2. A memorable final impression

An effective **conclusion** serves to tie up your ideas and leave a lasting impression. It's the finishing touch on a piece of writing, and it should leave the reader feeling satisfied.

Not surprisingly, a strong conclusion should include many of the same elements of a strong introduction. Ideally, it should:

- Contain a succinct, clear, and poignant message

- Reiterate key words or phrases from the passage

- Consider a memorable quote or question that encapsulates your main point(s)

- Redefine an important idea or detail in the passage

- Capture your perspective or point of view regarding the topic

Transition Words and Phrases

A key factor in effective writing and organization is how ideas *connect* to each other. The appropriate use of **transition words** and **phrases** in a piece of writing can make all the difference, and without them, a compelling piece with powerful ideas could turn into a rambling and incoherent mess that lacks authority.

Sometimes, writers use entire sentences to transition between ideas—and you should be ready to encounter these on the SAT® exam.

 Transition words provide key context clues for answering questions on the Writing and Language Test, so be on the lookout for them.

Different transition words and phrases perform different functions, and your ability to recognize when transitions are being used correctly—and when they're not—will likely be put to the test on the Writing and Language Test.

Review and master the following table, which will help you to be able to quickly and effectively tackle questions involving transitions on test day.

Function	Transitional Words and Phrases
Introduction	*to begin, first of all, to start with*
An addition	*also, furthermore, in addition, moreover, secondly*
Clarification	*in other words, that is to say, to put it another way*
Passage of time	*afterward, later, meanwhile, next, subsequently*
Examples	*for example, for instance, to demonstrate, specifically, to illustrate*
Cause	*because, since*
Effect	*as a result, consequently, therefore*
Comparison	*comparatively, in comparison, in similar fashion, likewise, similarly*
Contrast	*at the same time, however, in contrast, nevertheless, notwithstanding, on the contrary, yet*
Conclusion	*in conclusion, in short, to conclude, to sum up, to summarize, ultimately*

Organization for Clarity and Effect

No passage, no matter how well written, can simply rest on a powerful introduction, memorable conclusion, and strong transitions. For a piece of writing to be fully effective, every sentence and paragraph needs to be on target and well organized.

How can you effectively tackle these sorts of questions on the SAT® Writing and Language Test? It begins before you even reach the questions.

While you're reading each passage, keep your "editorial instincts" alert and sharp:

- Note the type of organization the passage follows.

- Get a sense of the structure and flow of the piece, which will help you identify any glaring inconsistencies or illogical organization.

Familiarize yourself with the following common organizational formats:

- **Chronological:** information is organized by the time that the events occurred (can be forward or reverse)

- **Sequential:** often used when describing a process, information is organized by the order in which the steps or parts occur

- **Order of importance:** information is organized by its relative value or importance (can be most to least important, or vice versa)

- **Compare and contrast:** often used when writing about two or more things, wherein one is discussed, then another to compare it with, and so on

- **Cause and effect:** often used to describe a particular result, and the events or reasons behind why that result occurred

- **Issue/problem and solution:** in this type of organization, a central dilemma is discussed, followed by strategies for addressing/fixing the problem

DEVELOPMENT QUESTIONS

On the SAT® Writing and Language Test, you'll encounter various questions regarding **development,** which will task you with identifying, revising, adding, and deleting key elements of the passages provided to ensure each piece of writing achieves its intended purpose.

On the test, you'll have to make important decisions about the following:

- **Proposition questions:** The *main topic elements* of each passage, including *topic sentences, thesis statements*, and *core claims* made by an author

- **Support questions:** The *supportive elements* of each passage, which includes *supportive information* and *details* that bolster a writer's central ideas or claims made in a piece of writing

- **Focus questions:** The *relevant elements* of each passage, which requires you to make judgments regarding whether or not information presented *supports*, *detracts*, or is *irrelevant* to an author's purpose and central claims

- **Quantitative information questions:** Supplemental *quantitative elements* for a given passage; you'll encounter graphical information related to specific passages on the Writing and Language Test, and you'll need to make determinations regarding their *purpose*, *accuracy*, and *level of effectiveness* in relation to the passages. These graphical elements can take the form of *graphs, charts, tables, illustrations*, etc.

These core elements lie at the heart of every piece of writing and are essential tools for any author to effectively convey his or her intended meaning and message—and this holds true for the passages you'll encounter on the Writing and Language Test.

For each of these elements, you'll need to make critical, analytical decisions to ensure each passage communicates its core points in the clearest and most effective way possible, with relevant support and a sharp focus.

Let's take a closer look at each development question type you'll encounter on test day and how best to attack each of them.

PROPOSITION QUESTIONS

An effective SAT® Writing and Language Test passage contains the following elements, all designed to communicate and support the piece's intended meaning:

- A clear and compelling thesis statement
- Effective topic sentences
- Compelling and relevant contextual claims

On the Writing and Language Test, you'll be tasked with making decisions on adding, revising, and deleting material, as well as answering analytical and comprehension questions involving topic sentences, thesis statements, and core claims made by an author. These questions will test your ability to identify the main ideas of a passage and whether an author's attempt to convey his or her intended messaging was successful, or if revision is required.

Let's take a closer look at each of these elements and how to effectively tackle related questions on the SAT® Writing and Language Test.

Thesis Statement

A thesis statement is a brief statement designed to succinctly convey an author's main point or claim. For example, a simple thesis statement for an essay might be as follows:

Thesis statement: *The sailfish is without peer when it comes to speed in the ocean.*

The piece of writing that follows this thesis statement—if written well—should be designed to support this notion regarding the sailfish. Whenever you begin a piece of writing, you should always have a main idea in mind, as this will lie at the very core of why you're writing the piece in the first place.

Here's an example of a Proposition question similar to one you may encounter on test day:

Assembly lines are used in virtually every type of product manufacturing conceivable. Complex, labor-intensive items can be assembled quickly and effectively through the assembly line process. The assembly line process maximizes individual task specialization and minimizes time spent on a given task. This money- and time-saving innovation revolutionized how businesses operate and meet consumer demands.

Which choice best reflects the main idea of the paragraph?

A. Every company that has embraced the assembly line process has found great success.

B. America utilizes the assembly line process more than any other country in the world.

C. The assembly line process has made manufacturing more efficient and cost effective.

D. Industrialized nations look forward to the next big manufacturing innovation.

In this question, we're on the lookout for a thesis statement that best summarizes all of the points in the paragraph. Perhaps you recognize a suitable answer immediately among the answer choices. If so, great—select it and move on to the next question. If you need more time, try eliminating incorrect answer choices to help you arrive at the correct answer. Choice A is incorrect—this is a big speculative leap and it's likely not true that every company that has embraced the assembly line process has found great success. Choice B is another assertion that's unsubstantiated by the information in the paragraph. Choice D, while possibly true, is beyond the scope of the paragraph. That leaves us with choice C, which appropriately reflects the main idea of the paragraph—that the assembly line process has made manufacturing more efficient and cost effective. **The correct answer is C.**

 When you run into trouble on a question, try eliminating as many incorrect answer choices as possible to help increase your chances of arriving at the correct answer.

Topic Sentences

Topic sentences can be considered the "thesis statements" of the paragraphs in which they appear—they communicate the main ideas of each of the paragraphs that make up a given piece of writing.

Each paragraph—including the **introduction,** the **body paragraphs,** and the **conclusion**—will likely have an identifiable idea designed to deliver its core point and purpose and support the piece as a whole.

Building on the thesis statement in the previous example, here's a sample topic sentence:

Thesis statement: *The sailfish is without peer when it comes to speed in the ocean.*

Topic sentence: *Sailfish have been known to reach speeds of nearly 70 mph.*

Notice that the topic sentence *directly supports* the thesis statement. In essence, one of the reasons why *the sailfish is without peer when it comes to speed in the ocean* is because *they have been known to reach speeds of nearly 70 mph.*

Core Claims

A core claim is a point or assertion that a writer is trying to make in his or her writing, which—when delivered effectively—relates directly back to both the topic sentence of the paragraph in which it appears and the thesis statement of the entire passage.

Claims can be found in persuasive, argumentative, and informative passages and can also take the form of a **counterclaim,** which is an *opposing* point of view or assertion to that of an author's.

When handled effectively, directly addressing counterclaims in a piece of writing is an effective tool for providing a comprehensive analysis of an issue or argument.

Building on the thesis statement and topic sentence in the previous example, here's a sample claim:

> **Thesis statement:** *The sailfish is without peer when it comes to speed in the ocean.*
>
> **Topic sentence:** *Sailfish have been known to reach speeds of nearly 70 mph.*
>
> **Claim:** *Due to their incredible speed, sailfish are incredibly difficult for fishermen and predators alike to catch.*

Notice how the claim made here directly supports *both* the topic sentence of the paragraph in which it would appear and the overall thesis statement.

Let's look at a possible counterclaim and how an author might address it within a passage:

> **Counterclaim:** *Some scientists claim that swordfish are the fastest fish in the ocean.*
>
> **Response to counterclaim:** *However, there are numerous accounts of sailfish outswimming swordfish in the water.*

A nuanced, well-developed essay will *not* shy away from directly addressing a counterclaim—it will not only mention it, it will also have a satisfying response to it.

You *don't* have to agree with an author's core claims—your job is to determine if the author effectively communicated his or her intended point of view and to make needed revisions to ensure that this is done as well as possible.

Check for a Stem

Proposition questions on the Writing and Language Test often—though not always—appear with a question stem, asking you to make a key decision about specific text, either currently within the passage or within the question and/or answer choices. A typical question stem could be as follows:

> *Which of the following sentences should be deleted to reinforce the author's point of view that sailfish are the fastest swimmers?*

Use this signal to help you quickly identify this question type and determine the best approach for getting the correct answer.

Support Questions

Any passage worth the words that were used to write it will include sufficient support and details to bolster the author's point of view and claims. These are the subordinate ideas that lend reinforcement to the larger central ideas in a piece of writing and can include relevant facts, research, details, data, figures, and examples.

 Support questions on the Writing and Language Test will often include the word *support* or a close synonym. When you encounter this, you'll likely know what type of question you're dealing with.

On the Writing and Language Test, you'll be tasked with making decisions on adding and revising supportive textual material, deleting nonsupporting material, and answering analytical and comprehension questions involving relevant support.

Let's take a look back at the sailfish passage and our previous central claim:

Thesis statement: *The sailfish is without peer when it comes to speed in the ocean.*

Here are a few examples of supportive claims for this main idea, as well as one claim that fails to support it. Can you identify the claim that fails to provide relevant support?

Support A: *Sailfish have large, sail-like dorsal fins that aid them in moving swiftly through the water.*

Support B: *Their smooth, elongated bodies help them glide quickly through the water.*

Support C: *Their fast reflexes and rapid metabolisms help them react and pivot quickly when swimming.*

Support D: *Sailfish are capable of changing color to reflect their mood.*

As you might have guessed, choice D fails to support the central claim that sailfish are the swiftest fish in the ocean. Although this information *does* relate to the sailfish and *does* provide an interesting contextual fact, the fact that sailfish can change color *does not* directly support the thesis statement that they are the fastest fish. **The correct answer is D.**

 When making judgments regarding which material to keep, revise, add, or delete from a passage, *proceed with caution*—and make sure you know *exactly* what each question is asking!

Focus Questions

Recognizing appropriate, effective, and necessary background information within a passage and eliminating the existence of irrelevant, tangential, or redundant information is a common question type on the Writing and Language Test.

Remember, your goal on test day is to improve the passages you'll encounter, which includes text relevance and focus. Every writer—and every SAT® passage—has a focus, and information provided can either serve to support that focus or detract from it.

Let's refer back to our sailfish example and take a look at how focus can come into play.

Thesis statement: *The sailfish is without peer when it comes to speed in the ocean.*

Topic sentence: *Sailfish have been known to reach speeds of nearly 70 mph.*

Claim: *Due to their incredible speed, sailfish are incredibly difficult for fishermen and predators alike to catch.*

Let's focus on our topic sentence for a moment, which provides a central claim for one of the paragraphs that would comprise an entire passage with the following central claim: *The sailfish is without peer when it comes to speed in the ocean.*

[1] Scientists have recorded sailfish at speeds of approximately 70 mph. [2] The recording tools that these scientists have used reflect the most accurate and reliable devices and methodologies available. [3] Swordfish are also fast aquatic creatures that have been recorded at high speeds. [4] The unique anatomy and physiology of the sailfish reflect a design built for achieving the amazing water speed that they have been measured to reach.

Which of the following sentences in the paragraph should be eliminated to maintain the focus of the paragraph?

A. Sentence 1

B. Sentence 2

C. Sentence 3

D. Sentence 4

Were you able to determine the sentence that's a bit off focus? **The correct answer is C.** The other sentences *directly* relate to the topic sentence (sentence 1) and maintain the focus of the paragraph. However, sentence 3 provides tangential information and should be deleted.

When you read each passage, make note of anything that seems off, including redundant words and phrases and text that seems completely off-topic or irrelevant to the central ideas of the passage. Chances are it's *not* a coincidence, and you'll come across it again when you're answering the questions. If you're already familiar with an issue and are ready for it, you'll likely save yourself some time finding the correct answer.

 Test takers who are successful on test day don't run away from challenging questions; they tackle them head on! When you confront a tough question on the SAT® exam, break it down, use your analytical skills, and hunt down the correct answer!

QUANTITATIVE INFORMATION QUESTIONS

As previously mentioned, some of the passages on the Writing and Language Test will be accompanied by an associated informational graphic, which will provide relevant quantitative information pertaining to the passage topic.

Let's refer back to our sailfish example. The following informational graphic might accompany a passage with the following central thesis: *The sailfish is without peer when it comes to speed in the ocean.*

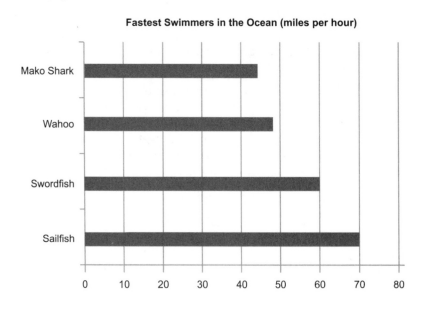

Fastest Swimmers in the Ocean (miles per hour)

The following question might appear in relation to this informational graphic:

[1] The sailfish is without peer when it comes to speed in the ocean. [2] They possess an **1** unproven ability to accelerate and achieve incredible water speeds. [3] Sailfish have been known to reach speeds of nearly 70 mph. [4] Due to their incredible speed, sailfish are quite difficult for fishermen and predators alike to catch.

1 Based on the information provided in the passage, what would be the most effective revision to the underlined text?

A. NO CHANGE

B. unloved

C. unsubstantiated

D. unrivaled

Based on the data in the informational graphic, we can see that no other aquatic creature can attain the top speed that sailfish are capable of reaching. This speed has been substantiated by the information in sentence 3, so choices A and C are incorrect. *Unloved* does not fit given the context of the sentence, so choice B is also incorrect. **The correct answer is D**—the informational graphic indicates that the speeds sailfish are capable of in water are *unrivaled*.

Be prepared to encounter at least one informational graphic on test day—these can take the form of tables, charts, graphs, or illustrations, and the information itself in the graphic can take a variety of quantitative forms. You'll be tasked with analyzing and interpreting the data provided and determining how it relates to the passage and topic.

EFFECTIVE LANGUAGE USE QUESTIONS

Writing and Language Test questions that fall into the Effective Language Use category are designed to analyze how effectively authors make key language choices to achieve a variety of important goals, which include the following:

- **Syntax:** ensures that text in each passage is coherent and arranged properly, and delivers a logical flow of thoughts and ideas

- **Precision:** ensures that information in each passage is clear, focused, and to the point

- **Concision:** ensures that each passage is free from repetition and distracting wordiness

- **Style and Tone:** ensures that each passage maintains a consistent voice, mood, and effect

Let's take a closer look at each of the core areas of Effective Language Use.

SYNTAX

Syntax refers to the appropriate arrangement of words to create well-constructed sentences in a piece of writing. Without proper syntax, your writing would be a chaotic, unintelligible mess, leaving your readers confused, bewildered, and lost.

On the Writing and Language Test, you'll be tasked with analyzing and making key decisions regarding an author's use of syntax for the passages you'll encounter. Syntax questions often require you to analyze connections between related sentences; determine how sentences can be combined to enhance cohesion, emphasis, and flow; and make revisions to improve flow and cohesion.

Let's take a look at a practice Syntax question.

Antihistamines are a type of helpful pharmaceutical **2** drug. Antihistamines serve to effectively reduce the effects of common allergic reactions, including sneezing, itching, and runny nose. These chemical marvels are designed to suppress vascular permeability, which causes fluid to release into capillaries and tissues, causing the classic runny nose and watery eyes with which many individuals suffer. Antihistamines are commonly available for over-the-counter purchase in pharmacies.

2 Which of the following answer choices most effectively combines these two sentences?

- **A.** drug and serve
- **B.** drug who, serve
- **C.** drugs they;
- **D.** Drugs serve

The first two sentences of this paragraph contain the same subject (antihistamines) and can be effectively combined to reduce wordiness and maximize word economy. The only choice that effectively does this is choice A: *Antihistamines are a type of helpful pharmaceutical drug and serve to effectively reduce the effects of common allergic reactions, including sneezing, itching, and runny nose.* **The correct answer is A.**

 On the Writing and Language Test, your goal is *not* to revise the author's perspective or point of view to align it with yours, or vice versa. Remembering this when taking the test will help you save time and avoid some tricky answer choices that simply revise the author's intended meaning.

PRECISION

Language precision is often something you quickly recognize when you encounter it in a piece of writing. When we read something that's direct, precise, and on target, it's often easy to follow, memorable, and a joy to read.

Conversely, most of us would appreciate the opportunity to avoid a piece of writing that's vague, meandering, and generally imprecise—which generally makes for a confusing and frustrating reading experience.

Precision questions on the Writing and Language Test often ask you to make decisions regarding the use of words or phrases in order to appropriately convey an author's intended meaning. Here's a sample Precision question, similar to those you may encounter on test day.

> Schools all across the United States have undertaken an intriguing initiative in recent years. In addition to completing the requisite academic coursework, they are requiring students to fulfill a certain amount of hours volunteering for a cause or charity. This **3** <u>optional</u> volunteer service can be performed at a venue that reflects a specific concern or issue that a student is passionate about. This program has both ardent supporters and vociferous critics, and only time will tell if the goals of the initiative are attained or not.

3 **A.** NO CHANGE
B. mandatory
C. exhausting
D. droll

In this question, we're being asked to make a decision regarding precise word choice. As written (choice A), the underlined word *optional* adds a confusing element to the sentence, as we were just told in the previous sentence that this volunteer service was required. Clearly, a revision to the underlined word is needed here. Choices C and D are incorrect, as the adjectives in these answer choices (*exhausting* and *droll*) are not supported by the information in the passage. The most logical word choice to describe the volunteer service, which we've established is required, is *mandatory*, so **the correct answer is B.**

CONCISION

Strong writing reflects a thorough understanding of making concise and effective points in as few words as possible. Unnecessary or repetitive words, phrases, and sentences can turn a lean and mean piece of well-structured writing into a bloated, rambling, and confusing mess.

On the Writing and Language Test, you'll likely be tested on your ability to recognize and fix issues of verbosity and word redundancy in the passages provided. These types of questions are typically focused at the sentence level; you'll be tasked with identifying and eradicating wordiness to improve the flow of sentences and, as a result, improve the passages as a whole. However, you typically don't need to analyze the entire passage to handle these types of questions.

 If a question on the test involves the option to delete text, this is often a signal that there may be issues to address involving redundancy or wordiness.

Let's tackle a sample Concision question.

> [1] What are your thoughts on lowering the legal voting age in the United States? [2] At present, the right to vote is afforded to all citizens who are at least eighteen years old. [3] Some individuals would like to lower the legal voting age to sixteen. [4] Supporters of the notion to lower the voting age want to encourage younger individuals to be more engaged in the political process, and to take their civic responsibilities as citizens more seriously. [5] Do you have an opinion about the notion of changing the legal age to vote in America? **4**

4 Which of the sentences should be deleted in order to eliminate redundancy and maximize concision?

- **A.** Sentence 2
- **B.** Sentence 3
- **C.** Sentence 4
- **D.** Sentence 5

While reading this paragraph, did you note any information repeated multiple times? Sentence 1 poses an engaging question to readers regarding lowering the legal voting age—as mentioned earlier in the chapter, this is an effective way to begin a piece of writing. However, the paragraph concludes in the same way, with a question that's essentially the same one posed at the opening. This redundancy should be eliminated, so **the correct answer is D.**

STYLE AND TONE

When a writer is plotting out a piece of writing, he or she has to think about the audience, which will help set the appropriate style and tone. When you read a piece of writing, you should be able to determine how the writer feels about the topic, and how the writer wants to make his or her readers feel. Writers employ elements of style and tone to create their intended effects.

A writer shouldn't be using the same formal style and tone in a professional letter or technical academic journal article as used in a casual e-mail or friendly letter. The following is a list of common formal and informal writing categories that you should generally be familiar with. Try to quickly get comfortable with each type.

Formal	Informal
Technical journal	Blog post
Academic paper	Entertainment magazine article
Newspaper article	Fictional story
Scientific study	Novel
Professional correspondence	Personal essay
Educational textbook	Post on social media site
Professional presentation	Friendly e-mail or tweet

Passages on the Writing and Language Test won't necessarily announce the kinds of writing they are, but you'll be able to tell if they require formal or informal language based on how they're written. On test day, you'll be tasked with recognizing the intended style and tone of a passage and ensuring that it remains appropriately consistent throughout.

The following are the sorts of logical inconsistencies that you'll need to be able to recognize and fix on the Writing and Language Test:

- Does a writer shift between an active or passive voice in the passage?
- Does the writer use—or misuse—a specific stylistic flourish to create a certain effect on the audience?
- Does a writer seem like he or she is in favor of a particular topic, and then suddenly seem to take a negative stance without rhyme or reason?
- Does a writer establish a cheerful mood, and then suddenly things get dark for no logical reason?

Let's tackle a sample Style and Tone question:

[1] The town of Valleyview met with an unexpected tragedy today. [2] The Norvell dam, which protected the town from the raging waters of the Charlestown River, burst after years of erosion and neglect. [3] The surging water flooded nearby streets, displacing several homeowners and small business owners and causing millions of dollars in damage. [4] Benjamin Lacroix, the owner of the Valleyview

Barbershop on Beacon Avenue, just celebrated his store's 25th anniversary with a huge celebration and free haircuts for everybody. Simone Castra, the mayor of Valleyview, has declared a state of emergency for the town and is leading a concerted effort to address the unfortunate events following the dam burst. **5**

5 In an effort to maintain a consistent tone and mood, the author should consider deleting which of the following sentences?

- **A.** Sentence 1
- **B.** Sentence 2
- **C.** Sentence 3
- **D.** Sentence 4

This question requires you to recognize the serious tone of the paragraph, which is discussing the tragic recent flood that hit the town of Valleyview, and to identify anything that conflicts with the somber mood of the piece. Choices A, B, and C are all appropriate given the overall tone. Choice D, which talks about a joyous and happy celebration at the Valleyview Barbershop, conflicts with the overall tone and should be deleted. **The correct answer is D.**

STANDARD ENGLISH CONVENTIONS: AN OVERVIEW

Standard English conventions are the core rules and practices that lie at the heart of writing and language. They are the collectively agreed-upon guidelines for connecting words, constructing phrases and sentences, and conveying thoughts that effectively communicate your ideas to others. It's not difficult to see why this is such an important area—and one worth testing on an exam as important as the SAT®.

NOTE: Standard English Conventions and Expression of Ideas questions *do not* appear separately on the exam—these question types are blended together in the writing passages you'll encounter on test day.

Standard English Conventions questions on the Writing and Language Test fall into three main categories: Sentence Structure, Conventions of Punctuation, and Conventions of Usage.

Some of the questions you'll encounter will refer to underlined portions of text within the passages; others will ask you to consider adding, eliminating, or revising text within the passage to align the writing with the core rules of standard English writing—always with the goal of improving each passage and making it a more appropriate and effective piece of written communication.

We'll now take an in-depth look at the topics that comprise each of these three main categories, along with advice and strategies for tackling the types of questions you can expect to encounter on test day.

SENTENCE STRUCTURE QUESTIONS

Sentence Structure questions focus on identifying and fixing issues involving sentence construction and sentence formation. You can expect to encounter questions involving parallel structure; modifier placement; sentence boundaries including grammatically incomplete and ineffective sentences; inappropriate pronoun shifts; and inappropriate shifts in voice, mood, and verb tense. It may sound intimidating, but really, these questions simply will assess your ability to tackle concepts you've covered throughout your life—both in English/language arts classes and in the writing you do in your personal life—including letters, e-mails, texts, notes, and more. We all know the difference between a well-constructed sentence and a rambling, incoherent one and can tell which is more effective.

Let's take a look at a sample Sentence Structure question that you might encounter on test day:

> Dominic began his first day as a volunteer at the Cincinnati Zoo. He has been assigned to maintain the popular reptile exhibit. His will be cleaning the reptile tanks, fed the animals in the exhibit, and providing information and directions to customers. He's excited to be a part of the zoo's staff.

6 **A.** NO CHANGE
   B. feeding the animals
   C. feed the animals
   D. had fed the animals

This is a common parallel structure question. Sentences with correct parallel structure have all of their parts moving in the same tense and direction. While reading this paragraph, you may have noticed something awkward when you reached the underlined portion of the sentence. The verb *fed* is written in the *past* tense, while the other action words in the sentence (*cleaning* and *providing*) are in what is called the *future continuous* tense, reflecting the fact that Dominic will perform these activities regularly. The fact that these verbs don't have parallel construction is a problem, and here it's your job to find and fix such sentence structure issues.

Since the paragraph established that these responsibilities will be a regular part of Dominic's volunteer job moving forward, we can determine that the future continuous tense is correct for the action that occurs. If you know the correct verb form, select the answer choice and move on. If you need some more time, scan the answer choices. Choice C is the present tense and is incorrect—Dominic is not performing these activities at present. Choice D is the past tense and is also incorrect—these are not activities that Dominic has performed in the past.

The other two verbs end in *–ing*; perhaps this is a clue that our verb in focus needs the same treatment? *Feeding* (choice B) is indeed the correct tense of the verb. If you need to make sure, plug it into the sentence and check:

> His tasks include cleaning the reptile tanks, *feeding the animals* in the exhibit, and providing information and directions to customers.

The correct answer is B, and you can move on with confidence!

Bottom line: Following the rules of good sentence construction and formation helps ensure that your thoughts and ideas are properly communicated to others. The makers of the SAT® exam recognize how important of a skill this is, and the test is designed to make sure your skills in this area are well honed.

The questions you can expect to encounter will measure your ability to understand the relationships between and among clauses, the placement of modifiers, and shifts in construction. You'll also have to spot and fix fragments, run-ons, and incorrect sentence shifts—in pronouns, mood, voice, and more.

That's a lot to know for test day, but we cover it all in this chapter, along with comprehensive, targeted practice and review, to get you confident and ready.

CLAUSES

Just as you can't have a sentence without a subject and verb that express a complete thought, you can't have a sentence without clauses.

We'll let you in on a little secret: A subject and verb that express a complete thought is a clause. It's an **independent clause**, because it can stand on its own.

> **Independent clause:** *The vase falls.*

A clause that *can't* stand on its own, even though it has its own subject and verb, is a **dependent,** or **subordinate, clause**.

> **Subordinate clause:** *whenever the table shakes.*

A subordinate clause *needs* to be paired with an independent clause to be part of a complete sentence, like this:

> *The vase falls whenever the table shakes.*

There are four different sentence structures that you'll commonly encounter. Notice that each one *always* includes at least one independent clause.

A **simple sentence** has only one independent clause:

- *The faucet drips.*
- *The ceiling leaks.*

A **compound sentence** has two independent clauses that are typically joined in one of two ways:

1. With a **conjunction** (for example *if, and*, and *but*) to connect the clauses:
   - *The faucet drips, and the ceiling leaks.*

2. With a **semicolon:**
   - *The faucet drips; the ceiling leaks.*

A **complex sentence** joins an independent clause and a subordinate clause:

- *Whenever she does the dishes, the ceiling leaks.*

A **compound-complex sentence** has at least two independent clauses and one or more subordinate clauses:

- *Whenever she does the dishes, the faucet drips and the ceiling leaks.*

- *Whenever she does the dishes, the faucet drips; once the floor gets wet, the ceiling leaks.*

Be on the lookout for comma splices. A semicolon is the only punctuation that can join clauses without a conjunction. Using only a comma is known as a *comma splice*—and it is wrong.

CONJUNCTIONS

You may have noticed the important role that **conjunctions** play in various sentence structures. They are the words that connect clauses and phrases in sentences and help writers clearly and effectively communicate sentences with multiple thoughts and ideas.

When a conjunction joins independent clauses of equal importance, it is known as a **coordinating conjunction.**

For example:

The brownies were fantastic, but the cake was burnt.

In this compound sentence, *but* is the coordinating conjunction. If you divide the sentence before and after the coordinating conjunction, you will still have two independent clauses of equal importance:

For example:

The brownies were fantastic.

The cake was burnt.

If a conjunction joins a subordinate clause to an independent clause, it is known as a **subordinating conjunction.**

The vacation that I didn't want to take was actually amazing.

In this sentence, the subordinate clause is *that I didn't want to take*, which is not a complete sentence on its own. The subordinating conjunction is *that*.

Here are some other common coordinating and subordinating conjunctions that you can expect to encounter on the Writing and Language Test:

Coordinating Conjunctions			
and	for	or	yet
but	nor	so	

Subordinating Conjunctions		
after	since	whereas
although	that	wherever
as	though	whether
because	unless	which
before	until	while
even though	when	who
if	whenever	why

FRAGMENTS AND RUN-ONS

Two of the most common sentence structure errors are **fragments** and **run-ons**—be on the lookout for these on test day, and make sure you know how to fix them.

A **fragment** is a piece of a sentence and is not complete on its own.

For example:

Racing through the woods.

Who or what was racing through the woods? We'll never know until we fix this sentence fragment. This sentence needs a subject:

The hungry squirrel was racing through the woods.

Mystery solved! The subject-verb pair *The hungry squirrel was* rescued this sentence from the confusing fragment heap.

 Sometimes, writers intentionally break the rules and use fragments and run-on sentences creatively to achieve a particular effect, typically referred to as **creative license.** However, as far as the SAT® Writing and Language Test is concerned, fragments and run-on sentences are always wrong and need to be fixed.

Run-on sentences are the opposite of fragments, but they are just as incorrect. Much like the comma splice, run-ons occur when two independent clauses are incorrectly joined. In the case of a run-on sentence, the punctuation is missing.

For example:

The hungry squirrel was racing through the woods he was searching for acorns.

This run-on sentence needs the correct internal punctuation to join its first and second parts. We have several options to choose from to fix this, but let's try a semi-colon:

The hungry squirrel was racing through the woods; he was searching for acorns.

Now it's a clearly expressed thought!

MODIFIERS

Modifiers such as **adjectives, adverbs,** descriptive phrases, and clauses need to be placed correctly in sentences. Otherwise, you can end up with some *very* bewildering thoughts.

Two common modifier issues that you can expect to encounter on the Writing and Language Test are misplaced modifiers and dangling modifiers. Let's examine them more closely.

A **misplaced modifier** creates confusion because it's not placed next to the word it's supposed to modify.

For example:

Alice walked across the room because she didn't want to disturb her baby sister resting in the room below hers carefully.

In this sentence, the modifier *carefully* is not where it should be. In fact, its placement makes it seem as though *her baby sister* was resting carefully. How do you rest carefully? You have to be conscious and careful about where information is placed in sentences.

The adverb *carefully* would be put to better use modifying *walked*:

Alice walked carefully across the room because she didn't want to disturb her baby sister resting in the room below hers.

Excellent! In this sentence, the modifier *carefully* is no longer misplaced.

Dangling modifiers are often more confusing than misplaced ones. The object they are meant to modify is not in the sentence. Take a look at this sentence:

Excited about the trip, the suitcases were stacked by the door.

The modifier in this sentence is *Excited about the trip*. But there's a problem: We don't know exactly *who* was excited about the trip. This sentence's lack of a subject leaves the modifier dangling without anything to modify. A subject needs to be added to give the modifier something to modify, as follows:

Excited about the trip, Frankie made sure the suitcases were stacked by the door.

The addition of the subject *Frankie* gives the phrase *excited about the trip* something to modify.

On the test, make sure you choose the right subject for the modifier to modify. Read the passage very carefully so you can make the best selection.

PARALLEL STRUCTURE

Sentences with correct parallel structure have all of their parts moving cohesively and in the same tense and direction. You can't place a word or phrase that's going into the past alongside one that's moving into the future, for example. Parallel structure crumbles when groups of words combine different types of phrases, clauses, and parts of speech.

For example:

> On Friday afternoon, I will finish my homework, mow the lawn, and went to the movies.

This sentence begins by describing things that are going to happen in the future—*On Friday afternoon*, to be precise. Everything is smooth until that final phrase: *went to the movies*. It's written in the *past tense*, which violates the parallel structure of a sentence that is otherwise written in the *future tense*. Let's take a look at a revised version of the sentence:

> On Friday afternoon, I will finish my homework, mow the lawn, and go to the movies.

This version corrects the parallel structure by putting the phrase *went to the movies* into the future tense (*go to the movies*), where it belongs.

A sentence *does not* need to be written entirely in the same tense to be correct. It just needs to be structured correctly.

For example, the sentence *I ate a burrito yesterday, and I am going to eat a sandwich tonight* does not violate the rules of good parallel structure.

CORRELATIVE CONJUNCTIONS

You need to be mindful of parallel structure when dealing with correlative conjunctions. These are conjunctions that work in pairs: *either… or, neither… nor*, and *not only… but also*. Mixing correlative conjunctions is another way to violate parallel structure.

For example:

> Neither the suit or the hat matches my sense of style.

Oops! *Neither* indicates a negative, and *or* indicates a positive. So, what does this sentence mean? Do the suit and hat suit the writer's very particular tastes or don't they? We'll only know if the parallel structure is repaired:

Neither the suit nor the hat matches my sense of style.

Oh, this person doesn't like the two pieces of clothing. Good to know!

CONVENTIONS OF PUNCTUATION QUESTIONS

You're undoubtedly aware of the importance of good punctuation in writing. Without it, a piece of writing can devolve into a confusing mess.

Conventions of Punctuation questions focus on recognizing and adhering to the rules and standards of appropriate punctuation. These questions will test your ability to tackle a wide array of familiar punctuation issues—including the rules of within-sentence and end-of-sentence punctuation, plural and possessive forms of pronouns and nouns, proper use of nonrestrictive and parenthetical items, items in simple and complex lists, and unnecessary or superfluous punctuation.

Let's take a look at a sample Conventions of Punctuation question that you might encounter on test day:

> Valerie had to travel from Baltimore to Chicago for an important work conference this morning. Her plane landed safely, and she arrived at the airport on time. After retrieving her baggage, she needed to find a taxi that could take her to her hotel room. She went up to the information desk and asked the clerk, **7** "Where can I catch a taxi to my hotel!" The clerk gave her clear and careful directions to the nearest taxi stand.

 A. NO CHANGE

    B. "Where can I catch a taxi to my hotel."

    C. "Where can I catch a taxi to my hotel"

    D. "Where can I catch a taxi to my hotel?"

This question type, involving end-of-sentence punctuation, is found often on the Writing and Language Test. You'll need to know which type of ending punctuation is appropriate for a wide variety of sentences. Let's review the underlined quote in the paragraph. If you know what type of punctuation is needed here, that's great—select the answer choice and move on. If you need some more help, let's keep going. The appearance of the word *where* at the beginning of the quote gives us a valuable context clue—it tells us that we're dealing with a question. Now we know that we'll need a question mark to properly punctuate this sentence. Scan the answer choices, and find the correctly punctuated version. **The correct answer is D.** If you need to make sure, plug it into the sentence and check:

> *She went up to the information desk and asked the clerk, "Where can I catch a taxi to my hotel?"*

That's correct, and you can move on with confidence!

You can expect to encounter a wide array of punctuation issues within the writing passages—it will be your job to identify and fix them appropriately. This section covers the most frequently tested punctuation concepts—master these and make the most of the practice later in this chapter to help you reach your SAT® score goals.

END-OF-SENTENCE PUNCTUATION

Every sentence must eventually come to an end, which means that the one form of punctuation you will *always* see in every complete sentence is **end-of-sentence punctuation.**

These are probably the very first punctuation marks you learned about:

- **The period (.):** good for ending most declarative sentences
- **The exclamation point (!):** used for ending exclamations, which indicate extreme excitement
- **The question mark (?):** absolutely necessary for ending questions

 Make sure you know the right punctuation for the situation. A question can be asked excitedly, but it still needs to end with a question mark, not an exclamation point.

End-of-sentence marks are usually pretty straightforward. You probably already know that you shouldn't end a question with a period or an exclamation with a question mark.

These marks become slightly trickier when **quotation marks** are added to the punctuation mix. End-of-sentence punctuation usually belongs *inside* the quotation marks:

> Belle asked, "When should we arrive at the party today?"

Exceptions to the rules do occur, so be careful. For example, when the quotation marks indicate a title, and placing end-of-sentence punctuation within the marks might give the false impression that the mark is part of the title, then the punctuation mark is placed outside the quotation marks, as in this example:

> Have you seen the new movie, "No Time for Tomorrow"?

COMMAS

Let's continue with one of the most commonly misused forms of punctuation. Some writers overuse **commas,** and using them without rhyme or reason can make your sentences awkward or confusing.

Here's an example of a sentence with way too many commas:

> After, Jacob finished the final exam he breathed, a huge sigh of relief stretched, his arms and smiled.

It's quite a mouthful, and it's a bit difficult to figure out what's happening. Let's take a look at the corrected version:

> After Jacob finished the final exam, he breathed a huge sigh of relief, stretched his arms, and smiled.

This version is much easier to follow!

While there is the odd situation in which the use of a comma is up to the writer, there are almost always very definite rules for comma use. Let's look at some of the most important ones.

Introductory or Transitional Words and Phrases

Commas should be used to offset introductory words or phrases from the words that follow, as in the following example:

> <u>Unfortunately,</u> the headphones that Stella purchased online didn't work when they arrived.

Compound Sentences

Compound sentences consist of two independent clauses, which means that both parts of the sentence would be complete sentences on their own. Each independent clause in a compound sentence with a conjunction needs a comma to separate it.

For example:

> Gheeta had vegetable fajitas for lunch in the school cafeteria, but Laird doesn't like vegetables.

Gheeta had vegetable fajitas for lunch in the school cafeteria is the first independent clause. *Laird doesn't like vegetables* is the second independent clause. The conjunction is *but* and a comma is used to separate those clauses correctly.

Nonrestrictive Phrases

A nonrestrictive phrase is not essential to the meaning of the sentence. It should be separated with one comma if it comes at the beginning or end of the sentence and two commas if it is placed in the middle.

Read this sentence:

> My new silk sheets, which I received as a birthday present, are too small for my bed.

This sentence would still make sense without the phrase *which I received as a birthday present*. It would read as *My new silk sheets are too small for my bed*, which is a perfectly fine sentence. This means the phrase is nonrestrictive and should be enclosed in commas, like it is in the previous example. However, if that phrase were restrictive—or essential to the meaning of the sentence—no commas would be needed. (Example: *The new silk sheets I received as a birthday present are too small for my bed.*)

Series

Each item in a simple series or list should be separated by a comma.

For example:

> *Saul purchased a medium coffee, bagel, and home fries at the coffee shop yesterday.*

In this sentence, a comma also precedes the conjunction *and* (also known as a **serial** or **Oxford comma**), although this is not a hard-and-fast rule. Some writers prefer not to use that extra comma. So, the following sentence is also technically correct:

> *Saul purchased a medium coffee, bagel and home fries at the coffee shop yesterday.*

 The decision to place a comma before the conjunction in a series of items is up to the writer. Passages on the test use the comma before the conjunction, but you will not be expected to answer questions about such situations without concrete rules.

For more complex lists of items, **semicolons** are often used, as in the following example:

> *Each day after school, Lena goes to softball practice; feeds her dog, little sister, and parakeet; and brings her laundry, homework, and clarinet to her uncle's house.*

When multiple verbs refer to multiple items in a series within a single sentence, you can see how semicolons can come in handy to keep things organized.

Appositives

An appositive is a phrase that describes a noun. An appositive contains a noun or pronoun, and often one or more modifiers, and it appears directly before or after the noun it describes. When they are not essential to identifying the noun they modify, appositives need to be separated with commas.

For example:

> *Bruce, my new ferret, is a cute and furry pet.*

In this sentence, the appositive *my new ferret* is the appositive of the proper noun *Bruce*, and commas are used to separate it correctly.

If the appositive is essential to identifying the noun it modifies, no comma is needed.

For example:

> *My new ferret Bruce is a cute and furry pet.*

In this sentence, *Bruce* acts as the appositive for the common noun *ferret* and is essential to identifying which ferret is being referred to. No commas are needed.

Quotations

When quoting a complete phrase that someone said, quotation marks are needed and one or more commas are required to separate it from the rest of the sentence. See how the commas are used in these examples:

Bella declared, "That song was the best one I've heard all summer."

"That song was the best one I've heard all summer," Bella declared.

"That song," Bella declared, "was the best one I've heard all summer."

However, if that quotation includes end-of-sentence punctuation, a comma is not needed at the end of it.

For example:

"That song was the best one I've heard all summer!," Bella declared. (***Incorrect!***)

"That song was the best one I've heard all summer!" Bella declared. (***Correct!***)

APOSTROPHES AND POSSESSION

Apostrophes are most often used to indicate that a word is a contraction or to show possession in a sentence.

The correct use of apostrophes in **contractions** mostly depends on placing the apostrophe in the right place within a word:

Ca'nt (***Incorrect!***)

Can't (***Correct!***)

You'll also need to recognize when a word that looks like a contraction is not a contraction:

it's (***a contraction of it is***)

its (***the possessive form of it***)

Using apostrophes in possessive words is a little trickier. For the most part, the apostrophe will be placed before the letter -*s*:

Diane's purse

However, if the possessive word ends with an *s*, the apostrophe belongs after the -*s*:

the cactus' needles

This rule is different when a specifically named person is doing the possessing. For people whose names end in *s*, an apostrophe and an extra *s* is required:

Cyrus's new skateboard

When more than one noun is doing the possessing, only the last noun in the pair or list needs an apostrophe:

Dorian and Ella's sleepover party

When more than one noun is doing the possessing of different things, both nouns in the pair or list need an apostrophe:

Bill's and Alicia's paychecks

COLONS

Colons are typically used to introduce a list or series of examples:

Jeremy bought everything he needed for his upcoming backpacking trip: a canteen, hiking boots, a sleeping bag, and a tent.

Colons are also used to offset and emphasize an example:

My favorite novel offers a powerful lesson: revenge is often unexpected.

They can also be placed after a salutation in a letter:

To whom it may concern:

Colons can be used to separate a title from a subtitle in a piece of work like a book or movie:

Space Voyager: The Sequel

However, colons should *not* be used to separate objects and verbs or prepositions and objects:

Incorrect: *This new game is: boring.*

Incorrect: *Some ingredients that taste great on pizza are: pepperoni, mushroom, olives, and others.*

SEMICOLONS

Semicolons can be used in place of conjunctions in compound sentences, joining the independent clauses just as *and, or, but,* or *because* would:

I was terrified after watching the scary movie; I barely slept at all last night.

As previously mentioned, semicolons are also used in complex lists that contain items with commas to keep all those commas from becoming confusing.

This anniversary cake contains only the tastiest ingredients: chocolate, which I bought at the gourmet store; raspberries, which I grew in my yard; and fresh vanilla, which I got from the best market in town.

Dashes

Much like commas, dashes tend to get overused and misused. A big problem with dashes is that they're almost never *absolutely necessary* according to the rules of mechanics, so a lot of writers just aren't sure what to do with them. You're about to become one of the lucky few who know when to use them!

Like the colon, a dash can be used to offset and emphasize a single example:

> *My best friend in the entire world is loyal, fun, and brave—my dog, Oliver.*

Dashes are also useful for indicating a pause or interruption in dialogue, and two dashes can be used to separate an example or examples in the middle of a sentence:

> *The movie contained everything I like—action, intrigue, and romance—and I couldn't stop watching it.*

Parentheses

Sometimes, a few extra details are needed to make a sentence as informative as it can be—but those details aren't always easy to cram into the natural flow of the sentence. In such cases, parentheses are in order. Parentheses are often used to enclose additional examples that tend to be a little less relevant to a sentence than the ones you'd place between dashes:

> *My coworker Doug Lane (who is retiring at the end of the year) is delivering a major presentation to the senior staff this afternoon.*

Unnecessary Punctuation

Making sure that a piece of writing is free from unnecessary or incorrect punctuation is important to ensure that it contains no confusing errors and effectively conveys its intended meaning, thoughts, and ideas. Just as missing punctuation can lead to awkwardness and confusion, unnecessary punctuation can have the same effect. Let's look at an example:

Once, the wolf reached the peak of the high, cliff it howled at, the slowly, setting sun.

Don't be concerned if you had trouble reading this sentence. Did the wolf just howl once? What exactly is "the peak of the high"? The meaning and flow of this sentence is clearly being disrupted by its inappropriate punctuation. Its abundance of unnecessary commas makes it confusing and obscures its intended meaning. Commas are among the most overused—and misused—types of internal punctuation, and on test day you should always be on the lookout for unnecessary commas and other forms of punctuation. Let's look at a corrected version of our example:

Once the wolf reached the peak of the high cliff, it howled at the slowly setting sun.

This version is *much* easier to follow and understand.

CONVENTIONS OF USAGE QUESTIONS

Following the rules of sound grammar and usage is essential—in school, in life beyond the classroom, and on the SAT® exam. Conventions of Usage questions will test your ability to tackle some extremely important writing and language concepts—including the proper use of possessives and determiners, subject-verb agreement, logical comparisons, recognizing conventional English language expressions and their appropriate use, proper pronoun use, and correctly identifying and using frequently confused words.

Let's take a look at a sample Conventions of Usage question that you might encounter on test day:

The athletes stretch their limbs and prepare for the hurdle race. They take their positions on the track, size up the competition, and look out at the cheering crowd. The group of racers tense up and wait for the starting gun to fire. The gun fires, and the racers sprint toward the first hurdle. The fastest racer **8** leap over the hurdle first and lands on the other side. The other racers follow right behind. We'll know who the winning athlete is before long.

---

8 **A.** NO CHANGE

    B. leaps over

    C. leapt over

    D. leaping over

This is a common Subject-Verb Agreement question. Sentences with correct agreement have their subjects and verbs aligned in both form and tense. Let's take a look at the underlined portion of the sentence. A quick scan of the answer choices shows us that a variety of forms of the verb *to leap* are on display. This signals to us that it's our job to determine the correct verb form needed here. We first need to determine *who* or *what* is performing the action in order to determine the appropriate verb form for the sentence.

Here, the *fastest racer*, a singular noun, is presently leaping over a hurdle, so the present tense of the singular form of the verb *to leap* is needed.

If you know the correct verb form needed here, select the answer choice and move on. If you need some more time, let's move forward. Scan the sentence and see if we can find any more helpful clues. If you're looking carefully, you'll notice that another verb, *lands*, is also in this sentence. It isn't underlined, so we can safely assume that it's in the correct form. Scan the answer choices and see if you can find the correct singular present verb form for *to leap*. For this example, **the correct answer is B.** If you need to make sure, plug it into the sentence and check:

> The fastest racer leaps over the hurdle first and lands on the other side.

Everything is in agreement. You've found your answer.

These questions can appear in a variety of formats on the test—some will be obvious and others will be more subtle. This section covers the most essential usage concepts— the ones that you'll need to know and use on test day. Use the practice and review in this chapter to sharpen your skills and get test ready.

 While incorrect punctuation won't necessarily make a sentence sound wrong, poor grammar almost certainly will. Thinking about how sentences sound can help you select the best answers to usage questions.

Nouns

The subject of any sentence is most often a noun: the person, place, or thing performing the action that the sentence describes. Some Conventions of Usage questions on the Writing and Language Test will likely involve subjects of sentences, often in terms of how they agree with verbs or pronouns.

Before we discuss how nouns interact with other words, let's look at some specific noun forms.

Plural Nouns

The nice thing about nouns is that they really only have two general forms: singular and plural.

1. The **singular** form is the most basic: *goose*, *bird*, *otter*, *lampshade*, *mango*, and *mushroom*—these are all nouns in their most basic singular form.

2. Making a singular noun **plural** is often as simple as adding the letter s to the end (for example: *cat–cats*). Plural nouns get tricky only when they are *irregular*— hard-and-fast rules for creating irregular plural nouns are often tough to apply

to a language as complicated as English. We can't simply say that you're *always* safe adding *-es* to the end of all nouns that end in *-o* to make them plural. For example, the plural of *avocado* is *avocados*.

While you're not expected to memorize every single irregular verb for the SAT® exam, it's a good idea to familiarize yourself with some of the most common. Review the following table before test day to make sure you have a grasp on these verbs.

COMMON IRREGULAR PLURAL NOUNS		
Noun Ends With	**Creating the Plural Form**	**Examples**
-f	change *f* to *v* and add *–es*	**singular:** calf **plural:** calves
		singular: elf **plural:** elves
		singular: half **plural:** halves
		singular: leaf **plural:** leaves
		singular: shelf **plural:** shelves
		singular: thief **plural:** thieves
		singular: wolf **plural:** wolves
-fe	change *f* to *v* and add *–s*	**singular:** knife **plural:** knives
		singular: life **plural:** lives
		singular: wife **plural:** wives
-is	change to *–es*	**singular:** axis **plural:** axes
		singular: analysis **plural:** analyses
		singular: parenthesis **plural:** parentheses

COMMON IRREGULAR PLURAL NOUNS		
Noun Ends With	**Creating the Plural Form**	**Examples**
-o	add –es	**singular:** echo **plural:** echoes **singular:** hero **plural:** heroes **singular:** potato **plural:** potatoes **singular:** tomato **plural:** tomatoes
-ouse	change to -ice	**singular:** louse **plural:** lice **singular:** mouse **plural:** mice
-ss	add -es	**singular:** class **plural:** classes **singular:** boss **plural:** bosses
-us	change to -i	**singular:** alumnus **plural:** alumni **singular:** fungus **plural:** fungi

There are a few other variations of irregular plural nouns that do not involve changing the last letter or two of the singular form. Fortunately, most of these should be very familiar to you.

Nouns that require -ee- to be changed to -oo- for their plural form:

singular: foot	**plural:** feet
singular: goose	**plural:** geese
singular: tooth	**plural:** teeth

Nouns that require the addition or substitution of -en for their plural form:

singular: child	**plural:** children
singular: man	**plural:** men
singular: ox	**plural:** oxen
singular: woman	**plural:** women

Finally, there are the nouns that require no change whatsoever to become plural:

singular: deer	plural: deer
singular: fish	plural: fish
singular: offspring	plural: offspring
singular: series	plural: series
singular: sheep	plural: sheep
singular: species	plural: species

Collective Nouns

Collective nouns are interesting because they have some of the flavor of plural nouns since they seem to describe more than one thing.

For example:

- *A bunch of ants in a* **colony**
- *A group of buffaloes in a* **herd**
- *Several puppies in a* **litter**

However, while the individual nouns in these collections are plural (*ants*, *buffaloes*, *puppies*), the collections themselves are singular (*colony*, *herd*, *litter*). This means that collective nouns must *always* be treated as singular nouns. This will be particularly important when we deal with subject-verb agreement and noun-pronoun agreement in the next section.

Familiarize yourself with some common collective nouns. Remember, all of these nouns are singular, not plural:

army	corporation	flock	public
audience	council	group	school
band	department	herd	senate
board	faculty	jury	society
committee	family	majority	team
company	firm	navy	unit

AGREEMENT

When words in a sentence agree, things tend to go smoothly. When they don't, there can be trouble. You can ensure that the elements in sentences don't clash by recognizing when they are—and aren't—in agreement.

Subjects and verbs need to agree in terms of number. The same is true of pronouns and antecedents, which also need to agree in terms of gender.

Subject/Verb Agreement

Every complete sentence has a subject and a verb.

- The subject is the noun doing the action.
- The verb is the action that the subject is doing.

Simple, right? Actually, it can be—a sentence with just a subject and a verb can be really simple:

The wolf howls.

That sentence only has three words, but it's still a complete sentence because it has a subject and a verb. Just as important, the subject and verb agree: the singular subject *wolf* agrees with the singular verb *howls.* (That's right: The verb is singular even though it ends with the letter -*s*.)

Determining whether or not subjects and verbs are in agreement can get a little more complicated in sentences with compound subjects:

The wolf and the coyote howl.

Neither *wolf* nor *coyote* ends with an *s*, so they may not look plural, but they work together as a **compound subject** when joined with a conjunction (*and*). This means that they require a plural verb and, as you may have guessed, the plural verb does not end in an extra -*s*.

However, if the conjunction were *or* or *nor*, a singular verb would be required:

Neither the wolf nor the coyote howls.

Once again, the compound subject and verb are in agreement.

Subject-verb agreement can get confusing when there is a word or phrase between the subject and verb. Make sure you have identified the *entire* subject and verb correctly before figuring out whether or not they agree.

When dealing with collective nouns, the agreement rule depends on what the collective noun is doing. If every member of the collective noun is doing the exact same thing, it is operating as a single unit and the verb should be singular:

The committee meets on Tuesdays.

However, if all the members of that collective noun are doing their own things, those members should be specified and a plural verb is required:

After the meeting, the committee return to their offices.

NOTE: To avoid the confusion of deciding when to use plural or singular verbs with collective nouns, writers often force the verb to be plural by adding *members* or *members of* to the sentence:

After the meeting, the committee members return to their offices.

Pronoun/Antecedent Agreement

Pronouns and antecedents also need to play nice. A pronoun replaces a specific noun. Its antecedent is the noun the pronoun replaces. Since it would sound clumsy to say *Sara mows Sara's lawn*, most writers would replace the second *Sara* with a pronoun:

Sara mows her lawn.

Much better, right? In this sentence, *Sara* is the antecedent and the pronoun is *her*, a female pronoun. Both are in agreement in this sentence. It is also singular, which is appropriate since Sara is only one woman.

Now, if the sentence read *Sara mows his lawn* and we know that Sara is a woman, it would lack pronoun-antecedent agreement in terms of gender (unless, of course, if Sara is mowing some guy's lawn). If it read *Sara mows their lawn*, it would sound as if Sara is mowing a lawn owned by two or more people other than herself.

However, *their* would be necessary in a sentence with a **compound antecedent.** For example, maybe Sara co-owns her lawn with a friend named Ginnie. Then the sentence could read *Sara and Ginnie mow their lawn*. Compound antecedents are a bit more complicated when the conjunction is *or* or *nor* instead of *and*. In such cases, you will select your pronoun based on which antecedent it is nearest:

1. *Neither my friend nor my sons brought their coolers to the baseball game.*
2. *Neither my sons nor my friend brought his cooler to the baseball game.*

Both of these sentences are written correctly. Since the plural antecedent *sons* is closer to the pronoun in sentence 1, the plural pronoun *their* is required. Since the singular antecedent *friend* is closer to the pronoun in sentence 2, the singular pronoun *his* is required.

Now, if your antecedent is a collective noun, selecting the right pronoun depends on what the collective noun is doing and how it is doing it. If every member of the collective noun is doing the exact same thing as a single unit, the singular pronoun is needed:

*The lacrosse team faced **its** rival effectively.*

In this example, everyone on the lacrosse team is playing against the same rival, and the singular pronoun *its* is used correctly. However, if all of the members of that team are doing their own things, a plural pronoun is in order:

*The lacrosse team put on **their** uniforms quickly.*

Selecting Pronouns

Selecting appropriate pronouns, given the context of the sentences they will appear in, is another challenge you should be prepared to face on the Writing and Language Test.

Perspective will be a factor when figuring out the best way to use pronouns on test day. Let's look at a few essential rules:

- A **first-person pronoun** (*I, me, we, us*) is necessary when a writer is referring to herself or himself.

- A **second-person pronoun** (*you*) is needed when the writer is addressing the reader.

- A **third-person pronoun** (she, he, her, him, they, them) is needed when the pronoun refers to a third person who is neither writing nor reading the passage.

When sentences pair pronouns with nouns, choosing the right pronoun can be tricky. Which of the following examples is correct?

Wesley and I went to the movies.

Wesley and me went to the movies.

In such cases, try removing the noun and saying the sentence with just the pronoun: *I went to the movies* (**correct!**); *me went to the movies* (**incorrect!**). Chances are that the wrong pronoun will now seem more obvious to you.

Relative Clauses

Relative clauses are like adjectives: They exist to describe. Restrictive relative clauses cannot stand on their own. You can recognize a relative clause from the presence of a relative pronoun.

The relative pronouns *who, whom, whose,* and *that* all refer to people; the relative pronouns *that* and *which* refer to places and things.

The relative clauses in the following sentences are underlined:

> Mrs. Moritz, <u>who lives in the apartment complex across the street from mine,</u> just won the lottery.

> Alaska, <u>which is where we plan to visit next year,</u> is the largest state in the United States.

Reflexive and Interrogative Pronouns

When a subject needs a pronoun to refer to itself, a **reflexive pronoun** fits the bill. In fact, *itself* is a reflexive pronoun, as is any pronoun that ends with *self* or *selves*.

- There are five singular reflexive pronouns: *myself, yourself, himself, herself, itself*.
- There are three plural reflexive pronouns: *ourselves, yourselves, themselves*.

To interrogate is to question, and **interrogative pronouns** are used to ask questions.

- There are five main interrogative pronouns: *whose, who,* and *whom* refer to people exclusively; *what* refers to things exclusively; and *which* can refer to people or things.

Who vs. Whom

A common confusion regarding interrogative pronouns is when to use *who* and when to use *whom*.

- *Who* is used as the **subject** of a question (Example: *Who wants pizza for dinner tonight?*)
- *Whom* is used as the **object** of a question (Example: *To whom am I speaking?*).

The addition of the suffix *-ever* also creates six less common interrogative pronouns: *whatever, whichever, whoever, whomever, whosoever,* and *whomsoever*.

Possessive Pronouns

Apostrophes are used when indicating that a noun possesses something. More often than not, you can just add an apostrophe and an *-s* to the end of a word to make it possessive:

*That globe is **June's**.*

*There is a used spatula in **Helen's** sink.*

The extra *-s* is not necessary with a possessive noun that already ends in -s but is not someone's name:

*The **lions'** cubs played in the grass.*

*Those **plates'** designs are really beautiful.*

Pronouns, however, usually have their very own forms to show possession. Since pronouns such as *his, her, its, their, my, mine, yours, their,* and *theirs* already show possession, they don't need an apostrophe or an extra *-s*:

*The bookmark is **mine**.*

***Their** aunt is coming to the craft store with us.*

The only pronouns that do need that apostrophe and extra *-s* are *anybody, anyone, everybody, everyone, no one,* and *nobody*:

***Anybody's** guess is as good as mine.*

***Everybody's** time should be spent helping others.*

 Remember that *it's* is *not* the possessive form of *it*; it is a contraction of *it is.*

VERB TENSE

Verbs are words that refer to action, and their **tense** indicates *when* that action happened.

- Did the action already happen? If so, then the verb is in the **past tense.**
- Are you still waiting for the action to happen? If so, then the verb is in the **future tense.**

Past, present, and future are the most basic points in time. However, there are quite a few more than three verb tenses. Let's take a quick look at possible verb tenses:

- **Simple present tense** indicates an action happening now: *I am here.*

- **Present progressive tense** indicates an action happening now that will continue into the future: *I am walking.*

- **Present perfect progressive tense** indicates an unfinished action: *I have been working all day.*

- **Present perfect simple tense** indicates an action that occurred in the past but continues to be relevant: *I have never eaten lentils.*

- **Past perfect simple tense** indicates an action that occurred in the past but is now complete: *When Sherri woke up yesterday morning, she realized that she had missed her dental appointment.*

- **Past simple tense** indicates an action that happened already: *I laughed at his joke.*

- **Past progressive tense** pairs a past tense verb with a continuous verb ending in *-ing*: *I was laughing.*

- **Past perfect progressive tense** reflects on an ongoing action from the past: *By the 1990s, hip-hop had been a popular form of music for several years.*

- **Future simple tense** indicates an action that will happen later: *I will be at work by 9:00 a.m.*

- **Future progressive tense** indicates an action that will happen later and continue: *I will be volunteering all day on Sunday.*

- **Future perfect simple tense** indicates the completion of an action that will happen later: *I will have finished vacuuming the bedroom by noon today.*

- **Future perfect progressive tense** indicates an incomplete action that will happen later: *I will have been cleaning for four hours by the time my parents arrive.*

ADJECTIVES AND ADVERBS

As we've already established, the only completely essential elements of a sentence are its subject and verb.

For example, look at the following sentence:

The jaguar prowls.

Once again, this is a complete sentence. But is it a particularly *interesting* sentence? Writing a sentence with nothing but a subject and a verb is like making soup with nothing but water and tomatoes. Where are the other flavors, the words that give a sentence some unique and memorable character?

In a sentence, **adjectives** (words that describe nouns) and **adverbs** (words that describe verbs) add some extra sentence flavor. Think of them as the spices of a sentence.

Let's add some spice to our previous example:

The stealthy jaguar prowls silently.

Now there's a sentence that paints a more vivid picture! The adjective *stealthy* shows us that the jaguar may be tracking prey. The adverb *silently* shows us that the jaguar is likely a careful predator. It's certainly a more engaging sentence now.

Let's take a look at the different forms of adjectives and adverbs you should know before taking the SAT® exam.

Comparative and Superlative Adjectives

Big! Bigger! Biggest! Adjectives and adverbs change form when they are used to make a comparison.

The **comparative** form is used when comparing two things.

comparative adjectives	This piano is <u>larger</u> than the last one.
	Jen feels <u>more relaxed</u> than she did before she napped.
comparative adverbs	Today's lecture seemed to go by <u>more quickly</u> than last week's lecture did.
	Flo is taking her test preparation <u>more seriously</u> than she ever had before.

The **superlative** form is used when comparing three or more things.

superlative adjectives	Perry is the _weirdest_ fish I own.
	Alshad is the _tallest_ student in my class.
superlative adverbs	Out of everyone in the company, Candice works the _fastest_.
	This is the _slowest_ I have ever jogged.

As you may have noticed, simply adding -er to the end of comparative adjectives and -est to the end of superlative adjectives is not always enough. Once again, there are a number of exceptions you need to understand to use comparative and superlative adjectives correctly. Review the following:

Case	Adjective	Comparative	Superlative
One- and two-syllable adjectives ending in -e do not need an extra -e	close huge polite	closer huger politer	closest hugest politest
One-syllable adjectives ending in a consonant need to have that consonant doubled	big sad thin	bigger sadder thinner	biggest saddest thinnest
One- and two-syllable adjectives ending in -y need that -y changed to an -i	dry heavy tiny	drier heavier tinier	driest heaviest tiniest
Certain adjectives with two or more syllables remain the same but need the addition of _more_ for comparatives and _most_ for superlatives	beautiful complete important	more beautiful more complete more important	most beautiful most complete most important
Irregular adjectives require their own special alterations in the comparative and superlative forms	bad far good little many	worse farther better less more	worst farthest best least most

For comparative adverbs, adding _more_ is usually enough, and superlative adverbs usually only need _most_:

> I cried _more quietly_ than Davonne did.

> The scooter runs _most smoothly_ when it has a full tank of gas.

As you may have guessed, there are exceptions to this rule, but don't worry—there aren't as many exceptions for adverbs as there are for adjectives. Basically, any adverb that does not end in -ly should be treated the same way you would treat it if it were being used to modify a noun instead of a verb.

Adverb	Comparative	Superlative
bad	worse	worst
far	farther	farthest
fast	faster	fastest
good	better	best
hard	harder	hardest
little	less	least
long	longer	longest
loud	louder	loudest
many	more	most
quick	quicker	quickest
soon	sooner	soonest

One thing you need to make sure of on the Writing and Language Test is that comparatives and superlatives are actually being used to make a comparison.

You may have seen an advertisement that boasts, *Our product is better!* Well, your product is better than what? Obviously, the implication is that the product is better than other similar products, but the comparison is incorrect and incomplete if that information is not stated directly, as follows:

Our product is better than other similar products!

This may not be the catchiest slogan in the world, but it is a complete comparison. Remember that incomplete comparisons are incorrect when you're reading Writing and Language passages on the SAT® exam.

CONVENTIONAL EXPRESSIONS

For some students, conventional expressions, or **idioms,** can be confusing because they use words to mean something other than their literal meanings.

For example, if you were to *pull the wool over someone's eyes*, you probably would not *literally* grab a wool scarf and pull it over that person's eyes. However, you may *deceive* them, which is the idiomatic meaning of *pull the wool over someone's eyes*. See what we mean? Idioms can be tricky.

Idiom questions on the Writing and Language Test often require you to identify mistakes in their wording. So, even if you don't know what the idiom *bite off more than you can chew* means, you may still have heard it before, and you should be able to recognize that *bite off more than you can see* is not a correctly composed idiom (you may also deduce that biting with your eyes is both difficult and uncomfortable).

Here are some other common idioms that you may encounter:

Idiom	Meaning
Actions speak louder than words	What one does is more important than what one says.
Back to the drawing board	Time to start all over again!
Barking up the wrong tree	Making the wrong choice
Beat around the bush	Avoid the topic
Bite off more than you can chew	Take on too large of a task
Costs an arm and a leg	Very expensive
Cry over spilled milk	Complain about something that cannot be changed
Feel under the weather	Feel ill
Has a lot on the ball	Is very competent
Hit the sack	Go to bed
Kill two birds with one stone	Accomplish two tasks with a single action
Let sleeping dogs lie	Do not provoke a potentially unpleasant situation
Let the cat out of the bag	Reveal a secret
Piece of cake	Easy
Take with a grain of salt	Not take something too seriously
The whole nine yards	Everything

A good way to become familiar with a wide variety of idioms is to read a lot in your daily life. Writers love to use idioms, and the more you see them, the more comfortable you'll be in facing them on test day!

PREPOSITIONAL PHRASES

Prepositions indicate time and direction and are pretty straightforward. Prepositional phrases, however, are a bit less straightforward. In fact, they're very similar to idioms in that they cannot be explained with simple rules—you just have to get familiar with them and decide what works best.

As the old lesson goes, a **preposition** is anywhere a mouse can go: *over, under, sideways, down, in, out, at, from, above, to, inside, outside, before, after, forward, toward,* etc.

A prepositional phrase combines a preposition with one or more words. For example, *at home* is a common prepositional phrase. Technically, there is nothing grammatically wrong with saying *in home* (*I didn't go to the park last weekend; I was in home*); however, it simply isn't common to say *I was in home,* and you'll need to be aware of the most commonly used prepositional phrases on test day.

Here are a few common prepositions you should remember:

among friends	at work	in the grass	in your mind
at home	at the beach	in the room	on the lawn
at the office	in my heart	in the tree	on the road
at play	in the doorway	in the window	on the roof
at school	in the family	in the yard	over the top

FREQUENTLY CONFUSED WORDS

The English language contains many frequently confused words—words that may look or sound alike but have completely different meanings, so using them interchangeably in your writing can have serious negative consequences. You may encounter these tricky word pairs on test day, and should be able to correctly identify the correct word required in a sentence given the context.

Here are a few common frequently confused words that you should be aware of—and on the lookout for—on test day:

accept	to receive something
except	the exclusion of something
advice	a recommendation to follow
advise	to recommend something
affect	to influence (*verb*); an emotional response (*noun*)
effect	a result (*noun*); to cause (*verb*)
allude	to make an indirect reference to
elude	to successfully avoid
altogether	thoroughly
all together	everyone or everything in a single place
accent	a pronunciation common to a region

ascent	the act of rising or climbing
assent	consent or agreement
brake	a device for stopping a vehicle
break	to destroy into pieces
coarse	feeling rough
course	a path or an academic class series
complement	something that completes another thing
compliment	praise or flattery
conscience	a sense of morality
conscious	awake or aware
dessert	final course in a meal, typically sweet
desert	to abandon
desert	a dry and sandy area
die	to lose life (*verb*); one of a pair of dice (*noun*)
dye	to change or add color to
hear	to sense sound using an ear
here	in this particular place
hole	an opening
whole	a complete and entire thing
its	the possessive form of *it*
it's	a contraction for *it is*
lead	a type of metal substance (*noun*); to guide (*verb*)
led	past tense of *to lead*
loose	not tightly fastened
lose	to misplace
metal	a type of hard substance
medal	a flat designed disk, often given in recognition of an accomplishment
mettle	courage or spirit
peace	free from war
piece	part of a whole
pedal	the foot lever of a vehicle used to generate power
petal	part of a flower
peddle	to sell
personal	intimate, or owned by a person
personnel	employees or staff
plain	simple and unadorned
plane	to shave wood (*verb*); an aircraft (*noun*)

precede	to come before
proceed	to continue
presence	attendance
presents	gifts
principal	foremost (*adj.*); head figure of a school (*noun*)
principle	a moral conviction or basic truth
reign	to rule
rein	a strap to control an animal (*noun*); to guide or control (*verb*)
right	correct, or opposite of left
rite	ritual or ceremony
write	to put words on paper
sight	scene or picture
site	place or location
cite	to document or quote
stationary	standing still
stationery	a type of writing paper
than	besides
then	at that time, or next
their	possessive form of *they*
there	in a specific place
they're	contraction for *they are*
through	finished, or into and out of
threw	past tense of *to throw*
thorough	complete
to	toward
too	also, or very (used to show emphasis)
two	number following one
weak	not strong
week	seven consecutive days
weather	climate conditions
whether	if
where	in which place
were	past tense of *to be*
which	one of a group
witch	female sorcerer
whose	possessive of *who*

who's	contraction for *who is*
your	possessive of *you*
you're	contraction for *you are*

LOGICAL COMPARISONS

People make comparisons all the time—both in their daily lives and in writing. The key to making logical comparisons is to make sure that the things being compared are similarly balanced and equivalent. But what happens if we make an **illogical comparison?** Illogical comparisons occur when dissimilar or illogical things are compared, leading to an awkward or confusing result—as in the following example:

> Both Jerome and Patricia have new dogs. Jerome and Patricia took their new dogs to the veterinarian and had them weighed. According to the vet's scale, Jerome's dog is heavier than Patricia.

According to the last sentence of this paragraph, *Jerome's dog* and *Patricia* were weighed on the vet's scale. That certainly doesn't sound right, does it? A review of the earlier portion of the paragraph confirms this—Jerome's dog and Patricia's dog were weighed on the vet's scale. We have an illogical comparison to fix. Let's take a look at a corrected version:

> Both Jerome and Patricia have new dogs. Jerome and Patricia took their new dogs to the veterinarian and had them weighed. According to the vet's scale, Jerome's dog is heavier than Patricia's dog.

Much better—the problem is solved, the illogical comparison is fixed, and all is well. Be on the lookout for illogical comparison's on the SAT® Writing and Language Test, and be prepared to fix them.

Now you should have a better sense of the main topics and types of Writing and Language questions that you'll likely encounter on the test. As we've said before, thorough practice and review are your best strategies for test day success. Let's quickly tackle some practice questions in the context and format that you'll encounter them on test day—alongside a complete passage.

ATTACKING WRITING AND LANGUAGE PASSAGES AND QUESTIONS

Let's start small and then work our way up. The first passage includes five questions that are designed to test your skills with Expression of Ideas and Standard English Conventions questions. The second passage is a full-length passage that includes an informational graphic. Read the passages carefully, and answer the associated questions to the best of your ability. When you're finished, review the answers that follow as well as the strategies used for arriving at the correct answers. Best of luck!

Questions 1–5 are based on the following passage.

The Lumière Brothers: A Journey on Film

Today, we take the existence of movies and films for granted, but in the final years of the nineteenth century, moving pictures were truly rare and special creations, and the artistic medium contained only a small handful of creative pioneers. Among those trailblazing individuals whose hearts, minds, and talents were captured by the possibilities of film stood Auguste and Louis Lumière, French brothers who were among history's first filmmakers and auteurs.

The Lumière brothers were born in 1862 in eastern France, to parents who ran a small photo portrait studio; the brothers toiled in the studio for long hours throughout their childhood. This early exposure to film perhaps served as inspiration for the young duo's later path in life. Their **1** journey into filmmaking and trek through movie making started relatively late in life—the brothers didn't start to create their "moving pictures" until around the age of 30. Unlike today's feature films, which typically run in excess of 2 hours, the early works of the Lumière brothers each lasted under a minute, the brief output a result of the primitive film technology available at the time. Their first film, *Workers Leaving the Lumière Factory*, ran only 46 seconds long.

Over the next several years, they created a series of captivating short films, each one portraying a slice of contemporary late-nineteenth century life (such as *Cordeliers Square in Lyon* and *Blacksmiths*) or a whimsical snippet that captured the attention of the Lumière brothers (see *Horse Trick Riders*). The brother's creative film output culminated in a paid public exhibition—possibly the first public movie screening in history—of ten of their motion pictures at the Grand Café in Paris in 1895. This **2** inconsequential event brought the Lumière brothers immediate recognition and acclaim. Following their screening at the Grand Café, the brothers toured the world with their short films, which included stops in London, New York, Brussels, Montreal, and Buenos Aires.

Despite the accolades given to the Lumière brothers and **3** his moving pictures, they considered their journey into filmmaking as somewhat of a brief novelty, which ended around 1905. Their focus and ambitions turned to their other significant contributions—innovations in the technology used to make movies and color photography processing. Among their work in these areas **4** will be their version of the cinematograph, an early motion picture film camera that also served as a printer and film projector, which the Lumière brothers held a patent for and recorded their first film with. The brothers eventually found great success as manufacturers of photographic products in Europe through the Lumière company. **5**

1.
A. NO CHANGE
B. journey into filmmaking started
C. journey into filmmaking or trek through movie making had started
D. journey into both films and movies, as well as treks, started

2.
A. NO CHANGE
B. groundbreaking
C. geographic
D. humorous

3.
A. NO CHANGE
B. her moving pictures
C. its moving pictures
D. their moving pictures

4.
A. NO CHANGE
B. is their
C. will be his
D. was once their

5. Which of the following would make an effective concluding sentence to the passage?

A. The Lumière brothers enjoyed their lives in France, were devout family men, and each lived happy and to a ripe old age.

B. Filmmaking has moved on since the days when the Lumière brothers were making moving pictures, and these days they are little more than a curious footnote in cinematic history.

C. Although their foray into film-making was short-lived, their early films and innovative contributions to film technology have helped shape the medium for all of those who have followed in their footsteps.

D. The Lumière brothers' legacies are those of unrivaled filmmakers—even though it has been over a century since their first film, nothing since has matched its scope or sheer creativity.

Questions 6–15 are based on the following passage.

The next time you're in a supermarket, take a close scan of the shelves—you might be amazed at the great abundance and wide array of available products on display, many of which were unavailable just a few years ago. You may be surprised to learn that many of the **6** items available for purchase that you could buy, from produce to meat and others, are the result of genetic modification or contain genetically modified ingredients. According to the **7** food, scientists and companies responsible for creating these genetically modified organisms (GMOs), these manipulations are designed to benefit consumers. Others feel that profits are the real reason behind GMOs, and question their safety. What exactly are these GMOs that have created such a fractious debate?

GMOs are commonly defined as organisms who have had some aspect of their genetic material manipulated or altered through the use of genetic engineering—including the addition, mutation, or deletion of genes, or by promoting the natural transfer of genetic material. GMOs per se is not a new concept. The selective breeding of desirable traits in domesticated animals for ideal household pets, for example, is a type of manipulation that has been around for centuries. GMOs have also been used extensively in the pharmaceutical and medical research fields for decades. However, genetically modified food is a relatively newer concept. Genetically modified crops and animals targeted for human consumption began obtaining the Food and Drug Administration's (FDA) official approval in the 1980s, and the number of GMOs available for consumer purchase worldwide—and the amount of land used to grow GM crops—has been **8** decreasing steadily ever since. Predictably, GMO proliferation and use has had a divisive societal effect, with fierce and vocal proponents and detractors making their points of view well known. **9**

Those in support of GMOs claim that they are safe for consumption—or at least point to the fact that no evidence regarding short- or long-term ill effects of ingesting GMOs has been found. They also claim that careful and targeted genetic manipulation can make the products available to consumers bigger, taste better, and more resilient to the potential ravages of **10** time weather temperature and insects. They also claim that strategic initiatives that take advantage of genetic modification can help reduce world hunger and meet the demands of nations that are ill-equipped to feed their citizens. Some critics of GMOs designed for human consumption claim that there has not been enough research to support the notion that they are fully safe for long-term, continued ingestion. Critics also claim that government approval of GMOs in the absence of sufficient irrefutable data regarding their safety simply represents years of **11** failed lobbying by powerful and well-funded groups that represent the interests of big business. Some also argue that this is simply a way for major corporations to boost their profits, using genetic manipulation to create greater food supplies faster and that last longer, and at cheaper costs, all at the expense of the consumer. The trend towards healthy eating continues to grow, as evidenced by the massive increase in the number of organic foods now available for purchase. **12**

A key point of contention in the debate regarding genetically modified foods pertains to the labeling of these items. Critics of ingestible GMOs argue that all modified food should be clearly and carefully labeled so that consumers are aware of what **13** they are potentially purchasing—and can make informed decisions regarding the foods they purchase and eat. They are pushing for an FDA mandate that would require compulsory labeling for all such foods; similar regulations exist in many countries worldwide. Supporters of GMOs claim that labeling can have a negative coercive effect, possibly signaling consumers that foods labeled as GM are somehow unsafe. They also claim that complex regulations in other countries might inhibit the ability to openly sell items with GMO labeling. With no consensus regarding these issues on the horizon, this complicated and highly contentious issue, representing billions of dollars in annual food sales across the globe, will likely be debated in the public spotlight for years to come. **14** **15**

Land Area Use for Genetically Modified Crops in U.S.A. (1996–2009)

	2.8	12.8	27.8	39.9	44.2	52.6	58.7	67.7	81.0	90.0	102.0	114.3	125.0	134.0
	1996	1997	1998	1999	2000	2001	2002	2003	2004	2005	2006	2007	2008	2009

■ USA

* in millions of hectares

6 **A.** NO CHANGE
B. available purchasable and buyable items
C. items available for purchase
D. items that you can buy that are available for purchase

7 **A.** NO CHANGE
B. food scientists
C. food; scientists
D. food—scientists

8 Based on the information provided in the chart, the most appropriate choice for the underlined phrase is

A. NO CHANGE
B. increasing steadily
C. rapidly fluctuating
D. unchanged

9 Which of the following sentences would make an effective transition between paragraphs 2 and 3?

A. GMOs are also used by the pharmaceutical industry to make medicines.
B. GMOs are not receiving enough attention, given the seriousness of the issue.
C. What else that you purchase is the result of targeted genetic manipulation?
D. Let's take a closer look at both sides of the debate on this hot-button issue.

10 **A.** NO CHANGE
B. time, weather, temperature, and insects
C. time weather, temperature; and insects
D. time; weather temperature, and, insects

11.
A. NO CHANGE
B. ineffective
C. successful
D. unwanted

12. To make paragraph 3 most logical, which sentence should be deleted?

A. They claim that careful and targeted genetic manipulation can make the products available to consumers bigger, taste better, and more resilient to the potential ravages of weather, temperature, and insects.

B. They also claim that strategic initiatives that take advantage of genetic modification can help reduce world hunger and meet the demands of nations that are ill-equipped to feed their citizens.

C. Some also argue that this is simply a way for major corporations to boost their profits, using genetic manipulation to create greater food supplies faster and that last longer, and at cheaper costs, all at the expense of the consumer.

D. The trend towards healthy eating continues to grow, as evidenced by the massive increase in the number of organic foods now available for purchase.

13.
A. NO CHANGE
B. he is
C. she is
D. they have been

14. The author is thinking of adding the following sentence to support the passage:

Adding GMO labeling to food will cost millions in additional manufacturing costs annually.

Where is the most effective place to add this sentence?

A. Paragraph 1
B. Paragraph 2
C. Paragraph 3
D. Paragraph 4

15. Which of the following would be an appropriate title for the passage?

A. GMOs: The Perfect Way to End World Hunger
B. GMOs: Making Foods Better
C. GMOs: Progress or Danger?
D. GMOs: Buyer Beware!

ANSWER KEY AND EXPLANATIONS

1. B	4. B	7. B	10. B	13. A
2. B	5. C	8. B	11. C	14. D
3. D	6. C	9. D	12. D	15. C

1. **The correct answer is B.** This is a concision question, and like every question you'll encounter on the Writing and Language Test, you should first identify what's being asked of you before attempting to answer it. A good strategy for starting is to quickly scan the answer choices. Here, you'll see a series of variations of the under-lined phrase in the passage, which should signal to you that you're being asked to make a word choice decision and that some-thing *may* be wrong with the sentence as written. Now we know what we're dealing with! Which answer choice fixes this issue? This question is at the heart of a key strategy for attacking Writing and Language Test questions—the correct answer will always be the choice that best improves the passage. Make all of your deci-sions with this in mind. A quick way to test it is to plug in the correct answer and see if it works: *Their journey into filmmaking started relatively late in life—the brothers didn't start to create their "moving pictures" until around the age of 30.* Choice B eliminates the redundancy without affecting the author's intended meaning— thereby improving the passage. As written, choice A contains the original redundancy problem. Choices C and D confuse or alter the meaning of the sentence and do not fix the redundancy.

2. **The correct answer is B.** This is a classic word choice precision question; the varied selection of words among the answer choices should signal to you that you're dealing with a word choice question. Again, for these and other types of questions on the Writing and Language Test, context is key. Let's examine the sentence that contains the underline in question. What's the main idea of the sentence? It highlights the movie exhibition event at the Grand Café in Paris, which we are told is possibly the first public movie screening in history. That's certainly a monu-mental event. Which adjective best describes this? As written (choice A), *inconsequential* would seem to have the opposite intended meaning. Choices C and D don't fit within the context of this sentence, and are also incorrect. Choice B, a *ground-breaking* event, works well given the context of the sentence, and is the correct answer.

3. The correct answer is D. This is a common sentence structure question; here, you're being asked to determine the appropriate pronoun for the underlined portion of the sentence, given the context. We can quickly determine the question type we're dealing with based on a scan of the answer choices, which contain a series of varying pronouns. How do we determine which one is right for this sentence? Our next step is to determine the antecedent—the noun that the pronoun is meant to replace. In this sentence, the noun in question is the *Lumière brothers*, a plural noun. Therefore, we need a plural pronoun. Choice A, B, and C are incorrect—they're all singular pronouns. Choice D contains the appropriate plural noun given the context—*their*—and is the correct answer.

4. The correct answer is B. In this question, you're being tasked with determining the appropriate verb tense in the underlined portion of the sentence, given the context. The sentence under review details the contributions of the Lumière brothers in the area of film technology. Remember that contributions, innovations, or inventions, such as the version of the cinematograph that the Lumière brothers are responsible for, don't expire or recede just because they happened in the *past*—the work of the Lumière brothers is *still* their work, even though it may have happened a long time ago. Let this fact guide you as you to determine the appropriate tense of *to be* for this sentence. Based on what we just covered, you can eliminate choice D—*was once their* would indicate that the Lumière brothers' version of the cinematograph was once their work but is no longer, which is illogical. As written (choice A), the verb *will be* is in the future tense, which would indicate that the work of the Lumière brothers hasn't happened yet, This is illogical, as the Lumière brothers lived a long time ago, so we can eliminate this answer choice. Choice C is also in the future tense but contains a change in pronoun—be careful of sneaky answer choices that could serve as an obstacle between you and the correct answer. We know that proper verb tense is the issue here, and that the future tense is incorrect, so we can eliminate this choice and move on. This leaves us with the correct answer and the correct present tense, as this is still the Lumière brothers work in the area.

5. **The correct answer is C.** Here's a classic strategy question that's asking you to make a decision on the best way to conclude the passage. A great first step for tackling this question is to quickly ask yourself, "What makes an effective essay conclusion?" Remember what we covered in this chapter—a strong essay conclusion is often a poignant and memorable wrap-up of the main themes and ideas that lie at the core of the written piece. Referring back to our notes, this passage is *an informational biographical snapshot of Auguste and Louis Lumière, French brothers and filmmakers.* The concluding paragraph *covers their later years, including their technological innovations and business successes.* Do any of the answer choices capture the spirit of these central ideas? This sentence refers to the Lumière brothers' lasting legacy on filmmaking and film technology, which effectively ties back to the main idea of the passage. Choice A makes conclusions about the later years of the Lumière brothers that may or may not be true. Choice B runs counter to the spirit of the passage by saying that the Lumière brothers "are little more than a curious footnote in cinematic history." Choice D is incorrect because it makes a subjective claim about the work of the Lumière brothers that the author of the passage hasn't made.

6. **The correct answer is C.** This question is designed to gauge your ability to identify superfluous or inappropriate text within a piece of writing, in an effort to enhance the overall economy of the passage. Let's take a closer look at the sentence in question, and the underlined portion in particular. If you read the sentence as written (choice A) and something seemed a bit awkward, your instincts are sharp—the phrase "items available for purchase that you could buy" does not require the redundant "that you could buy," since "items available for purchase" covers it. Choice C fixes the redundancy: *You may be surprised to learn that many of the items available for purchase, from produce to meat and others, are the result of genetic modification or contain genetically modified ingredients.* Choices B and D fail to fix the redundancy and introduce additional confusion into the sentence.

7. **The correct answer is B.** In this question, you're ability to recognize and eliminate unnecessary punctuation is put to the test. As covered in this chapter, commas are among the most overused and misused types of internal punctuation. In this sentence as written (choice A), an unnecessary comma creates a strange confusion—*according to the food* would lead us to believe that the food had an opinion, which is illogical. Choices C and D swap out the comma for a semicolon and an em-dash, respectively—but they are both incorrect. Semicolons are used to separate related independent clauses in a sentence, or to separate items in a complex list, neither of which we have here. Em-dashes are used to create a long pause or highlight key information in a sentence, which is not appropriate here. Choice B effectively removes the unnecessary punctuation and improves the sense and flow of the sentence, and is the correct answer: *According to the food scientists and companies responsible for creating these genetically modified organisms (GMOs), these manipulations are designed to benefit consumers.*

8. **The correct answer is B.** An analysis of the infographic provided reveals a clear trend regarding the amount of land used for growing genetically modified crops—it has been steadily increasing worldwide for years. The underlined portion of the sentence as written (choice A) provides the opposite of the intended meaning. Choices C and D also don't reflect the information provided in the chart. Choice B is the correct answer: the amount of land used to grow GM crops has been increasing steadily.

9. **The correct answer is D.** This question is tasking you with determining how best to effectively transition between paragraphs and ideas within the passage. Here, we are searching for an effective transition sentence between paragraphs 2 and 3. The best approach is to capture the core ideas of each of these paragraphs, and figure out which sentence best serves as a bridge between the ideas. Paragraph 2 discusses the background and evolution of GMOs. Paragraph 3 highlights the core points of GMOs supporters and detractors. Which sentence best serves to bridge these two core notions? Choice D is the most effective transition, moving readers from the background information in paragraph 2 to the debate issues covered in paragraph 3.

10. The correct answer is B. This question is testing your ability to correctly separate items in a simple list with the appropriate punctuation within a sentence. The sentence as written (choice A), which fails to separate the list items with any punctuation, is a run-on and is incorrect. Choice B correctly fixes the problem and separates the items in this simple list with commas: *They also claim that careful and targeted genetic manipulation can make the products available to consumers bigger, taste better, and more resilient to the potential ravages of time, weather, temperature, and insects.* Choice C and D fail to separate all the list items with commas correctly, and intersperse semicolons with commas. Semicolons are used to separate items in more complex series of lists, and are incorrect here.

11. The correct answer is C. In this question we're trying to determine the appropriate word choice for the underlined portion of the sentence. Again, searching for context clues can help us arrive at the correct answer. We're told early on in the sentence that this is a claim made by critics of GMOs, which is a key clue. They argue that although there is an absence of sufficient irrefutable data regarding the safety of GMOs,

they were still given approval—this would indicate that groups lobbying on behalf of the companies that created GMOs were *successful*, so choice C is the correct answer. It wouldn't be logical to state that they *failed* or were *ineffective* (choices A and B) given the context of the sentence, and we haven't been given sufficient information to assume they were *unwanted* (choice D).

12. The correct answer is D. This question is asking you to make a strategic decision regarding information in the passage—specifically, determining what information *doesn't* belong in a paragraph based on context. After reading the paragraph, try and determine what its primary purpose is. Paragraph 3 focuses on both sides of the GMO debate, including the core points of supporters and detractors of genetically modified foods. Scan the sentences among the answer choices and try to determine the sentence that least supports this core focus. Choice D focuses on healthy eating and organic foods—not GMOs—and is the best choice for deletion. The other sentences among the answer choices are more closely aligned with the main idea of the paragraph.

13. **The correct answer is A.** In this question, you're tasked with determining the correct pronoun and verb for the underlined portion of the sentence. Let's begin by tackling the pronoun in question. The first step in determining proper pronoun usage is to figure out the *antecedent*—the noun or nouns that it is replacing. In this sentence, the underlined pronoun replaces *consumers*, a plural noun.

Is there a plural pronoun among the answer choices that can replace *consumers*? The sentence as written (choice A) contains a suitable plural pronoun (*they*) to replace *consumers*, as well as a suitable verb in the correct present continuous tense—which refers to the *modified food* that consumers are currently potentially purchasing and could potentially purchase in the future. Choices B and C are incorrect because they both utilize singular, gender-specific pronouns (*he* and *she*), which are inappropriate to replace the plural noun *consumers*. Choice D is incorrect because even though *they* is a suitable plural pronoun, the verb phrase *have been* is in the past tense, which is incorrect for this sentence—the addition of GMO labeling is meant to make current and future consumer purchases safer, *not* past purchases.

14. **The correct answer is D.** This question is asking you to determine the most effective place to add supplementary information to the passage. The sentence being added discusses the potential monetary effect of adding GMO labeling to food. Which paragraph in the passage covers this issue? Paragraph 4 (choice D) discusses this specific issue in the GMO debate, and is the correct answer.

15. **The correct answer is C.** In order to determine an appropriate title for the passage, we need to first determine the main idea of the piece—and then come up with a succinct way to capture it. The passage discusses the raging debate regarding GMOs. Which of the answer choices best captures this idea? Choice C is the correct answer—those who support GMOs consider them a step forward and those opposed to GMOs consider them a potential danger, and "GMOs: Progress or Danger?" best captures this. Choice A is incorrect, as the piece does not claim that GMOs are the perfect way to end world hunger. Choices B and D are also incorrect, as the piece does not take the position that GMOs make foods better or are dangerous.

SUMMING IT UP

- The **Writing and Language Test,** one of two tests that comprise the Evidence-Based Reading and Writing section, lasts **35 minutes** and contains **44 questions** that will task you with making qualitative editorial decisions designed to improve the writing passages included in the exam.

- The purpose of this test is to gauge your abilities to read critically, recognize errors and weaknesses in writing, and make substantive fixes to improve written work.

- The two core topic areas on the SAT® Writing and Language Test are **Expression of Ideas** and **Standard English Conventions.**

- **Expression of Ideas** questions assess your ability to recognize and address key structural issues that impact the overall effectiveness of a piece of writing, including **organization, development,** and **effective language use.**

- **Organization** questions are designed to assess how well you can make decisions about effective *grouping*, *distribution*, and *arrangement* of ideas at the word, phrase, sentence, and paragraph levels. These will include the following question types:
  - **Logical sequence questions:** These questions will test your ability to recognize if information provided in the passage—either a word, phrase, sentence, or paragraph—is in the correct and most effective order, and if it isn't, you'll be tasked with fixing it.
  - **Introductions, conclusions, and transitions questions:** These questions will test your ability to recognize the proper use and placement of information to *introduce, conclude,* and *connect* ideas within a passage, and to effectively move between related ideas between paragraphs in a passage.

- **Development** questions will task you with *identifying, revising, adding,* and *deleting* key elements of the passages provided, in an effort to ensure that each piece of writing achieves its intended purpose. These will include the following question types:
  - **Proposition questions:** These questions address the *main topic elements* of each passage, including *topic sentences, thesis statements,* and *core claims* made by an author.
  - **Support questions:** These questions address the *supportive elements* of each passage, which include *supportive information* and *details* that *bolster* a writer's central ideas or claims made in a piece of writing.
  - **Focus questions:** These questions address the *relevant elements* of each passage, which require you to make judgments regarding whether or not information presented *supports, detracts,* or is *irrelevant* to an author's purpose and central claims.

- **Quantitative Information questions** address *supplemental quantitative elements* for a given passage. These graphical elements can take the form of *graphs, charts, tables, illustrations,* etc., and you'll need to make determinations regarding their *purpose, accuracy*, and *level of effectiveness* in relation to the passages.

- **Effective Language Use** questions are designed to analyze how effectively authors make key language choices to achieve a variety of important rhetorical goals, which includes the following:
  - ○ **Syntax:** Ensures that text in each passage is coherent and arranged properly, and delivers a logical flow of thoughts and ideas
  - ○ **Precision:** Ensures that information in each passage is clear, focused, and to the point
  - ○ **Concision:** Ensures that each passage is free from repetition and distracting wordiness
  - ○ **Style and Tone:** Ensures that each passage maintains a consistent voice, mood, and effect
- Within *each* of these two core skills areas, questions on the Writing and Language Test will measure your skill levels in the following areas:
  - ○ **Words in Context:** These questions will gauge your mastery of effective and appropriate word choice, based on context within the passages provided. Your vocabulary should be sharp for test day, and you'll need to be able to use available context clues to make decisions that impact **tone**, **style**, and **syntax**, with the goal of improving a given piece of writing.
  - ○ **Command of Evidence:** These questions are designed to test your ability to grasp how effectively a piece of writing conveys ideas and information, and to make critical improvements in these areas: to enhance meaning, sharpen a claim or argument, and provide appropriate details and support.
- **Analysis in History/Social Studies and in Science** are topic areas in which the SAT® exam will measure your ability to critically read, comprehend, and analyze passages—and to make key decisions on how best to improve them.
- **Standard English Conventions** questions test mechanics issues like sentence structure, punctuation, and language usage.
- **Sentence Structure** questions focus on identifying and fixing issues involving **sentence construction** and **sentence formation.** You can expect to encounter questions involving parallel structure, modifier placement, sentence boundaries including grammatically incomplete and ineffective sentences, inappropriate pronoun shifts, and inappropriate shifts in voice, mood, and verb tense.
  - ○ **Independent clauses** contain a subject and a verb and make sense on their own. **Subordinate clauses** do not contain a subject-verb pair and must be linked to an independent clause to be correct.
  - ○ **Fragments** are partial sentences that lack either a subject or a verb. They are grammatically incorrect.

- **Run-on sentences** are grammatically incorrect compound or complex sentences that fail to link their parts with the necessary conjunction or punctuation.
- **Modifiers** are words and phrases that describe. **Misplaced modifiers** are not placed next to the words they are supposed to modify. They are grammatically incorrect. **Dangling modifiers** fail to modify any word at all because the object they are meant to modify is not in the sentence.
- **Parallel structure** occurs when all groups of words in a sentence are written in the same tense and form. When such words are not in the same tense or form, the sentence is grammatically incorrect. Failing to pair correlative conjunctions correctly also violates parallel structure.

• **Conventions of Punctuation** questions focus on recognizing and adhering to the rules and standards of appropriate punctuation. On test day, you can expect to encounter a wide array of punctuation issues: within-sentence punctuation, including dashes, colons, and semicolons; plural and possessive forms of nouns and pronouns; end-of-sentence punctuation including periods, exclamation points, and question marks; the correct use and display of parenthetical, tangential, and nonrestrictive items in a sentence; correctly displaying items in a series, utilizing commas and semicolons for simple and complex lists; and addressing unnecessary and superfluous punctuation.

- **End-of-sentence punctuation** includes the period, the exclamation mark, and the question mark. When a sentence ends with quotation marks used to indicate dialogue, the end-of-sentence punctuation is placed *within* the quotation marks. If the quotation marks indicate a title and placing end-of-sentence punctuation within the marks might give the false impression that the mark is part of the title, the end-of-sentence punctuation is placed *after* the closing quotation marks.
- **Commas** are used to separate introductory words and phrases, clauses in compound sentences, non-restrictive phrases, items in series, appositives, and quotations.
- **Apostrophes** are used to separate letters in contractions and indicate possession. When indicating possession, an apostrophe is usually followed by the letter *-s*. However, no extra *-s* is necessary if the possessing word ends in *-s* and is not someone's name.
- **Colons** are used to introduce a list of items or offset an example.
- **Dashes** are used to offset examples and indicate a pause or interruption in dialogue.
- **Parentheses** often enclose tangential or bonus information that cannot be fit into a sentence naturally.
- Making sure that a piece of writing is free from **unnecessary punctuation** is important for ensuring that it conveys its intended meaning, thoughts, and ideas.

• **Conventions of Usage** questions focus on identifying and adhering to standard writing and language practices. You should be prepared to tackle questions involving possessives and possessive determiners including contractions and adverbs, issues involving subject-verb agreement, appropriate pronoun use for clarity, appropriate and logical comparisons of like versus unlike terms, recognizing standard conventional English language expressions and their appropriate use, and correctly identifying and using frequently confused words.

- **Plural nouns** do not always end with -s; there are several variations among plural nouns depending on the words' letters. **Collective nouns** are not plural nouns; they are singular.
- **Subjects and verbs** are in agreement when they are in the same form. They both need to be either singular or plural and not a combination of both forms.
- **Pronouns and antecedents**—the words for which the pronouns stand in—need to be in agreement. They need to agree in terms of number, gender, and person.
- **Relative pronouns** signal relative clauses, which are used to describe nouns; **reflexive pronouns** refer back to their subjects; **interrogative pronouns** are used when asking a question; **possessive pronouns** show ownership.
- **Verb tense** indicates when the action the verb describes takes place.
- **Comparative adjectives and adverbs** are used when comparing two things. They usually end in -er. **Superlative adjectives and adverbs** are used when comparing three or more things. They usually end in -est.
- **Idioms** use words to mean something other than their literal meanings.
- **Prepositional phrases** combine a preposition with other words to indicate direction and time. Their particular word often depends on common usage.
- You may encounter **frequently confused words**—words that may look or sound alike but have completely different meanings—on test day. Be prepared to correctly identify the correct word required in a sentence, given the context.
- **Illogical comparisons** occur when dissimilar or illogical things are compared, leading to an awkward or confusing result.

CHAPTER 6: THE SAT® ESSAY

OVERVIEW

- A Brief Introduction to the SAT® Essay
- Scoring
- Prompts and Essays
- Managing Your Time
- An Essay Walk-through
- Essay Writing Practice
- Summing It Up

The SAT® Essay is an optional section of the SAT® exam, so it may be wise to spend the little preparation time you have focusing mainly on the other sections of the test. However, the SAT® Essay may still be important to the colleges to which you are applying, so if you plan on taking it, there are some important things you will want to know before test day.

This chapter won't bog you down in details. It will just give you a quick and clear overview of the SAT® Essay, how it's formatted, and what you will be expected to cover in order to get a top score. This is of particular importance since the SAT® exam changed not too long ago. Whereas the old essay required you to provide your own opinion on an argumentative passage, you are now expected to *analyze* an argumentative passage.

This chapter will give you some valuable information to help you through the SAT® Essay:

- The format of the essay
- How the prompt is worded
- How your essay is scored
- A walk-through of a sample prompt, so you know what you will have to analyze in your essay

- Examples of advanced, proficient, and inadequate essays responding to that prompt
- Tips for making the most of your time

There's no time to lose, so let's begin.

A BRIEF INTRODUCTION TO THE SAT® ESSAY

 Be sure to find out whether or not your preferred college requires you to take the SAT® Essay. You don't want to opt out of the Essay only to find out that your preferred college requires it.

As we've already stated, the SAT® Essay is optional, so unless your school requires it, you don't have to take it. However, if you do opt in, you can expect to do the following:

- Take it after the multiple-choice sections of the test.
- Read a prompt and a 650- to 750-word reading passage similar to the kinds of argumentative passages you will read on the SAT® Reading Test.
- Analyze that argumentative passage.
- Include evidence from that passage in your essay.

You will have 50 minutes to complete your essay.

SCORING

Your essay will receive a score in each of the three following categories: reading, analysis, and writing.

1. The **reading score** measures how well you comprehended the passage.

2. The **analysis score** measures how well you analyzed its argument.

3. The **writing score** measures how well you wrote your analysis.

NOTE: Your three SAT® Essay scores aren't combined with each other or the score you receive for the multiple-choice sections of the test.

Two scorers will grade each category of your essay (reading, writing, and analysis) on a scale of 1 to 4, with 1 being the absolute worst and 4 being the absolute best. Each number from 1 to 4 has a specific meaning:

Score	Meaning
4	Advanced
3	Proficient
2	Partial
1	Inadequate

The final score you will receive for each category will be the sum of the two scorers' marks, which means the grade you see will actually be on a scale of 2 to 8. For example, if you receive a total of 6 in reading, 5 in analysis, and 8 in writing, the score you receive will look like this:

6/5/8

PROMPTS AND ESSAYS

Now that you have the basics of how the essay is given and scored, let's go more into what you are expected to include in your essay. First, you should familiarize yourself with the prompts given. Then, we'll discuss how to approach your reading and writing during the time allotted on test day.

THE SAT® ESSAY PROMPT

The SAT® Essay prompt is always basically the same. It requires you to analyze the argument an author makes in a reading passage.

The prompt given to you on test day will look a lot like this:

As you read the passage below, consider how (the author) uses

- evidence, such as facts or examples, to support claims.

- reasoning to develop ideas and to connect claims and evidence.

- stylistic or persuasive elements, such as word choice or appeals to emotion, to make the ideas strong and convincing.

The argumentative prompt passage follows these initial directions. Next comes the specific task, which will look a lot like this:

> Write an essay in which you explain how (the author) builds an argument to persuade his/her audience that (author's claim). In your essay, analyze how (the author) uses one or more of the features listed above (or features of your own choice) to strengthen the logic and persuasiveness of his/her argument. Be sure that your analysis focuses on the most relevant features of the passage.
>
> Your essay should not explain whether you agree with (the author's) claims, but rather explain how the author builds an argument to persuade his/her audience.

 TIP Read the prompt as it appears in this chapter very carefully so you won't have to waste time getting familiar with it on test day.

The prompt passage can be about any topic, but it will always make an argument. That means the author is giving her or his opinion on a topic and trying to convince the reader that this opinion is the right one.

Your essay will analyze how the author makes that argument and how effective that argument is based on the evidence the author includes. To make your own essay well-supported and persuasive, you will have to include evidence from the prompt passage. That evidence may be direct quotes or accurate paraphrases of the author's main points or, ideally, both. The scorers will want to see some variety in your work.

As you read the prompt passage, take note of the following factors:

- The author's main argument
- How the author uses evidence to support that argument
- What kind of evidence the author uses (expert testimony, statistics, surveys, personal opinions, etc.)
- How the author uses language and tone to get her or his point across
- How convincing the overall argument is based on the evidence and language the author uses

 TIP You may want to take notes addressing each of these factors as you read the prompt passage. Those notes may actually serve as a good outline for your essay.

YOUR ESSAY

You've probably written a lot of essays throughout your school career. The SAT® Essay is no different. It will still need to be a complete and well-organized piece of writing with the standard essay elements. As they specifically pertain to the SAT® Essay, these elements are:

- An **introductory paragraph** that introduces the argument you will be analyzing while hinting at how you plan to analyze it. (Is the argument well reasoned as a whole? Is it poorly reasoned?)

- **Body paragraphs** that analyze the prompt passage thoroughly and thoughtfully. This is where you will explain the tactics the prompt author uses, how well reasoned and effective they are, and how the author uses evidence to support his or her ideas. Three paragraphs is generally a good length for the body of an effective essay.

- A **concluding paragraph** that wraps up or sums up the main findings of your analysis. Here, you will be clearer about whether or not the prompt passage is effective than you were in your introductory paragraph.

 To save time and stay on track when writing your essay, create an outline of what you plan to discuss in your introduction, body, and conclusion before you begin.

The details you choose to include in the introduction, body, and conclusion will have the most bearing on your analysis score, but they will also affect your reading score. The details show how well you read and understood the prompt passage. For example, misquoting the prompt passage or suggesting that the author said something he actually did not say will cost you points in reading. So be sure to read the prompt passage carefully!

Be sure to leave yourself time to edit the first draft of your essay to make sure it contains no errors and that you've used language as effectively as possible. This will help you to get a top score in writing. While editing, make sure your essay:

- Has a clear introduction, body, and conclusion

- Uses precise vocabulary words to make your points as clearly as possible

- Uses varied vocabulary and sentence structure so that your essay is interesting to read

- Contains no errors in language, grammar, spelling, mechanics, syntax, or structure

- Maintains a consistent tone

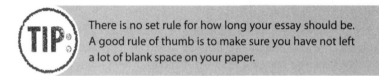
MANAGING YOUR TIME

While it might seem like 50 minutes is plenty of time to write your essay, you won't actually be spending that entire time writing. There's a lot more that goes into the essay, such as reading, taking notes, and editing. Don't worry, though, because there's a simple schedule you can follow to ensure you manage your time effectively on test day.

Any time you practice essay writing before your actual SAT® exam, and then again on test day, try to allot your time in the following way:

Total test time	50 minutes
Reading the prompt and taking notes	10 minutes
Outlining	5 minutes
Writing	25–30 minutes
Editing	5–10 minutes

AN ESSAY WALK-THROUGH

Now that you have a general idea of what you will read and have to write on the SAT® Essay, let's get specific by looking at examples. First, you'll read a prompt similar to the kind of prompt you will read on test day. Then, we'll show you a sample essay response. Finally, we will actually walk you through the essay to give you an idea of how scorers might rate each of its paragraphs in terms of reading, analysis, and writing. This will give you a better idea of the kinds of things you'll want to accomplish in your essay on test day and how the scorers might respond to it.

CAUTION
Remember that the essay scorers are not tasked with evaluating your opinion on the topic the prompt passage discusses. You may feel the urge to give your personal opinions if you strongly disagree with the prompt passage's argument, but you must have some self-control. Turning your analytical essay into an argumentative one will cost you points.

THE ESSAY PROMPT

As you read the passage below, consider how A.A. Milne uses

- evidence, such as facts or examples, to support claims.

- reasoning to develop ideas and to connect claims and evidence.

- stylistic or persuasive elements, such as word choice or appeals to emotion, to add power to the ideas expressed.

The following passage is adapted from "State Lotteries" by A.A. Milne.

The popular argument against the State Lottery is an assertion that it will encourage the gambling spirit. The popular argument in favour of the State Lottery is an assertion that it is hypocritical to say that it will encourage the gambling spirit, because the gambling spirit is already amongst us. Having listened to a good deal of this sort of argument on both sides, I thought it would be well to look up the word "gamble" in my dictionary. I found it next to "gamboge," and I can now tell you all about it.

To gamble, says my dictionary, is "to play for money in games of skill or chance," and it adds the information that the word is derived from the Anglo-Saxon *gamen*, which means "a game". Now, to me this definition is particularly interesting, because it justifies all that I have been thinking about the gambling spirit in connection with Premium Bonds. I am against Premium Bonds, but not for the popular reason. I am against them because (as it seems to me) there is so very little of the gamble about them. And now that I have looked up "gamble" in the dictionary, I see that I was right. The "chance" element in a state lottery is obvious enough, but the "game" element is entirely absent. It is nothing so harmless and so human as the gambling spirit which Premium Bonds would encourage.

We play for money in games of skill or chance—bridge, for instance. But it isn't only of the money we are thinking. We get pleasure out of the game. Probably we prefer it to a game of greater chance, such as *vingt-et-un*. But even at *vingt-et-un* or baccarat there is something more than chance which is taking a hand in the game; not skill, perhaps, but at least personality. If you are only throwing dice, you are engaged in a personal struggle with another man, and you are directing the struggle to this extent, that you can call the value of the stakes, and decide whether to go on or to stop. And is there any man who, having made a fortune at Monte Carlo, will admit that he owes it entirely to chance? Will he not rather attribute it to his wonderful system, or if not to that, at any rate to his wonderful nerve, his perseverance, or his recklessness?

The "game" element, then, comes into all these forms of gambling, and still more strongly does it pervade that most common form of gambling, betting on horses. I do not suggest that the street-corner boy who puts a shilling both ways on Bronchitis knows anything whatever about horses, but at least he thinks he does; and if he wins five shillings on that happy afternoon when Bronchitis proves himself to be the 2.30 winner, his pleasure will not be solely in the money. The thought that he is such a skilful follower of form, that he has something of the national eye for a horse, will give him as much pleasure as can be extracted from the five shillings itself.

This, then, is the gambling spirit. It has its dangers, certainly, [but] it is not entirely an evil spirit. It is possible that the State should not encourage it, but it is not called upon to exorcise it with bell, and book, and candle. I am not sure that I should favour a State gamble, but my arguments against it would be much the same as my arguments against State cricket or the solemn official endowment and recognition of any other jolly game. However, I need not trouble you with those arguments now, for nothing so harmless as a State gamble has ever been suggested. Instead, we have from time to time a State lottery offered to us, and that is a very different proposition.

Write an essay in which you explain how A.A. Milne builds an argument to persuade his audience that state lotteries may or may not be a form of gambling. In your essay, analyze how Milne uses one or more of the features listed above (or features of your own choice) to strengthen the logic and persuasiveness of his argument. Be sure that your analysis focuses on the most relevant features of the passage.

Your essay should not explain whether you agree with Milne's claims, but rather explain how the author builds an argument to persuade his audience.

 In general, if any of your essay's paragraphs contain fewer than three sentences, they could probably use more information.

Sample Essay

Now it's time to look at a sample essay responding to this prompt. Read the sample essay in its entirety first. Then we will walk you through it with paragraph-by-paragraph notes on the essay writer's reading, analysis, and writing skills.

Is buying a state lottery ticket gambling? This is the essential question at the heart of A.A. Milne's essay "*State Lotteries.*" In responding to whether or not a state-run lottery is a form of gambling, Milne uses novel evidence and adopts a witty tone to get his argument across.

At first, Milne holds back on his personal opinion of whether or not state lotteries constitute gambling to go to a very direct source regarding this question. Instead of consulting some authority on morals, ethics, or law, he uses his handy, every day dictionary to find out what this basic reference book has to say about the big question. He does so not by looking up *lottery* but by looking up *gamble*, which the dictionary defines as a "game" that involves "chance." While he concludes that "chance" is an element in playing the state lottery, he says that the fact that playing the lottery has little in common with playing games exempts it from being gambling. He concludes that playing the lottery then has more in common with buying Premium Bonds than gambling.

Milne then goes into more detail to support his dictionary-based conclusion that playing the state lottery is not gambling. He introduces a comparison between horse racing and playing the lottery to further his argument, and here he uses humor more obviously to get us, his readers, on his side. One subtle humorous trick is giving the horse in his example a funny name: the illness Bronchitis. Getting us to giggle is a good way to loosen us up to go along with the author.

The author uses another subtle trick to make us follow his argument by referring to readers in the second person. In paragraph three, he starts referring to us as "you" to get us to relate to his argument better. This personal touch makes it seem as though we're not merely being lectured at but are almost having a conversation with the author.

Interestingly, although Milne seems to be moving toward a final conclusion that a state lottery is not a form of gambling, he introduces a touch of doubt in the final paragraph, suggesting that maybe it is gambling and should be banned. Ultimately, he just seems against the idea of the state being involved in any kind of game because that makes playing games "solem" when they should be "jolly." So in the end, A.A. Milne does seem to get his point across but without beating we readers over the head with it: the problem with a state lottery is not that it may be a form of gambling, but that it takes the fun out of games of chance.

ANALYSIS

Now that you've read the essay as a whole, we're going to break it down to see both what the essay writer did right and how this essay could be better.

First let's take a look at the introduction.

> *Is buying a state lottery ticket gambling? This is the essential question at the heart of A.A. Milne's essay "State Lotteries." In responding to whether or not a state-run lottery is a form of gambling, Milne uses novel evidence and adopts a witty tone to get his argument across.*

Here is an analysis broken down into the three scoring sections graders will use with your essay on test day.

Reading: The introduction is not the best place to get an idea of how well the essay writer read the prompt passage, but there are no mistakes here, and the writer seems to have a good general idea of the point of Milne's passage.

Analysis: Again, there is not much room for analysis in an introductory paragraph, but the essay writer does make some good general analytical observations about how Milne uses "novel evidence" and a "witty tone to get his argument across." This essay is off to a good analytical start.

Writing: The writing here is fine with well-varied language and sentence structure. Beginning the essay with a question is a valuable trick for getting the scorers engaged in the essay. The introduction is a bit too brief and blunt (identifying the question as Milne's "essential question" lacks subtlety), but it's fine overall.

Next, let's look at the body paragraphs, one by one.

> *At first, Milne holds back on his personal opinion of whether or not state lotteries constitute gambling to go to a very direct source regarding this question. Instead of consulting some authority on morals, ethics, or law, he uses his handy, every day dictionary to find out what this basic reference book has to say about the big question. He does so not by looking up "lottery" but by looking up "gamble," which the dictionary defines as a "game" that involves "chance." While he concludes that "chance" is an element in playing the state lottery, he says that the fact that playing the lottery has little in common with playing games exempts it from being gambling. He concludes that playing the lottery then has more in common with buying Premium Bonds than gambling.*

Reading: The first paragraph of the body gets more into the details of Milne's passage, and the essay writer seems to have read it carefully. There are no errors. The description of how Milne consulted his dictionary is accurate. This paragraph suggests that the essay writer has strong reading skills.

Analysis: This is where the essay writer is a bit weak in the first body paragraph. The writer spends too much time repeating details from Milne's essay without analyzing them closely. The only real analytical detail in this paragraph is the suggestion that Milne's use of a dictionary is novel.

Writing: The essay writer makes up for any analytical shortcomings with effective writing. Perhaps in an effort to mirror the tone of Milne's passage, the essay writer uses a light-hearted, witty tone while contrasting the "handy, every day [sic] dictionary" with the kind of "authority on morals, ethics, or law" the reader may have been expecting Milne to consult. Once again, the essay writer's grasp of sentence structure, vocabulary, and grammar is strong.

> *Milne then goes into more detail to support his dictionary-based conclusion that playing the state lottery is not gambling. He introduces a comparison between horse racing and playing the lottery to further his argument, and here he uses humor more obviously to get us, his readers, on his side. One subtle humorous trick is giving the horse in his example a funny name, the illness Bronchitis. Getting us to giggle is a good way to loosen us up to go along with the author.*

Reading: The essay writer is going to lose some points with this paragraph for asserting that Milne uses the comparison between playing the state lottery and horse racing "to support his dictionary-based conclusion that playing the state lottery is not gambling." In fact, Milne uses this comparison to introduce the idea that playing the state lottery may actually be a form of gambling, since horse racing is an acknowledged form of gambling that has little in common with playing games.

Analysis: The essay writer makes a good point in this paragraph about how Milne uses humor to appeal to readers. There isn't a lot of analysis going on in this second paragraph of the body, but it is still effective.

Writing: Writing is still basically strong here, while the essay writer introduces a clever use of second-person writing (referring to readers as *us*) to further the appealing light-hearted and personal tone of the essay. Language gets a bit repetitive towards the end with too many uses of *us*—the essay writer could have mixed it up a little by substituting the word *readers* for one of those uses of *us*—but it is still effective overall.

> *The author uses another subtle trick to make us follow his argument by referring to readers in the second person. In paragraph three, he starts referring to us as* you *to get us to relate to his argument better. This personal touch makes it seem as though we're not merely being lectured at but are almost having a conversation with the author.*

Reading: This final paragraph of the body is short on details that show how well the essay writer read the passage. There are no more errors, though. This paragraph probably won't affect the essay writer's reading score much one way or the other.

Analysis: Here's another good catch by the essay writer. The analysis of how Milne uses the second person is astute and may have even inspired the essay writer's own use of that tactic in this essay.

Writing: Writing is generally fine. The essay writer made one basic grammatical error by ending a phrase with a preposition ("we're not merely being lectured at"), but the tone of the essay is casual enough that this may not affect the writing score too much.

Finally, let's examine if the author wraps up his or her thoughts in an effective way.

> *Interestingly, although Milne seems to be moving toward a final conclusion that a state lottery is not a form of gambling, he introduces a touch of doubt in the final paragraph, suggesting that maybe it is gambling and should be banned. Ultimately, he just seems against the idea of the state being involved in any kind of game because that makes playing games "solem" when they should be "jolly." So in the end, A.A. Milne does seem to get his point across but without beating we readers over the head with it: the problem with a state lottery is not that it may be a form of gambling, but that it takes the fun out of games of chance.*

Reading: Oops. The essay writer's past mistake comes back to haunt him or her. The first sentence of the conclusion repeats the error in the second paragraph of the body. Milne had actually already introduced the possibility that playing a state lottery is a form of gambling back in the third paragraph of the prompt passage. By repeating that error, the essay writer is probably going to lose some more points for reading.

Analysis: However, the essay writer's final point about Milne's true evaluation of playing the state lottery is well detected and reasoned. Quoting Milne directly—even just quoting a couple of words ("solemn" and "jolly")—is good use of evidence and strengthens the essay writer's final conclusion.

Writing: The essay writer ends the essay on a strong note in terms of writing. Use of the word "Interestingly" is a good way to start the paragraph by stoking the reader's interest (even if the essay writer's "interesting" point is incorrect), and ending it with a neat summary of Milne's final conclusion makes for a strong ending. There is one minor spelling error ("solem" instead of "solemn"), but it is a very rare mistake in terms of the essay as a whole.

So, after taking all of these assessments of the essay writer's reading, analysis, and writing skills into account, the scorers would most likely offer an overall score of:

5/6/7

That's a score of 5 for reading, 6 for analysis, and 7 for writing.

ESSAY WRITING PRACTICE

Now let's look at another sample prompt. First, try this essay on your own. Treat it as you would the actual essay on test day. Set a timer for 50 minutes, read the prompt (though you should already know what it says!), read the passage, and write your response.

If you have the time to do this before test day, it will definitely come in handy—you will be more used to reading, writing, and editing under time pressure when the real thing comes.

Following the essay, we've given you some examples to which you can compare your essay. This time, there will be three essays at three different levels: advanced, proficient, and inadequate.

Good luck!

As you read the passage below, consider how Noah Webster uses

- evidence, such as facts or examples, to support claims.
- reasoning to develop ideas and to connect claims and evidence.
- stylistic or persuasive elements, such as word choice or appeals to emotion, to add power to the ideas expressed.

The following passage is adapted from *Dissertations on the English Language* by Noah Webster.

Young gentlemen who have gone through a course of academical studies, and received the usual honors of a University, are apt to contract a singular stiffness in their conversation. They read Lowth's Introduction, or some other grammatical treatise, believe what they read, without examining the grounds of the writer's opinion, and attempt to shape their language by his rules. Thus they enter the world with such phrases as, *a mean, averse from, if he have, he has gotten,* and others which they deem *correct;* they pride themselves, for some time, in their superior learning and peculiarities; till further information, or the ridicule of the public, brings them to use the language of other people.

Such has been my progress, and that of many of my cotemporaries. After being some years in that excellent school, the world, I recommenced my studies, endeavored, not merely to learn, but to understand, the *a, b, c,* of the English language, and in 1783 compiled and published the First Part of my Grammatical Institute. The favorable reception of this, prompted me to extend my original plan, which led to a further investigation of the principles of language. After all my reading and observation for the course of ten years, I have been able to unlearn a considerable part of what I learnt in early life; and at thirty years of age, can, with confidence, affirm, that our modern grammars have done much more hurt than good. The authors have labored to prove, what is obviously absurd, viz. that our language is not made right; and in pursuance of this idea, have tried to make it over again, and persuade the English to speak by Latin rules, or by arbitrary rules of their own. Hence they have rejected many phrases of pure English, and substituted those which are neither English nor sense. Writers and Grammarians have attempted for centuries to introduce a subjunctive mode into English, yet without effect; the language requires none, distinct from the indicative; and therefore a subjunctive form stands in books only as a singularity, and people in practice pay no regard to it. The people are right, and a critical investigation of the subject, warrants me in saying, that common practice, even among the unlearned, is generally defensible on the principles of analogy, and the structure of the language, and that very few of the alterations recommended by Lowth and his followers, can be vindicated on any better principle than some Latin rule, or his own private opinion.

Some compilers have also attempted to introduce a *potential mode,* where they arrange those phrases that have the *auxiliary* verbs, as they are called, *can, may,* etc. But all the helping verbs are principal verbs, and the verb following them is generally in the infinitive. *I can go, he may write, we shall see,* &c. are only a customary ellipsis of *I can to go, he may to write, we shall to see;* and are no more a potential mode than *I dare go, we saw him rise.*

In the indeclinable parts of speech, all authors were mistaken, till Mr. Horne Tooke explained them: Our conjunctions are mostly verbs in the imperative mode: Our adverbs and prepositions are mostly verbs, nouns and adjectives, either separate or combined; and the proper definition of adverb and preposition, is, "a word, or union of words, without the ordinary rules of government." *Because* is a compound of the verb *be*, in the imperative, and the noun *cause*; *otherwise* is merely a corruption of *other ways*; *wherefore* is a corruption of the Roman *qua-re*, with the addition of *for*; *wisely* is nothing more than the two adjectives *wise like*. So that in many cases, the want of a space between two words, or of the usual rules of government, is the only circumstance that distinguishes them from ordinary nouns and verbs; that is, the only thing that makes them *adverbs* or *prepositions*; such as, *because, always, beyond, before, behind, forward, backward*. In short, had the English never been acquainted with Greek and Latin, they would never have thought of one half the distinctions and rules which make up our English grammars.

> Write an essay in which you explain how Noah Webster builds an argument to persuade his audience that following the rules of grammar too closely can hinder communication. In your essay, analyze how Webster uses one or more of the features listed above (or features of your own choice) to strengthen the logic and persuasiveness of his argument. Be sure that your analysis focuses on the most relevant features of the passage.
>
> Your essay should not explain whether you agree with Webster's claims, but rather explain how the author builds an argument to persuade his audience.

First Sample Essay: Advanced

A strong education in grammar and language is integral to strong communication skills, but is there such a thing as too much education in this area? Can an over-reliance on the rules of grammar and "proper" English actually make one a less effective communicator? According to Noah Webster in his *Dissertations on the English Language*, the answer may surprise you.

Webster begins his argument by expressing his most straightforward point: the fact that most people use language casually and not according to the strictest rules makes those who do speak according to those rules sound a bit foolish. Ultimately, the "ridicule" of the majority leads those rigid few to adopt that more casual form of language that most people use. However, the fact that Webster drops this point in the introduction of his essay shines a light on its obviousness. He will use the majority of his argument to get into more technical and less easy-to-grasp matters.

In the first paragraph of his argument's body, Webster cagily eases us into the discussion with a personal story. He tells about his own experiences as an everyday communicator, explaining that his observations and experiences have led him to "unlearn" much of his language education, though he could have provided more personal evidence to explain those experiences, such as an incident in which using "perfect" grammar caused him to suffer ridicule. Instead, he quickly moves on to the sharpest point of his essay yet, criticizing the authors of English grammar rules.

Here he provides more specifics, illustrating the confusion of an English grammar system that overly relies on Latin or even "arbitrary" rules. He explains the failure of grammarians to "introduce a subjunctive mode into English," which he supports with the observation that "people pay no regard to it." So, once again, he is showing that the majority of people ignore those rules of "proper" grammar.

In this second paragraph, Webster also makes a smart move to help his argument appeal to readers: he praises the "people" for being "right" in rejecting the arbitrary rules of grammarians. Readers who are not among these "people," who, themselves, always speak according to the strictest grammar rules, may feel embarrassed to not be among these "right" people and mend their ways with a more casual form of expression. Therefore, this praising of "the people" can have a doubly positive effect for Webster's argument.

With his next paragraph, Webster launches into a discussion of the problems with trying to enforce a "potential mode" and risks losing his audience with a more technical and disjointed approach. However, he returns to clarity by beginning his final paragraph with a very straightforward statement that sums up his argument ("all authors were mistaken") and supports this blanket statement with a quotation from a "Mr. Horne" who is likely an authority on the subject. After another somewhat technical tirade about imperatives, adverbs, and prepositions, Webster finishes off with another clear statement, blaming the influence of Greek and Latin on those muddled and "arbitrary" rules of grammar.

Webster seems to be addressing an academic audience, so the more technical parts of his argument may actually be perfectly clear to his intended readers. However, he may lose any less academic readers with some of his discussion. Nevertheless, there are enough clear statements about the "arbitrary" nature of English grammar rules, the unnecessary influence of Latin, and the most simple fact of all, that most people simply do not follow the strictest grammar rules, that the main thrust of Webster's argument should still be clear to any reader.

Score

Reading: The essay writer has clearly read the prompt passage very carefully. The details are accurate, as are the quotes used as evidence. The essay writer implies that he or she may not have understood some of the more "technical" portions of the prompt passage, but wisely does not risk misinterpreting them by focusing on how they affect the argument rather than what it all means.

Analysis: The essay writer analyzes every aspect of the prompt passage with insight, supporting evidence, and even suggestions on how the argument could have been stronger. She or he examines how Webster's clearest statements and subtle appeals to readers strengthen the argument and how certain unsupported statements and lapses into technical discussions might harm it.

Writing: Vocabulary and sentence structure are varied and used correctly. There are no misspellings. The introductory paragraph uses a series of questions to engage readers effectively. The concluding paragraph sums up the main points without being too blunt.

Final score: 8/8/8

SECOND SAMPLE ESSAY: PROFICIENT

Noah Webster sees a problem with how people who rely too much on their educations speak. He believes that following the rules of grammar too closely will cause the speaker to be ridiculed by her or his peers. The main problem, according to Webster is not the person speaking. It is the education that person recieved.

Webster starts his argument by talking a little about how he came to his conclusion about language: his own experiences and "observations." Then he explains the main problem with English language education: too much of it depends on Latin and "arbitrary rules." He says grammar educators tried to introduce the "subjunctive mode" and failed, which proves that they are not convincing enough to get all people to follow their rules.

There's a problem in the next paragraph. Webster starts talking about the "potential mode" and frankly, his arguement starts getting pretty hard to follow here. Frankly, I'm not even sure I followed it enough to comment on it. But that probably just proves that it's a problem.

After that paragraph I couldn't make heads or tails of, he started making sense again by saying that the authors of grammar rules are "all mistaken." This really makes him seem like an authority on grammar, and he makes his argument even stronger by quoting another authority: Mr. Horne. Frankly, I'm not sure I understood this quote either, but maybe that makes Webster's argument even stronger. He certainly made me feel like he was much smarter than me whenever his argument got too technical.

In the end, I think Webster made a very strong argument. Some of it was really clear, like when he was saying that most people do not follow the proper rules of grammar (true) and that he thinks there is too much Latin in English grammar. When it was less clear, he was probably just showing off what an expert on grammar he is, which just made his argument more convincing. *Dissertations on the English Language* is a very convincing argument against always using proper grammar rules.

Score

Reading: The essay writer generally displays good comprehension of the prompt passage. However, the several blunt admissions that she or he did not understand portions of the passage reveal that comprehension was not complete. Still, there are no embarrassing misunderstandings of the prompt passage.

Analysis: The essay writer does not go into exceptional depth with her or his analysis, but does make an attempt to deal with several aspects of the prompt passage, particularly the author's more technical discussions. However, there is a lack of consistency in the essay writer's analysis of the effect of those technical portions—at first, they are presented as a problem, and finally, and somewhat unconvincingly, as something that makes Webster's argument stronger. The second paragraph relies too much on restating information in the prompt passage without any meaningful analysis.

Writing: The essay writer only makes a couple of spelling errors and mostly follows the rules of grammar. Some of the vocabulary is overused (the word *frankly*, for example), but the writing is proficient, overall.

Final score: 6/6/6

Third Sample Essay: Inadequate

Webster writes about grammer and he says he thinks we should basically not use it anymore. I'm pretty sure this won't work. We'd end up with everyone just talking lots of nonsense all the time. Without proper grammer, we'd all sound ridiculus according to me. I think everyone should actualy study English really hard in school. I can't believe someone who is as obviously smart as Webster would say we shouldn't! He knows a lot about grammer based on this thing he wrote. It was like he was trying to trick us into speaking badly. I don't know why he would do that, but I'm not falling for it. I will continue to speak good. I will do it all the time. Every time.

So if you read something like this that tells you not to get an English education and just talk the way everyone does I say "don't do it"! You will be the one who ends up sounding silly. Just listen every time someone can't speak good and see how you feel.

Score

Reading: The essay writer misinterprets the prompt passage, concluding that Webster suggests people should not follow any rules of grammar at all, when he is actually suggesting that we should not follow them so strictly.

Analysis: Basing his or her analysis on a misreading of the passage really affects the essay writer's analysis, suggesting that Webster is making an argument he actually is not making. The essay writer injects too many personal opinions in the essay and too little clear and careful analysis of the prompt passage.

Writing: The essay writer makes numerous grammatical, mechanical, and spelling errors. The essay is much too brief, lacking a body between its weak introductory and concluding paragraphs.

Final score: 2/2/2

SUMMING IT UP

- The **SAT® Essay** is optional, but many colleges consider it when looking at applications. Always check the colleges to which you are applying to see if they prefer you complete the essay.

- On test day, the SAT® Essay section will come after the multiple-choice test sections. You will have 50 minutes to read the given material and complete the essay.

- You will read a prompt and a 650- to 750-word argumentative passage. Your response essay should analyze the passage and assess how well it makes its argument, including evidence from the given passage.

- Two graders will give your essay a **reading score** (how well you understood the passage), an **analysis score** (how well you analyzed the argument), and a **writing score** (how well you wrote your response). Scores will range from 1–4 in each of these categories. Your final score for each section is the sum of the two scores.

- The SAT® Essay assignment is always the same; it requires you to analyze the argument an author makes in a reading passage. Your essay should *not* explain whether you agree with the author's claims; it should **explain how the author builds an argument to persuade the audience.**

- In order to get a top score, you must include evidence from the original passage: direct quotes, a summary of the author's main points, or both.

- As you read the author's passage, take notes on the author's main argument and how the author uses evidence and specific language to back it up.

  1. Your essay should contain an **introductory paragraph** that introduces the author's main argument and lays out how you plan to analyze it; **body paragraphs** (aim for three) that fully analyze how the author presents his or her points of view and builds an argument; and a **concluding paragraph** that wraps up or sums up the main findings of your analysis.

  2. Leave yourself enough time to read over your essay and edit it. You can't really check while you're writing, so it's important you read it with fresh eyes, as a whole, to make sure you've made your main points and included evidence from the original passage.

  3. Aim to allot your time in the following way on test day:

Total test time	50 minutes
Reading the prompt and taking notes	10 minutes
Outlining	5 minutes
Writing	25–30 minutes
Editing	5–10 minutes

NOTES

NOTES